P9-CJQ-017
WITHDRAWN
JUL 01
DAVID O. McKAY LIBRARY
BYU-IDAHO

Middle West Country

Middle West Country

Text and Photographs by

WILLIAM CARTER

A SAN FRANCISCO BOOK COMPANY/HOUGHTON MIFFLIN BOOK

HOUGHTON MIFFLIN COMPANY BOSTON 1975

D 10 9 8 7 6 5 4 3 2 1

A brief portion of this book has appeared previously in *JD Journal.*

Library of Congress Cataloging in Publication Data

Carter, William, 1934–
Middle West country.

"A San Francisco Book Company/Houghton Mifflin book."
Includes bibliographical references and index.
1. Middle West. I. Title.
F351.C34 977 75-23209
ISBN 0-395-20732-0

This SAN FRANCISCO BOOK COMPANY/HOUGHTON MIFFLIN BOOK originated in San Francisco and was produced and published jointly. Distribution is by Houghton Mifflin Company, 2 Park Street, Boston, Massachusetts 02107.

Book design by Anita Walker Scott

Printed in the United States of America by The Lakeside Press, R.R. Donnelley & Sons Company.

Photo credits: Cecil Beeson Collection: 6 (bottom), 7 (top left), 193, 199, 209; Burton Collection, Detroit Public Library: 207; Department of Landscape Architecture, Iowa State University: 140–41; Des Moines *Register and Tribune:* 222, 269; Courtesy Ford Archives, Dearborn, Michigan: 8 (left center), 211; Grant Heilman: 10, 63, 119, 123, 125, 182, 190; Indiana Historical Society Library: 42; Library of Congress: 9 (top right and bottom), 32, 36, 49, 84, 91, 111, 118, 131, 170, 213; Miami University (Ohio): 197; Michigan Department of Natural Resources: 8 (lower right), 12, 67; Michigan Tourist Council: 254; Minnesota Department of Conservation: 20; Minnesota Historical Society: 92, 186; Missouri Historical Society: 140; Norwegian-American Historical Museum: 60, 61; Oakland Museum: 51, 81; Project Documerica: 114; Public Archives of Canada: 68; Southern Illinois University Press: 35; State Historical Society of Wisconsin: 6 (center), 7 (top right and bottom right), 8 (top), 65, 96, 184; USDA: 173.

FOR BETTY

Contents

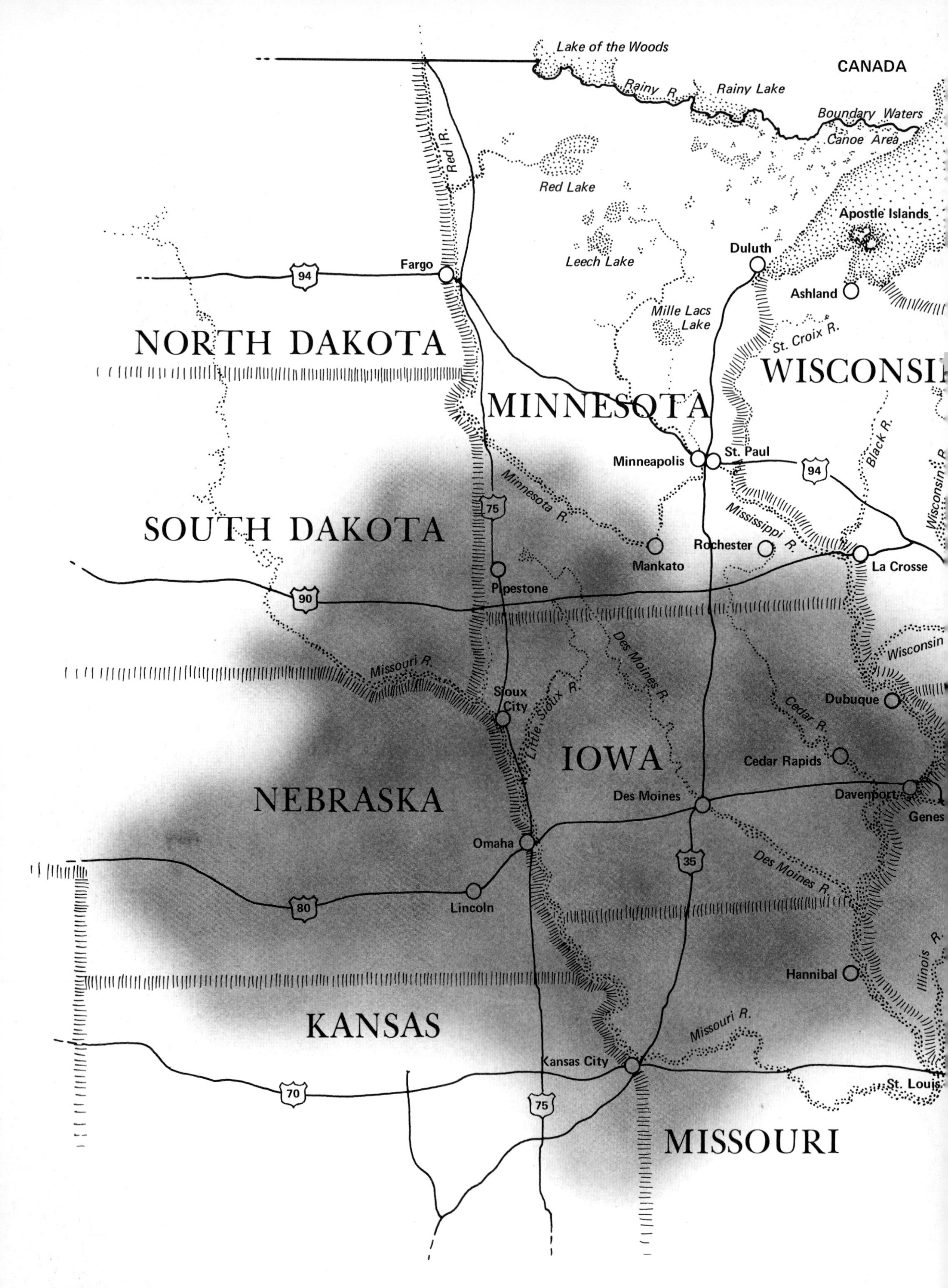
Lake of the Woods
CANADA
Rainy R.
Rainy Lake
Boundary Waters
Canoe Area
Red R.
Red Lake
Apostle Islands
Leech Lake
Duluth
Ashland
Fargo
94
Mille Lacs
Lake
St. Croix R.
NORTH DAKOTA
WISCONSI
MINNESOTA
Minneapolis
St. Paul
94
Black R.
Minnesota R.
75
Mississippi R.
Wisconsin R.
SOUTH DAKOTA
Mankato
Rochester
La Crosse
Pipestone
90
Des Moines R.
Wisconsin
Missouri R.
Sioux City
Little Sioux R.
Cedar R.
Dubuque
IOWA
Cedar Rapids
NEBRASKA
Des Moines
Davenport
Genes
Omaha
35
Des Moines R.
80
Lincoln
Illinois R.
Hannibal
KANSAS
Missouri R.
Kansas City
70
75
St. Louis
MISSOURI

Donald Dean

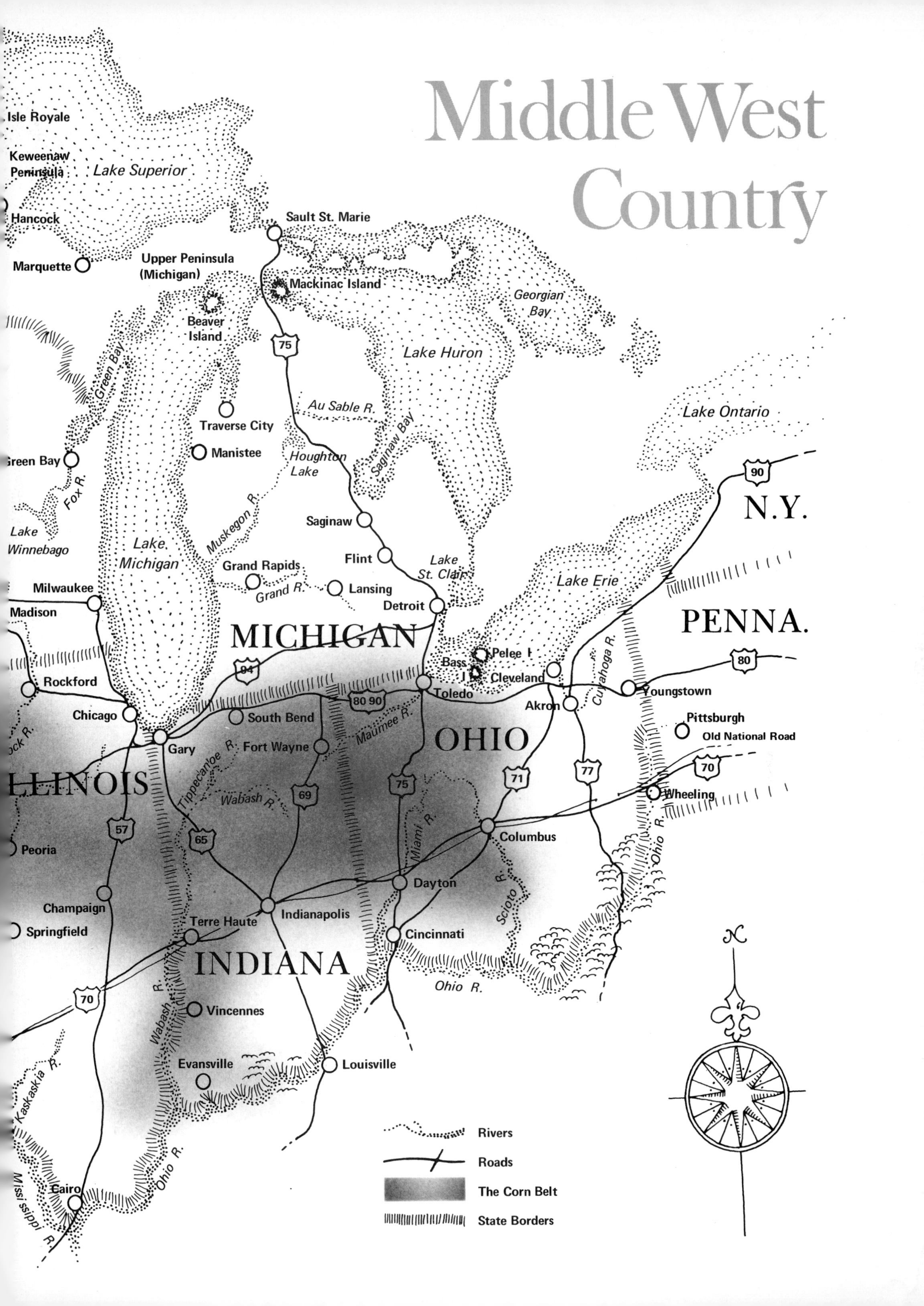

Middle West Country
Isle Royale
Keweenaw Peninsula
Lake Superior
Hancock
Marquette
Sault St. Marie
Upper Peninsula (Michigan)
Mackinac Island
Beaver Island
Georgian Bay
Lake Huron
Green Bay
Au Sable R.
Traverse City
Manistee
Houghton Lake
Saginaw Bay
Lake Ontario
Fox R.
Lake Winnebago
Muskegon R.
Lake Michigan
Saginaw
Flint
Lake St. Clair
Grand Rapids
Grand R.
Lansing
Detroit
Lake Erie
N.Y.
PENNA.
Milwaukee
Madison
MICHIGAN
Pelee I
Bass I
Cleveland
Cuyahoga R.
Rockford
Toledo
Akron
Youngstown
Chicago
South Bend
Pittsburgh
Old National Road
Gary
Fort Wayne
Maumee R.
OHIO
Tippecanoe R.
Wabash R.
Wheeling
Miami R.
Columbus
Ohio R.
Peoria
Dayton
Scioto R.
Champaign
Indianapolis
Springfield
Terre Haute
Cincinnati
INDIANA
Ohio R.
Wabash R.
Vincennes
Kaskaskia R.
Evansville
Louisville
Rivers
Roads
The Corn Belt
State Borders
Ohio R.
Cairo
Mississippi R.
N
94
80 90
75
69
65
57
70
71
77
90
80

Foreword

Why and Where

"WHY THE MIDDLE WEST?" people kept asking me. Their tones ranged from puzzlement to worried pride. While the coastwise intelligentsia were busy veiling their condescension, a Chicago manufacturer anxiously assured me that today's Corn Belt farmer has "soulful and creative feelings." Out in the small towns and farms, the conversations were simpler. Yet the voices carried a wonderment as to what on earth I could find to write about. Sure, it's a nice place to live, but . . . isn't it pretty much like everywhere else? And aren't people more or less the same everywhere? At first, such questions seemed discouraging. Then I began to see that they might really be provocative leads in helping me to define the character of the area. And if questions sometimes contained answers, I also found that some statements could open large new questions—as in Minnesota, where a man said, "New England is New England, the South is the South, and California is California. But the Midwest is America."

Why the Middle West? The weather alone would make a book. Or the superb soils; the vast watersheds; the unique woodlands. So, too, would the minglings of peoples who flowed in from the southern uplands, from New York and New England, from Germany and Scandinavia and elsewhere, clinging to certain ways and adapting to others.

For all the homogenization still going on, the Midwest, like America, remains something more than a melting pot. We are a people of strands and fibers and regions. Just try tracing the usage of "skillet" vs. "frying pan"; or follow the seeds scattered by the singing Methodists and fervent Baptists, the resolute Lutherans or staunch Quakers. Today, it's true, this "unmeltedness" is subtler than before. You won't find it on billboards, but behind clapboards, in the cracks and grooves of lives, which is where you'll find so much of the Middle West.

"Where *is* the Middle West?" Ah, that was always the other question. Innocently put, surely reasonable—and a bramble of dispute.

To start with, the dictionaries disagree. Webster says the Middle West extends from the Alleghenies to the Rockies. Random House hedges, giving the region a movable eastern boundary: "the Allegheny mountains, the E border of Ohio, or the E border of Illinois." American Heritage reverses this, calling the Middle West "a cultural and historical region of the United States extending roughly from Ohio westward through Iowa."

Professionals have come together to try to clarify the matter—and gone home agreeing to disagree. One professor mailed a questionnaire to 536 postmasters, asking simply, "In your opinion does your community lie in the Midwest?" The responses tended to give the term its broadest definition—from the Alleghenies to the Rockies. But sharp differences emerged. Typically, one Missourian penned, "I consider from the Mississippi River west through the plains states to be Midwest. Also we resent persons from Ohio and Indiana referring to themselves as 'Midwesterners' as actually they are 'Mideasterners.' "

Rather quickly, I learned to skate away from such thin semantic ice. Yet it is important to mention that the broader definition corresponds roughly to what geographers call the "upper Mississippi drainage basin," the vast tract of land that tilts down toward the Father of Waters from the Alleghenies, on the east, and from the Rockies, on the west, and that extends northward from the Ohio River to the Canadian border. Within this basin, the distinction between the humid, eastern portion and the subhumid, western part is a fundamental one.

In 1800, dense forests and tall-grass prairies blanketed most of Ohio, Indiana, Illinois, Iowa, Missouri, Michigan, Wisconsin, and Minnesota. Farther west, where the rainfall slackened and the grass grew shorter, the "true prairies" gave way to the treeless Great Plains. This difference was soon underscored dramatically by the white man's patterns of settlement. For a century following the Revolution, the woodlands and true prairies played host to the powerfully expansive energies of the new nation. Forests came down, log cabins went up. Along the rivers and lakes, commerce boomed, and great cities swelled on the shores. As the restless pioneer farmers kept pulling up stakes and moving on, other home seekers of a more patient bent, many of them immigrants, flooded in to take up permanent residence on the brown-black earth that would, under intensive cultivation, be transformed into the Corn Belt. By 1860, the rise of Illinois' Lincoln to the Presidency epitomized the style and growing power of the new West. But the lands beyond the Mississippi had yet to be settled, and partly over the question of whether slavery should be allowed in the Kansas and Nebraska territories, the Union was being torn in two. Ten years later, with the Civil War over, a series of homestead and land grant bills enacted, the railroads expanding, and new farm technologies rapidly appearing, the way was opened for a rush into the subhumid plains.

Here the pioneers faced new conditions. Farming and ranching, to be economic, had to be extensive. The scarcity of major rivers meant that shipments had to be by wagon or rail. Soils could be problematical, wells had to be sunk, and fencing was a major challenge. Since the area had little industrial potential, no great cities sprang up. And so a farmer who had come here to flee the "overcrowded" eastern prairies could gaze out over his expanses of waving wheat with the satisfaction that *these* wide-open spaces were not going to close in on him. Today, a century after the plains were opened, and two centuries after the nation's founding, Kansas, Nebraska, and the Dakotas remain the least populous Midwestern states, with only about sixteen persons to the square mile, whereas the other eight states average well over a hundred.

Why the Middle West? The question was also a personal one. As a Californian, I was sometimes thought to be an ex-Midwesterner bent on celebrating my origins. That assumption was wrong in fact but right in principle. I'm not, as Calvin Trillin has dubbed them, an "ExMid." Humorously describing the symptoms, this new-New Yorker concludes: "One thing I learned in high school in Kansas City is that Midwesternism cannot be created or destroyed, only changed in form."

The form, in my family, came via my grandparents on my mother's side. At forty, Grandpa Dailey had closed up his general store in Ohio and trekked west. When I was a small boy, he and I would chug slowly up the winding roads to the top of the Hollywood Hills, pausing to admire the view before dropping down into the San Fernando Valley. These days, of course, "the Valley" is a sea of concrete and glass, but in the early forties it was still open fields. We'd sit for hours in the tiny real estate office of a gruff, cigar-smoking man named Jessen. While a greasy fan fluttered well-thumbed maps and deeds, Grandpa and Jessen would go over and over the features of a repairable old house or fine avocado tract being offered for sale. Grandpa's instincts for the land, for democratic informality, and for careful, honest dealing were all, I think, very Midwestern.

Then we'd drive out across the dusty Valley, looking at acreage, figuring boundary lines, taking giant steps across the clotted dirt to pace off yards. For lunch we'd pull off under some eucalyptus trees at a field he owned. While he spread the blanket and unpacked the big hamper of food Grandma had packed at dawn, I'd run out and pick some ripe tomatoes. They were still hot from the sun as we squished our teeth into them. After lunch, in the drowsy summer air, we'd stretch out and have a nap.

It wasn't the Midwest, and it wasn't big corn or wheat country. But it was Grandpa himself, with his country-shy smile and proudly erect figure, his old Ohio expressions and loving way of tousling my hair, and the bushels of Ohio relatives who kept turning up—or, thrill of thrills, telephoning all the way from "back East"—through which I seemed to be picking up some Midwestern vibrations.

California was about to change beyond recognition, and so was I. So, in fact, was the world. But the more I came to see of it, the more I realized that I'll never outgrow those simple, warm days, or the memory of Grandpa Dailey's strong hands and upright character. At the age of forty, my journey back to his part of the country has been, indeed, a personal one. But it is more than personal: everywhere, it seems, there are signs that a nation that was once in such a hurry to discover the land is now turning back to discover itself.

Reversing the route of the pioneers, and driving from west to east across Nebraska, you note the transition from plain to true prairie in a hundred small ways. On the higher, drier ground near the Wyoming border, where the soil is low in acid but rich in lime, the open grazing land gives way reluctantly to small, tilled plots and scattered, poor-looking farmhouses. Through wind-whipped dust, the Intermountain Farm-Ranch Radio Network beams news of breeder-stock prices and rodeos. The year-round snow fences march in regiments, and the train tracks are never out of sight of the highway. Now and again a spinning windmill or lone grain elevator will punctuate the skyline. But so rare is a tree that a roadside stand, hunkering by a clump of cottonwoods, advertises, "EAT IN THE SHADE." The old sod houses are long gone, but if you look carefully you may spot a deserted cabin built of fieldstone. More common, yet equally forlorn, are the concrete-block cafés.

But gradually the green fields get bigger. Suddenly, at Sidney, you're in a real farm town, with tidy residential streets, a Deere dealer, a row of store windows hard to tell apart, and women clutching scarves over their curlers. East of Sidney, the land continues to get tamer. Plots expand, and the small-grain crops grow taller. Bright blue Harvestore silos smarten up the horizon. Boxcars lie on sidings, waiting to haul grain. Orderly haystacks and bales give the landscape a man-made look. Gone, now, are the distant mountains and powerful western vistas. You realize that while you were dropping from well over four thousand feet toward less than two thousand, your tires rolled over an invisible line—somewhere between North Platte and Kearney—dividing the high plains from the low plains.

Halfway across the state, the pace of life quickens with the traffic. There are more trees. The land is greener; less and less of it is allowed to lie untilled. Corn makes its debut—though it needs irrigation this far west. Red barns spring up. The radio sounds more urgent, bringing late market quotes on corn and soybeans and corn-fattened livestock. The Bible-belt stations are less dominant, and the news is less local, more regional. Near Lincoln, country churches start to poke their classic white steeples over the skyline. The soil is getting richer, the air more humid. Approaching Omaha, you realize you're already into big corn country, once the domain of the whispering prairie. And beyond the brown Missouri lie the green, folded flanks of Iowa.

It is that country, east of the Missouri, with which I shall be mainly concerned—east into Ohio and Michigan, southeast to the southern tip of Illinois, and north to the Canadian border. Yet some of what I say will apply, equally, to Kansas and the other plains states, whose small towns and farming traditions have much in common with those of the Corn Belt. And, clearly, it would be foolhardy to claim that one or the other region is the *real* Middle West.

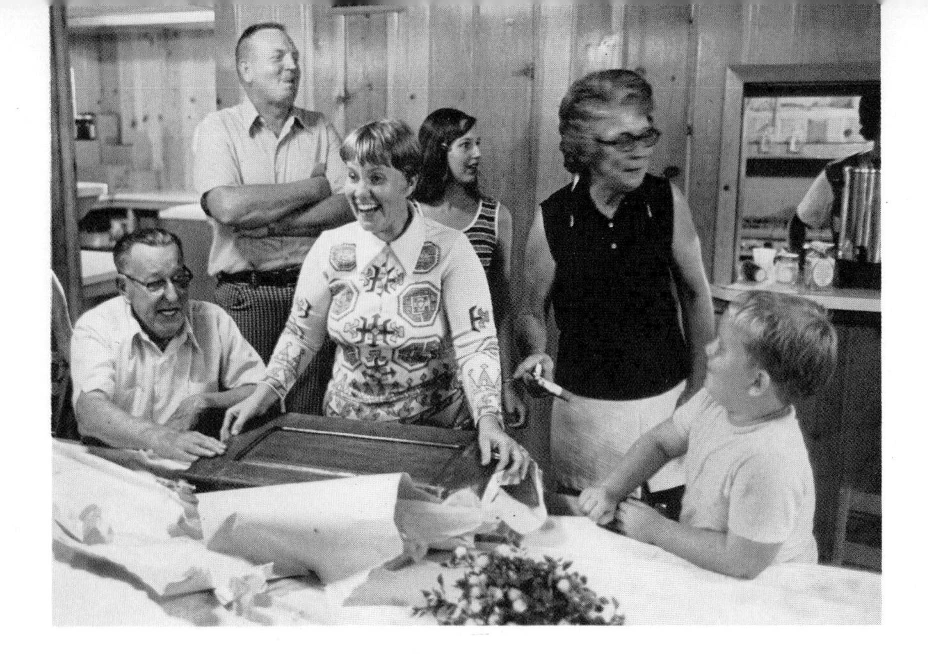

For Christ and Home and Country, I hereby enroll myself a member of
The Presbyterian Temperance Union
and promise with divine help to abstain from all intoxicating beverages and to use my influence to abolish the drink habit and the liquor traffic.
Name
Witness: Date

MILLGROVE
PRIMARY
GRADES
MILLGROVE
ADVANCE
GRADES
LIEBER &
HARDWARE,

Fritz Klemperer

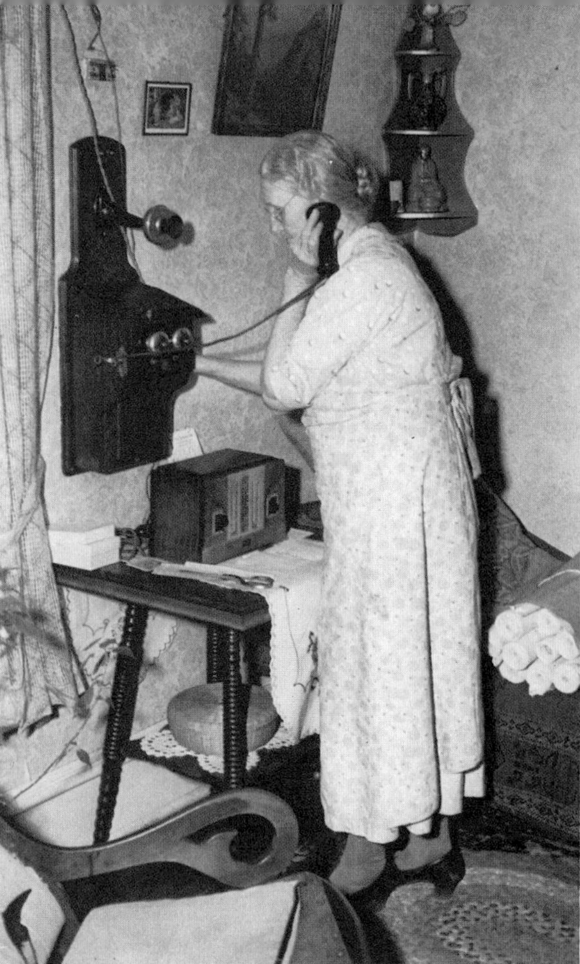

John Vachon

Arthur Rothstein

Grant H

Chapter One

Middle Ground

THE RURAL MIDDLE WEST is more than a physical area. It is a region of the heart. A home place: sometimes narrowly disapproving, but nurturing and loving, and preserving the style of the era before America moved away to the city. A place of ice cream socials on warm summer evenings, of the autumnal smells of fresh cider and burning leaves, of snowy silences pierced by the zip of sleds, of the dewy softness of a newborn calf. A place, as Robert McLaughlin writes, where "Frame houses, with front porches as ample as a grandmother's lap, are set back on wide lawns and hold memories of a creaking swing, the tinkle of a ukulele, the gleam of white dresses moving in and out of screen doors."

Loyalties are as firmly fixed to church, church group, and service club as they are to home, home town, home state. Church-going is taken for granted, as are neighborliness, boosterism, and family gatherings. Midwesterners and their far-flung progeny will travel incredible distances to be together at holidays, or to spend a few hours of artless conversation at a huge family reunion. In a small town, everybody turns out for the high school game; and for the next week, a player who did even moderately well will be told so whenever he shows his face downtown. If his behavior off the field also wins the approval

of the dominant middle class, he may be invited to speak at a Rotary luncheon. Homecomings bring out the whole town, too, inspiring snake dances, pie-eating contests, tearful Queens, sober Kings, and other luminaries such as "Miss Congeniality."

None of these Americanisms are exclusive to the Midwest. But it is here that they seem etched most deeply into the woodwork. Are they corny? Of course. Yet the values behind them are genuine. And these values are a refreshing alternative to the hard-sell, value-free vacuum of the mass society. Anyone who depends too heavily on the status symbols conferred by that society is likely to feel uncomfortable in a Midwestern village, or in the living room of a Corn Belt farmer unaware of such symbolism. Conversely, the country-bred Midwesterner, imbued with a sense of common belonging, and confident that good, plain-talking people are the same everywhere, may feel puzzled by the nuances prevailing in metropolitan areas—along Chicago's northshore commuter run, say, in such suburban havens as Glencoe and Winnetka, Lake Forest and Lake Bluff.

Across the rural Midwest, success is highly valued—but contentment and morality are rated just as high. The life expectancy is the longest in the nation, and the homicide rate the lowest. Less than an hour out of such jittery fortresses as Detroit, Gary, or Chicago, nobody thinks of locking his bike or car or front door.

To such coziness there is, to be sure, a cooler side. Contentment slips easily into dulling complacency. Making little provision for exceptionality, the Middle West country has often failed to make its more gifted sons and daughters feel welcome. So they tend to leave. As for some others who remain, but don't quite fit, writers like Sherwood Anderson and Edgar Lee Masters have shown us how external conformity can be but a thin cover for internal pain. Today, to be sure, there are powerful countertrends throughout the Middle West. But they remain countertrends—separate and embattled. The small towns and farms are just not going to bend toward sophistication as easily as the rest of America.

This is, of course, part of their charm. Yet one result has been that the region's authors have had too uneasy a relationship with their home ground to have produced any generally agreed-upon classic dealing with the mainstream of Midwestern country life. Rölvaag's *Giants in the Earth,* the great story of prairie settlement, belongs more to Norwegian literature than to American. *Huckleberry Finn* is unquestionably a Midwestern classic; but, like the novels of Cooper and Hemingway, it portrays escape from the social mainstream. Warm, skillful, and full of praise for the pioneer spirit, Willa Cather has been loved by generations of readers. Nonetheless, others have continued to insist that she underplays the harsher facts of prairie life.

Many a Hoosier, if not the literary establishment, remains stoutly proud of Indiana's own Booth Tarkington, who gave us memorable accounts of an early, genteel Indianapolis. Yet the Hoosier state scarcely claims Theodore Dreiser, who deserted it to write pessimistic novels about big-city problems. Sinclair Lewis did confront the small town head-on, but bitterness kept him from seeing much beyond his own Babbitts and Kennicotts.

While the pettinesses of Midwestern life remain easy targets, there are deeper and finer qualities on the farms and in the towns than the regional fiction has been able to exemplify. This is a serious loss, to our literature and to our understanding.

You can look at the flatness of the Middle West—or at its variety. Take the Midwestern farmer. If he is anything, he is his own man. I've been a guest in one farm home where the merest mention of alcohol would touch off a diatribe, and in another where the basement was stocked with a dozen varieties of home brew. In Illinois I chatted with a hog man whose world was literally bounded by the visible horizon; in Michigan I talked with another who had been all the way to Denmark and Switzerland to study new farrowing practices. One soft-spoken corn-and-cattle farmer, with yearly receipts well into the six figures, explained that he refuses government subsidies on principle and would risk losing an entire crop rather than go near his combine on a Sunday. Whereas his neighbor, planting about the same acreage, winked and assured me nobody can survive like that these days. All this on the richest farming ground in the world.

It is a ground attributable, in large measure, to ancient glaciers. They sculpted much of the variety, as well as the flatness, which you notice in crossing the land. Before the glaciers, the Midwest was submerged by a shallow inland sea. Very slowly, the land rose out of the water. In the warm climate, tropical forests bloomed profusely. Then, as if rejecting this destiny, the land sank back again, to be covered with layers of sand, mud, and the enriching lime of crushed seashells. Over millions of years, this process repeated itself again and again. Immense pressures gradually compacted the decaying forests into seams of coal. By the time the inland sea retreated for the last time, dinosaurs had been displaced by warm-blooded creatures. And as the Rockies rose in the West, the older Appalachians were being partly eroded down onto the central lowlands.

Steadily, the climate turned colder. From what is now Canada, a great hand of ice, thousands of feet thick, shoved its way south. Pulverizing mountains and filling in valleys, it leveled the landscape. Its

untold tons of debris included dirt scraped out of the hard-rock "Laurentian Shield" to the north and limestone scoured from the Great Lakes area. From all this the glacier fashioned a thick, rich layer of soil which it spread smoothly over the prairies.

At last, along a U-shaped trace just above the Ohio and Missouri rivers, the icy fingers halted and began to retreat. Like the sea, the glacial sheets came again—at least four times in all. Yet each time they stopped short of where they had been before, marking the limits of their probe with "moraines"—long heaps of dirt, gravel, and other debris, which still can be seen. The glaciers, as well as the soils left by each, have been named Nebraskan, Kansan, Illinoian, and Wisconsin (though they bear little relation to any state boundaries).

The icing on the cake is something called "loess." In spring and summer the melting glaciers would flood the Mississippi, Missouri, and other river valleys with silty water. Later in the year the water would dry up, leaving the silt, or loess. Fine as flour, the loess was blown aloft by the prevailing northwest winds, then sifted down over

Betty Carter

the glacial lands. This final dusting gave the soil a crowning touch of fertility. To this day, the loess still thickens in the directions from which it came—toward the main river valleys and toward the northwest. One of the best places to see it is on the brown bluffs above the Missouri, between Nebraska and Iowa.

Heading north from the Ohio River, you soon discover that the variety carved by the glaciers is matched by a diversity of the peoples who live on the land. At the southern limit of the earliest ice sheet, the old, eroded hills were settled by southern uplanders and still resound to their rich hillbilly palaver. Northward, as the land stretches out, the southern mood fades into the measured briskness of the enterprising Yankees and midlanders and Germans who first dragged their plows through the sticky prairie sod. These days their heirs may be harvesting more than twenty million bushels of corn and soybeans to a single county. Moving up past the industrial belt to the sandy soils of the forest and lake country, you meet people with names like Lundstrom or Oleson, who remind you that their ancestors found this land of gentle summers and fierce winters not unlike Scandinavia.

Speaking of the weather—everyone does in the Midwest—no other region of the United States can match this one for sheer drama. There are, of course, a few colder spots in winter, and a few hotter ones in summer. But not many. And none with such wild extremes or sudden changes. One dismayed visitor went so far as to recommend that the Midwest be expelled from the temperate zone, since its "climate varies between that of central Russia in winter and that of Singapore in summer." As for variability, Chicago has long advised out-of-towners: "If you don't like our weather, wait ten minutes." Those who don't appreciate such uncertainty can always try the high plains: " 'Does the wind blow this way all the time?' a greenhorn visitor once asked. 'No, mister,' a plainsman replied. 'It'll maybe blow this way for a week or ten days, and then it'll take a change and blow like hell for a while.' "

Both plains and prairies have what is called a "continental" climate: located far from the moderating oceans, they experience a cold winter, hot summer, and brief spring. But in a large area around the Great Lakes, special forces are at work. Here, as it happens, four major inbound air masses are constantly on a collision course. Veering in from the northeast, north, northwest, and south, these clashing armies of atmosphere cause blizzards and tornadoes, and eventually droughts and floods, as well as gentler phenomena like unseasonable balmy spells.

To all of this, the Great Lakes add their own dramatic effects. In the fall, their shimmering surfaces continuously emit so much heat that, could it be harnessed, a single day's energy transfer would be enough to supply the nation's entire power needs for a year. Not surprisingly, these inland seas exert a strong influence on the climate of the lands adjoining them. Moving aloft, the warm lake air sets up a rotary turbulence which, in turn, causes autumn winds to blow. Although most of the Midwest is free of the heavy fogs that often engulf our ocean coasts, fog does form over and around the Great Lakes and along the Ohio and Mississippi channels. In spring, the lakes' cool water delays the onset of high temperatures; and in fall, their warming effect delays the frost. This moderating influence creates an ideal climate for fruit growing in such lakeside areas as Wisconsin's Door County and the long strip running north from Kalamazoo and St. Joseph, Michigan. In summer, residents of towns like Evanston or Muskegon or Toledo can hope for cooling lake breezes. But westerly winds sweeping across the lakes also pick up a great deal of moisture, which they often dump onto the land as rain or snow. Unexpected squalls may thus strike towns as far apart as Sault Ste. Marie, up at the junction of Lakes Superior and Huron, and Gary, Indiana, down at the southern tip of Lake Michigan. Damp lake winds hitting the southern shore of Lake Erie have been known to blanket Cleveland with eight inches of snow in an hour.

Even though such complexities make the weather hard to cope with, the Midwestern climate has proven, in general, highly beneficial to man. As we shall see, its very changeability has had a stimulating effect on human achievement—on that old-fashioned vim-and-vigor still driving a region whose biggest city long ago adopted the motto *I Will.* More concretely, the Midwestern weather has a direct bearing on the U.S. economy and on stomachs around the world. So perfect for corn are the Midwest's growing season and precipitation patterns that a single inch of rain at a critical time in July can boost the nation's corn output by half a billion bushels. Since the corn is to be fed to hogs and cattle, that inch is immediately translated into lower meat prices on the forward markets. Too much rain, on the other hand, can be ruinous. But, of course, neither the grain speculator nor the farmer ever knows whether it will rain at all—or if it does, when it will stop.

And yet it is the smaller things that often remain most vividly in your mind:

On a summer night in Iowa, tossing and turning on an airless sleeping porch, with the temperature and humidity both in the eighties. While,

beyond the screens, the fine green stalks grow so fast they will be inches taller by morning. Filaments of lightning that dance along the horizon like witches, whacking kettledrums and flinging rain-veils. Orange-and-black Monarch butterflies, blue dragonflies, pesky mosquitoes and gnats. Up near the porch light, a spotted Luna Moth.

In spring, the loving familiarity with which a farmer squats, scoops up a handful of black earth, and lets it sift through his fingers to prove it has just the right moisture for a nice early planting. Later, the anguish that seizes him at the sight of blowing hail that may sever the stalks of his corn like knives. In October, the anxious way he peers from his upstairs bedroom window at the first hint of dawn, hoping this will be the day the muck has dried enough to get his machinery into the fields to start picking.

Spring again! The basement recreation room has been magically transformed into a wading pool, breathing mildew and soggy wool. The indelible memory of seeing flood refugees wandering through the streets of your town, in a state of shock, seeking any kind of shelter.

On upper Michigan's Keweenaw Peninsula, gaping up at a snow-measuring stick rising into the sky like a totem pole. Being told the folks here had twenty-five feet of snow in 1969.

Remember that freak storm that closed your school and let you go tobogganing on the hill? Or how about the ice storm? Poles and

power lines collapsing by the hundreds under the huge weight. Bringing havoc—and a frail loveliness: a world of glittering tinsel, branches crashing like glass, maple buds encased as rare jewels. No electricity. People helping each other. The newspaper saying how miraculous there had been no injuries in either Centerville or Ottumwa.

"It's not the cold, it's the windchill."

Chains clattering, snow tires sizzling. Avoiding the snowplow's spray and wondering which car-shape is yours.

For the pioneers: the ague, the shakes, the insect-borne epidemics and locust swarms. Frozen livestock, capsized rafts, wind blustering through crudely chinked cabins. Then, in March, survival. Pa jerks the latchstring, stomps a boot on the threshold, declares: "I reckon we wintered it out."

Dehumidifiers in bedrooms, air conditioners in tractor cabs, bulky furnaces in tiny cafés, a crop-spraying plane settling over ruler-straight rows. Families diving for tornado shelters, canoe-laden campers jamming northbound freeways out of suffocating Minneapolis. In Dayton, a spring sale on mittens and overshoes; in Kankakee, a "pre-Xmas special" on bass rods and outboard motors. Farmers, unable to afford

FRENCH
FRIES

Betty Carter

their own advice, saying the ideal crop rotation would be corn, soybeans, and Florida.

Ten miles up, feathery cirrus clouds wisp across the Arctic blue. Then, on the horizon, beyond your neighbor's antenna, vague dark smudges turn into rolling thunderheads. But through most of the long summer days, only frothy cumulus, dragging their shadows over the prairies like a magic lantern show.

Indian summer. Sensing changes of light and temperature, the trees slacken their juices. Sap slows. Stems seal off. Green chlorophyll decomposes, turning leaves red and gold. But in the crispy air, human hearts quicken. Boot on pigskin, smell of leaf-smoke, *thuck-thuck-thuck* of the busy combine. Cool nights at last! Dairy Queen closes next week. Go scuffling through the leaves, take down the screens, be sure and phone the fuel oil man. "Get that dog off the playing field!" Ruffled grouse in the damp Wisconsin underbrush. Hoarfrost in Michigan, apples in Ohio, pumpkins in Illinois. Red moon under the St. Louis arch.

Like a fulcrum between the flatness and variety stands another Midwestern quality—"middleness." Among the five major sections of the United States, only this one touches all the others—the East, the South, the Southwest, and the West. That factor, plus an unrivaled system of watercourses, roads, rail lines, and airports, have made this the hub of the nation's transportation and distribution networks. The westward-creeping population center of America is also in the Midwest: by the 1970s it had reached St. Clair County, Illinois. The Census Bureau defines it as "the point at which an imaginary flat, weightless, and rigid map of the United States would balance if weights of identical value were placed on it so that each weight represented the location of one person."

This notion of balance is deeply relevant to the Middle West. Rooted, sensible, and devoted, the section acts as a kind of balance wheel for America's more exotic tendencies. In industry and agriculture the Midwest is big, basic, and remarkably well balanced. In football, the Big Ten rely not on a flashy aerial attack, but on ball control and a basic ground game. A salesman covering this territory will tell you that a patient, sincere, feet-on-the-ground approach sells better than a New York-style facade. Toughened by adversity, but seldom either paralyzed by tradition or mesmerized by growth, the Midwest will always look for the *workable* solution.

The Midwestern farmer, however individual he may be, is a man of many skills. Not the least of these is money management: a capitalist in bib overalls, he constantly figures cost-effectiveness and sometimes trades on the commodities exchanges. In this he is very different from most other farmers in the world, who constitute a peasant class. As a family farmer, he is also distinct from the plantation owners of the Old South or the corporate agriculturalists of Hawaii and California. Neither peasant nor planter, he possesses many attributes of both. He belongs, in short, to the same broad middle class as the local banker who lends him money, the dealer who sells him seed, and the café owner who serves him coffee.

Every human community, of course, makes its social distinctions. In small towns, as we shall see, these often show up in who belongs to which church. The farmers, too, compete in subtle ways. But democracy is such a persistent value in the rural Midwest that no one likes to spell out these differences, especially to an outsider.

"Aren't people more or less the same everywhere?" The question is a very American one. It is rooted in the glowing faiths of the middle century—the nineteenth—when the nation was new, and the Midwest was being settled. In the cities, social distinctions would widen and class strife would appear: cities everywhere tend to become like cities everywhere. Not so the countryside. Where the ground remains uncovered, the roots are more visible.

Chapter Two

The Seeds

WHEN THE NATION WAS BORN, the Middle West was still virgin territory. The Indians, like the passenger pigeons and prairie fires, lived there within nature's balance. A few Jesuits, French traders, and others had long since built small outposts; and a tiny stream of settlers had just begun to trickle toward the Ohio Valley. But the land's real treasures remained her own.

Then, with dazzling suddenness, the Midwest was wedded to the strapping young U.S.A. In less than a century her abundant earth would be seeded with an entirely new character. And she, in turn, would transform America.

The time was ripe. Throughout the western world it was a century of ferment, marked by deep changes in man's relation to man, and in his relation to nature. The old social orders were breaking up. Progress and individualism were in the air. While poets sang the virtues of undefiled nature, scientists penetrated its secrets and industrialists bent it to their will. It was a century of energetic forward motion, and nothing summed this up better than the image of the locomotive hurtling onto the prairies.

Polperro House at Mineral Point, Wisconsin, a mid-nineteenth century Cornish miners' village

If the Middle West was a fertile field, planted in a remarkable season, its human character sprang from the seeds themselves—the pioneers.

Their odyssey, beginning in the years preceding the Revolutionary War, forms a uniquely American tale.

While the Colonies grew restless under the rule of England, a new breed of Americans were already chafing under the dominion of the eastern establishment. Hardy, independent, and God-fearing, the backwoods farmers shunned the aristocratic and increasingly commercial atmosphere of the Atlantic seaboard. Seeking good land they could afford, these restless pioneers scattered ever deeper into the hinterland until they found the way west blocked by the Allegheny Mountains.

The thirteen Colonies had long been clustered into three broad groupings. The villages of Puritan New England stressed piety, equality, and conformity. In Virginia and the Carolinas, a rather fluid Anglican aristocracy presided over a plantation culture supported by slavery. Based around Quaker Philadelphia were the Middle Colonies, comprising a mixed society noted for its pragmatism and tolerance. Communication among the Colonies was quite limited, for they remained separate social and political entities. However, the farmers of the interior, cut off from the restraints of the traditional East, moved freely across colonial boundaries. Facing common problems of survival on a primitive frontier, the backwoodsmen needed no declaration of independence to evolve an informal democracy of their own.

Although the eastern establishment feared these "radicals" and "savages," its efforts to bring them under control only created lasting resentments on both sides. Pressures on the frontiersmen kept increasing. By the late eighteenth century, America's population was doubling every generation. For the men of the wilderness, the message was clear: they would have to cross the mountains. In the fertile, well-watered Ohio and Mississippi valleys they could hope to find true independence and prosperity.

Yet the rugged Alleghenies were more than a physical barrier. The French had spent a century and a half taking possession of the huge interior of the continent, from Canada to the Gulf of Mexico, only to be expelled from the lands east of the Mississippi by the British in 1763. In the generation after that, a few colonial Americans had ventured through the mountain passes. But settlers had been inhibited from entering the West in any great numbers by a host of forces: foreign intrigue, governmental and land problems, the Revolutionary War, a head-on clash of powerful interests such as fur traders and land speculators, and—above all—the deep-seated hostility of the Indians. By 1795, however, skillful diplomacy, coupled with General "Mad

Split-rail fence, Lincoln's New Salem, Illinois

Anthony" Wayne's military triumphs over the Indians in Ohio and Indiana, had led to a series of treaties that effectively cleared away most of these barriers.

The rush was on, and it was soon accelerated by the policies of a President who was strongly sympathetic to the West and to the small farmer. Most significantly, in 1803 Thomas Jefferson negotiated the Louisiana Purchase, an act of diplomacy that brought the huge, unexplored territory from the Mississippi to the Rockies under the U.S. flag. Although he himself was an aristocratic planter and politician, Jefferson believed the family farmer to be the moral backbone of the nation. He wrote:

Those who labour in the earth are the chosen people of God, if ever he had a chosen people, whose breasts he has made his peculiar deposit for substantial and genuine virtue. It is the focus in which he keeps alive the sacred fire, which otherwise might escape from the face of the earth. Corruption of morals in the mass of cultivators is a phaenomenon of which no age nor nation has furnished an example. It is the mark set on those, who not looking up to heaven, to their own soil and industry, as does the husbandman, for their subsistence, depend for it on the casualties and caprice of customers. Dependence begets subservience and venality, suffocates the germ of virtue, and prepares fit tools for the designs of ambition . . . While we have land to labour, then, let us never wish to see our citizens occupied at a workbench, or twirling a distaff. Carpenters, masons, smiths, are wanting in husbandry; but, for the general operations of manufacture, let our workshops remain in Europe. It is better to carry provisions and materials to workmen there, than bring them to the provisions and materials, and with them their manners and principles. The loss by the transportation of commodities across the Atlantic will be made up in happiness and permanence of government. The mobs of great cities add just so much to the support of pure government, as sores do to the strength of the human body. It is the manners and spirit of a people which preserve a republic in vigour.

This pastoral, agrarian ideal was not original with Jefferson. It derived in a general way from the growing romantic movement, and more specifically from his own reading of pastoral poets as far back as Virgil and the Greeks. But it was Jefferson who sounded it most ringingly to American ears, and who translated it into a policy of westward expansion. Predictably, it was welcomed by an electorate 90 per cent of whom lived on the land. The Jeffersonian blend of rural morality and agrarian economics would run like a refrain through America's formative middle century—and persist to this day in the mind of many a Midwestern farm boy.

Shouldering their axes and long rifles, the men of the back country trudged west into the mountain passes. Despite their readiness to mingle, striking regional variations had developed along the thousand-mile Allegheny frontier—character differences that were about to be replanted in Midwestern soil.

It was in the North that continuity with the coastal settlements had been most clearly maintained. Life in the colonial hinterlands had continued to center around New England–style villages, carefully laid out in advance of their occupancy. While the roughhewn uplanders might startle their Puritan forebears with their nonconformist ways, they remained Yankees at heart. Now, heading for the Middle West, whole congregations or villages would sometimes march together, "intact with pastors and school masters and deacons," and solemnly bound by a civil and religious covenant. Thus did Norwalk, Connecticut, father Norwalk, Ohio; Granville, Massachusetts, conceive Granville, Ohio; and Pittsfield, Massachusetts, spawn Pittsfield, Illinois. The fine farmlands available in the virgin wilderness remained, of course, the great attraction. But mixed with this motive, for many New Englanders, was a desire for moral purification through a shared commitment to "begin again." Remarking on the founding of Hudson, Ohio, by zealots from New Haven, historian Richard Wohl explains that while Hudson "might, in many ways, be more primitive and ruder than New Haven, yet, in another way, it was the Connecticut original in purer form, undiluted and undistracted by modern worldliness and the change encroaching on the east."

By contrast, the interior regions of the middle states and the South had been peopled mainly by immigrants. In Pennsylvania and New York lived a hardworking, peace-loving group of Germans known as the Pennsylvania Dutch. Skilled, efficient farmers, they had arrived penniless, but soon prospered; and they would give the agricultural frontier such useful concepts as the covered wagon and the large cattle barn. Also pouring into the New World through the ports of Pennsylvania was a tide of Scotch-Irish—discontented Scotsmen who had previously moved to northern Ireland. When they reached the back country, some of these settled near the Germans. But more were deflected south and west, particularly into western Virginia and Carolina, which, unlike New England, had offered freedom of worship to Presbyterians. As historian Ray Allen Billington observed, "the Scotch-Irish built their crude cabins, raised their large crops of children and their small crops of corn, and succumbed rapidly to the forest environment. 'The clothes of the people,' wrote a visitor to one of their villages, 'consist of deer skins, their food of Johnycakes, deer and bear meat.' . . . Bold, devout, shrewd men, hating Indians and easterners with impartial vigor, and determined to 'keep the Sabbath and everything else they could lay their hands on,' the Scotch-Irish made ideal pioneers in the westward march."

It was these backwoodsmen who first breached the mountain barrier in force. The vital Cumberland Gap had been discovered in 1750, and for years glowing reports had been filtering back from lusty adventurers who loved the abundant woodlands of "Ol' Kaintuck." One party, suddenly stumbling onto Daniel Boone, had found him "lying on his back and singing so loudly for the sheer joy of his wilderness life that they believed when they first heard him they had discovered some strange new animal." Paced by the intrepid Scotch-Irish, land seekers hurried through the Gap in such numbers that by 1800 there were already 220,000 of them in Kentucky. More swarmed across the fertile plains and forests of Tennessee.

Yet, though southern Appalachia still lilts to their folk songs, these roving frontiersmen were not the ones to put down deep roots. In

Thomas Hutchins conducted an official survey of the Midwestern wilderness, and he published his reports in 1778. His map of southwestern Illinois showed the area's early French influence.

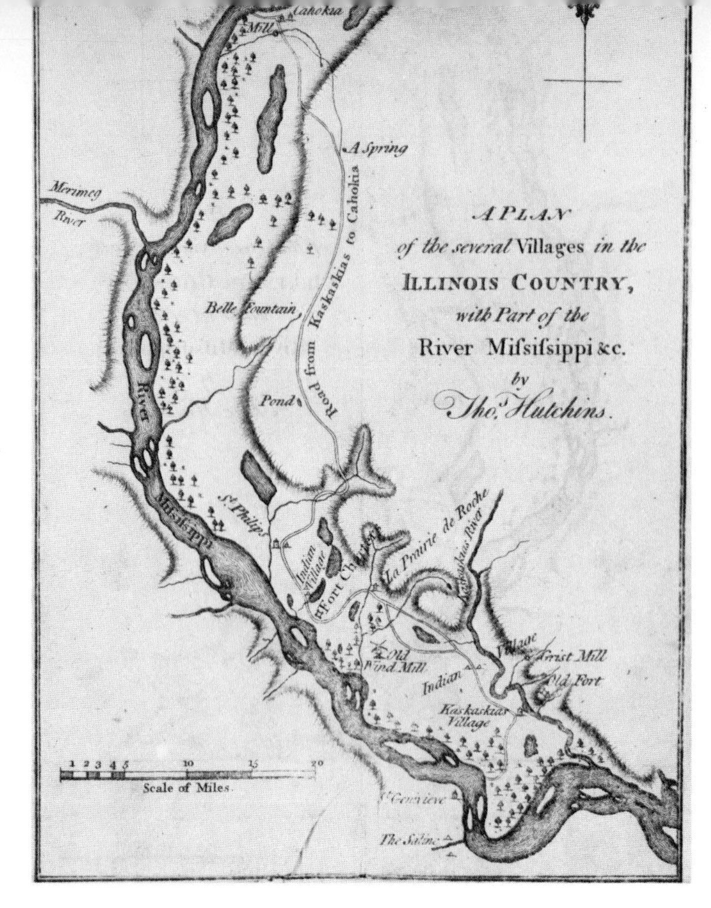

their tiny cabins in the woods, they might remain two or three years with only the vaguest notion of where they were. Then, instead of continuing to expand their small clearings, they would suddenly pull up stakes on word of better prospects somewhere else. "We lived the same as the Indians," remembered Abe Lincoln's cousin, Dennis Hanks, who must have seen many of the red men. Like many another fervent westerner, he added, " 'Ceptin' we took an interest in politics and religion." Soon these Kentucky pioneers were forging northward over the Ohio River at such a rate that Ohio's population zoomed from a mere 45,000 in 1800 to over 250,000 twelve years later. In 1816, when little Abe was nine, his family, too, made the move across the broad, sparkling river.

Since the dense hardwood forests north of the Ohio were still peppered with hostile Indians, few of the early settlers dared to venture very far from the riverbanks. Yet they gravitated north along Ohio tributaries such as the Muskingum, the Scioto, the Miami, and the Wabash, with its old French settlement at Vincennes. Others, following the Ohio southwest, reached its junction with the Mississippi and turned north. Along the shores they found enfeebled colonies of French settlers, and small trading villages like Cahokia, Kaskaskia, and Ste. Genevieve. But for the ambitious American farmers, the prime destination was a rich floodplain, south of the village of St. Louis, which became known as "the American bottom." As a result of this spreading influx, Indiana, with a population of 25,000, and Illinois, with 13,000, qualified as separate territories before 1812.

Yet Ohio was still the center of activity. As if to counter the invasion from the south, a log village in Pennsylvania, calling itself Pittsburgh, dispatched an endless flotilla of picturesque flatboats down the Ohio. Bobbing slowly past the Yankee townsite of Marietta, the French settlement at Gallipolis, and the little port of Cincinnati, those boxlike vessels carried entire farm families with their cows and horses, their butter churns and haystacks and fluttering clotheslines. But because the shallow flatboat was dependent on the current for propulsion, it could only be used going downstream. So, at the end of its journey, the clumsy craft was taken apart and its boards and nails used to build the family's first home in the wilderness.

Big commercial flatboats, loaded with oak barrel staves and farm produce or whiskey, also floated by. Manning the sweeps were tough river traders, their minds on the profitable markets of New Orleans.

Less professional travelers were frequently awestruck by the unspoiled beauty of the Ohio. Wrote one: "Sometimes we were in the vicinity of dark forests, which threw a solemn shade over us as we glided by; sometimes we passed along overhanging banks, decorated with blooming shrubs which timidly bent their light boughs to sweep the passing stream; and sometimes around the shore of an island which tinged the water with a reflected landscape." Others enthused over the effects of moonlight on the water and the deep shadows cast by the bluffs. Along the banks bright redbud caught the traveler's eye, and below the Scioto there were wild cane and pecan. Thomas Ashe, an Englishman, called this "the most beautiful river in the universe."

And the Ohio teemed with life. Kentucky cardinals seemed to converse with one another across the broad stream. Vividly hued Carolina paroquets flitted among the tree branches. Buffalo were a common sight, especially on the Kentucky side, where they loved the wild peas, rushes, and salt licks; sometimes they would swim out to small islands to munch on the lush new grass. Near Marietta, boatmen reported the river to be "completely overrun with immense quantities of black and gray squirrels," which, migrating from shore to shore, sometimes scampered up the oars to rest on the boats. One diarist recorded that "the flocks of wild geese and ducks which swarm upon the stream, the vast number of turkies, partridges, and quail we saw upon the shore, and the herds of deer or some other animals of the forest darting through the thickets afforded us constant amusement."

Of increasing importance, as well, was a man-made artery known as the National Road. Farmers and merchants in both the East and the West had early pressed for better two-way transportation across the Alleghenies. In 1802 Congress had passed the Ohio Enabling Act, which set aside 5 per cent of the proceeds of its Ohio land sales for road building. In 1806, after much politicking, Baltimore was selected as the eastern terminus of a new east-west route that would pass through Cumberland and Washington on its way to Wheeling. A dozen years later, the road was carrying the U.S. Mail and much more. As the interior of Ohio began developing, the National Road was extended to Zanesville and on to Columbus. Dotted with rough-and-ready taverns, it had reached Indianapolis by 1850 and was soon pushed to Vandalia, then the capital of Illinois. Primarily a freight route for the stout old Conestoga wagons, the National Road was gradually eclipsed by the railroads. In the automobile age it perked up as bustling U.S. Route 40. After the opening of Interstate 70, however, the venerable artery settled back again to become a quiet country lane.

All through the nineteenth century, the great waves of westward movement would suddenly be interrupted. Some of these slackenings were caused by financial distress—as during the depressions of the late 1830s and early 1870s. At other times, political events would temporarily stem the flow of home seekers.

One such event was the War of 1812. The red man had been learning to resent the white for many reasons. Underlying all of them was the loss of his hunting grounds, which spelled the loss of his whole way of life. If the Indian had to choose, he much preferred the trappers and fur traders to the farmers. The woodsmen merely used the forests; the conquering settlers cut them down. The British, for their part, were only too happy to make common cause with the natives in order to defend their own lucrative Great Lakes fur trade from the threat of advancing settlement. Challenged by the Indians and British, the Americans rallied around William Henry Harrison in a series of indecisive engagements in northern Indiana, northern Ohio, and southeastern Michigan. Finally the Indian leader Tecumseh was killed in battle, and the British were driven into Canada. The American triumph was unofficial but effective. It reopened the Midwest, and in particular it cleared the north-central portion for settlement.

Held back for three years, a tidal wave of impatient pioneers now

William Horrell

Junction of the Ohio and Mississippi Rivers, showing Missouri at lower left and top; Cairo, Illinois, at center; and Kentucky at extreme right

flooded across the Alleghenies. This tide, too, would ebb, but never for long. So vast were the Midwest's untapped resources—and so persistent were the forces prompting thousands to flee the East, the South, and Europe—that for two generations the heartland drew unprecedented numbers of settlers. Land developers and steamboat agents, revivalists and abolitionists, town boosters and Jeffersonian idealists—all painted such rainbows over the upper Mississippi Valley that in the years preceding the Civil War it became, for many, the resplendent "Garden of the World." The aggressive frontiersmen systematically shoved the Indian, the buffalo, and the frontier itself toward the Mississippi, and then across it, and across Iowa and Missouri to the very edge of the Great Plains. Behind them, the land-hungry settlers flooded in. By 1840 they comprised fully one third of the American population.

The Midwest was hurrying from infancy to muscled adolescence.

In its first years, this onrush was not greatly different from the influx that had preceded the War of 1812. Southern uplanders, still in the majority, filled the bottomlands of the unglaciated southern counties, then began overflowing into the forested hills and uplands between the river valleys, especially in Indiana and Illinois.

Instinctively, the southerner trusted the dappled forest but feared the cold glare of the open prairie, which looked to him like a greatly magnified Kentucky "barren." Not only did the forest provide such basics as fuel, water, shelter, and abundant game, but backwoods wisdom had taught the buckskinned pioneer to judge the fertility of the soil by the kinds of trees it grew. His aim was self-sufficiency, rather than cash profits. And so, once the hard, familiar work of chopping and girdling the trees, burning the stumps, and splitting the rails was accomplished, he tended to adopt an easygoing way of life.

A wry humorist, he loved fiddling, dancing, storytelling, corn whiskey, and horse trading. His attitude toward education ranged from indifference to sarcasm. Yet he might convert to one of the fundamentalist sects sweeping the West, such as the Disciples of Christ, a Baptist offshoot. Liking his religion simple and emotional, he might herd his

Nineteenth century emigrants descending the Ohio on a flatboat

family many miles across the rough countryside to experience the shoutings and seizures of a torchlit camp meeting. With equal enjoyment he listened to the spreadeagle oratory of stumping political candidates. He moved frequently and took few earthly possessions with him. But his mind was richly embroidered with forest lore. As Walter Havighurst wrote:

> In the twilit country superstitions flourished. Prairie people would never have as many dreads and omens as those of forest settlers. A dog crossing a hunter's path meant an aimless hunt and an empty-handed return to the clearing—unless a man hooked his fingers together and pulled until the dog disappeared. Hogs must be slaughtered in the waxing of the moon or the bacon would shrivel. A bird alighting on a window ledge, a new moon seen over the shoulder, a dog baying at an old diminished moon, a cough of a horse, the sight of a sloughed snakeskin or a dead snake—these common things were freighted with good and evil. Signs of the moon governed all planting. There were strong forces in the wild land; by signs and gestures people hoped to enlist or appease them.

Today, the southern forester scarcely survives in pure form. Yet the lower edge of the Middle West is still tinctured with his spirit—especially in the unglaciated hill country of Indiana, Illinois, and Missouri. Traveling south, you begin feeling it about where the cafés start serving apple butter and homemade biscuits-and-gravy. Even to the north, you occasionally hear of a little band of hillbilly types, getting by on a subsistence level somewhere beyond the outskirts of town, and, as one lady remarked, "doin' voodoo and all that funny stuff in the woods." The same lady could remember being terrified, as a child in the 1920s, by the sight of burning crosses in central Illinois.

From the first, the strenuous-minded northerners who guided their flatboats down the Ohio found the backwoodsmen to be shiftless, superstitious no-counts. The southerners returned the compliment by calling the Yankees cold and greedy, dull talkers, and obsessed with "improving" everything. While the southerners still held sway in the Illinois legislature, they took a swipe at the invading Yankee peddlers by charging them fifty dollars for a license to sell clocks—this at a time when a liquor license went for only two dollars.

One Yankee answer was to maintain quiet moral superiority—as one guidebook put it, to "mingle freely and unsuspiciously with his neighbors, and while he sinks his manners to their level, strive to bring up their habits, by successful example, to the New England standard."

In the meantime, the Yankee might hope to overcome the listless, thriftless infidel by sending for more of his own breed. In 1834, the Reverend Moses H. Wilder, of the village of China, in southern Indiana, flashed this plea eastward:

We want 3 intelligent Pious Farmers who love souls to emigrate and settle among us. One could buy a farm now owned by a Baptist Universalist drink[ing] Preacher who is a deadly enemy to everything like improvement price say $500. Another could in another neighborhood purchase a farm now owned by a *campbelite* and when he moves away their strength is gone in the neighborhood—$600.

All this was but a symptom of a deeper struggle which had, in a sense, begun two centuries earlier among the Stuartists and Cromwellians. The Scotch-Irish southerner lived in a warm world of family ties and emotional coloration, centered on his self-contained homestead. But the enterprising Yankee, to whom "a friend is more valuable than a relative," envisioned a rational world of contractual relationships, in which the farmer became a unit of specialized production in the widening web of a commercial society. The opposing styles would interpenetrate in a thousand subtle ways as the Midwestern character gradually jelled.

Even today, this sometime marriage of styles can be detected in the differing words Midwesterners use. Northern terms like "pail," "range," and "sweet corn" are typical of Michigan and Wisconsin, and of the northern counties of Ohio, Indiana, and Illinois. But as you move south, these words are gradually replaced by "bucket," "stove," and "roasting ear." More precisely, speech experts have found that three broad bands of word usage, stemming from the old colonial groupings, cover the whole eastern half of the United States. It was because the westering migrants tended to keep to their original zones of latitude that the speech areas of the eastern seaboard were carried into the Middle West. But, as we have seen, some mixing also occurred, particularly in the middle zone. And as the pioneers pushed farther west, there was more mingling of peoples and their words.

Beyond the Mississippi, real confusion sometimes sets in. A South Dakota housewife admits, "I just use *quilt.* I know one of 'em is supposed to be a comforter, but I never know which one." Occasionally, one researcher, after being told by a husband that the thing you fry eggs in is a frying pan, would hear the wife call from the kitchen, "No, it ain't. It's a skillet."

In states like Indiana, where the northern and southern styles fought it out for dominance, word usage may still carry important overtones. Terre Haute is an interesting case because it sat astride two "middle" migration routes, the National Road and the Wabash River. Midland words therefore tend to predominate, but there is a plentiful admixture, as well, of northern and southern forms. As a sign of which group gained the upper hand in central Indiana, Terre Haute's current system of social stratification, like that of some other mid-sized Midwestern communities, decrees that the Yankee dialect is prestigious, the southern one inferior.

Many Indianans, on the other hand, are proud of that certain "backwoodsiness" implied in the word "Hoosier." For example, W. L. McAtee compiled an "affectionate and reverent" lexicon of terms he remembered from his Grant County boyhood of the 1890s. These include country pronunciations like "agin," "allus," and "ketch"; words like "clum" (climbed), "bullyrag" (to domineer), and "piece" (short distance); and expressions such as "another county heard from" (a comment on an unexpected remark, especially from a child), and "Anyone who would kick about that would kick about being hung."

In 1817, an observer gave an unforgettable account of the river of humanity pouring west across Pennsylvania:

Old America seems to be breaking up and moving westward. We are seldom out of sight, as we travel on this grand track towards the Ohio, of family groups, behind and before us, some with a view to a particular spot, close to a brother, perhaps, or a friend who has gone before and reported well of the country. Many, like ourselves, when they arrive in the wilderness, will find no lodge prepared for them.

A small wagon (so light that you might almost carry it, yet strong enough to bear a good load of bedding, utensils, and provisions, and a swarm of young citizens, and to sustain marvelous shocks in its passage over these rocky heights) with two small horses, sometimes a cow or two, comprises their all, excepting a little store of hard-earned cash for the land office of the district, where they may obtain a title for as many acres as they possess half-dollars, being one-fourth of the purchase money. The wagon has a tilt, or cover, made of a sheet or perhaps a blanket. The family are seen before, behind, or within the vehicle, according to the road or weather or perhaps the spirits of the party . . . Often the back of the poor pilgrim bears all his effects, and his wife follows, naked-footed bending under the hopes of the family . . .

This influx through Pennsylvania and New York was swelling so dramatically that by the 1830s the northerners had begun to outnumber the southerners. Whether they came from the tired soils of the midland states, or from the stony fields of New England, these migrants soon proved that they were more interested in "civilizing" the land—and making profits on it—than were the roughhewn uplanders. They were also less afraid to locate out on the edges of the forest and in those "oak openings" and other zones where trees and grasslands mingled. At first the little prairie patches served as grazing spots that everyone used in common. Then, little by little, the grass succumbed to the plow. But this advance was soon halted by the true, open prairie, a treeless grassland that widened like a wedge from western Ohio across Indiana, Illinois, Iowa, and the edges of the states bordering Iowa. Though rich, the prairie sod was so entangled with tough grassroots that it discouraged cultivation until after the dissemination of John

Deere's self-scouring steel plow in the late 1840s. The pioneers who gazed out at the sea of grass were equally disheartened by its lack of wood, water, transportation, and protection from the howling winter winds.

Since the Sauk, the Sioux, and other northern tribes had continued to retreat westward, the settlers' attention turned to the good farmlands lying north of the open prairies. A significant factor in this northward shift was the opening of the Erie Canal from the Hudson River to Lake Erie: travelers preferred the Erie packet boat to the grueling Appalachian trek or the perilous float down the Ohio. By 1833, a regular passenger line plied Lake Erie from the bustling port of Buffalo to the suddenly resuscitated French village of Detroit. The population of Michigan grew a startling seventeenfold during this decade, and those counties of Ohio, Indiana, and Illinois that adjoined the Great Lakes grew twice as fast as those touching the Ohio River. The soggy village known as Chicago housed fewer than two hundred souls in 1833. Then suddenly, in that one year, it was overrun by twenty thousand anxious emigrants on their way to the virgin farmlands. Seized with visions of future greatness, speculators sent land values skyrocketing. More and more jerrybuilt stores kept popping up along Clark and Lake streets. Jammed with ships, the Chicago River docks were a jumble of grain elevators, lumber yards, factories, shipyards, and warehouses which had sprung up to handle the massive resources of the new inland empire. Already, Chicago was on the way to becoming the largest grain market in the world.

From the Great Lakes ports the migrants fanned out into the hinterlands. The prized spots for these northern pioneers were not the forests but the river valleys—such as the prairies near the Rock and Illinois rivers in Illinois, and the oak openings and "prairie rondes" of Michigan's Kalamazoo Valley. Conservative New Englanders found southern Michigan especially attractive. While many moved as individuals or single families, some still brought their community with them. Vermontville, Michigan, was an example. Planning a "pious migration," its Vermont-born residents had earlier drawn up a constitution specifying such villagey appointments as a parsonage and a New England town square. A scheme to distribute land among the settlers imposed strict limits on the size of anyone's plot. And before an applicant was allowed to join the covenant, he had to survive a stiff-necked inquiry into his moral character. Perhaps these careful Vermonters reasoned that Providence had spread that ocean of grass farther south

Wedding party on the Wabash and Erie Canal, 1872

in order to insulate their prim towns from the sulphurous emotings of the southern backwoodsmen.

Another choice locale for New Englanders was the northeastern corner of Ohio, known as the Western Reserve. Originally owned by the State of Connecticut, it had been partly deeded to homesteaders whose coastal properties had been ruined by the British during the Revolutionary War. The rest was sold to a speculative land company, which promoted and developed the region. Today, you can still see Connecticut repeated in the town squares, white churches, and charming homes of villages like Painesville and Chardon. But the delicate princess of Federal architecture east of the Appalachians is the First Congregational Church at Tallmadge, near Akron. It was built between 1822 and 1825 by Lemuel Porter, a talented joiner who had emigrated from Waterbury, Connecticut, some years earlier.

Still another landmark of the Western Reserve is Oberlin, one of the string of small, distinguished liberal arts colleges including Kenyon, Earlham, Wabash, Beloit, and Grinnell, that grace the upper Midwest. Founded by a Presbyterian preacher and an Indian missionary in 1833, it blended a vigorous type of Calvinism with shockingly liberal positions on important issues of the day. Shortly after its establishment, Oberlin became the first coeducational college in the world. And it displayed its abolitionist sentiments in no uncertain terms by opening its doors to Negroes.

The courage of that stand in the 1830s can be gauged by the virulence of the opposing view. In 1836 the Reverend Elijah P. Lovejoy was hounded out of St. Louis for publishing editorials against slavery. Moving to Alton, Illinois, he tried to remind his readers that the Constitution guaranteed freedom of the press. Angry mobs replied by smashing Lovejoy's presses three times. Finally, in 1839, they murdered him.

Among the earliest and most consistent opponents of slavery were the Quakers. Themselves persecuted by the Puritans when they attempted to settle in New England in the seventeenth century, the Quakers became concentrated in the Midlands, but later spread throughout the Colonies. During the eighteenth century they became somewhat ingrown—withdrawing from worldly diversions, insisting on plain speech, dressing quaintly, and willingly becoming known as a "peculiar people." By the early nineteenth century, however, many were beginning to emerge from clannishness into activism. One large group in Virginia and the Carolinas became disgusted by slavery and abruptly sold all their lands, worth up to twenty dollars an acre, for less than six. They moved to Ohio's Miami River Valley, and from there many pushed on to the Whitewater Valley around Richmond, Indiana. Quakers kept pouring west from all the eastern states until, by 1845, Pennsylvania, which had once counted over fifty thousand of them, was down to less than nine thousand, and Indiana, after gaining over thirty thousand, could claim the largest Quaker Yearly Meetings in the world.

In the 1820s these gentle activists organized the Underground Railroad, which would eventually funnel some 75,000 slaves to freedom. From three crossing points on the Ohio River, three "main lines" converged at a "grand central station"—the home of Levi and "Aunt Katie" Coffin in Fountain City, a Quaker village just north of Richmond. Well preserved down to the present day, and furnished in the style of the original period, this modest, two-story brick dwelling is well worth a visit. Coffin himself recalled his twenty years as "station master" with humor and fondness:

> We knew not what night or hour of the night we would be aroused by a gentle rap at the door. That was the signal announcing the arrival of a train of the Underground Railway, for the locomotive did not whistle or make any unnecessary noise. I have often been awakened by this signal, and sprang out of bed and opened the door. Outside in the cold or the rain, there would be a two-horse wagon loaded with fugitives, perhaps the greater part of

them women and children. I would invite them in a low tone to come in, and they would follow me into the darkened house without a word, for we knew not who might be watching or listening. When they were all safely inside and the door fastened I would cover the windows, strike a light and build a good fire. By this time my wife would be up and preparing victuals for them, and in a short time the cold and hungry fugitives would be made comfortable.

But whether, and how, to admit blacks into Indiana, Illinois, and Ohio were hot issues before 1860. Since slavery had been forbidden by the Northwest Ordinance of 1787, that question did not arise here as it did in the explosive debate over Kansas and Nebraska. Nonetheless, there were some indentured servants north of the Ohio. And by the 1850s, southern-drawling white farmers, fearing black competition, persuaded the legislatures of Indiana and Illinois to bar Negro emigration into those states.

But the idea that the WASPish character of today's Corn Belt could be traced to such actions seems a dubious one. Not until long after the Civil War were southern blacks prompted to move north in any important numbers. By then, the great magnet was not the farm but the factory. Particularly after 1900, the Negroes, like southern whites and other groups, sought jobs in the dockyards, blast furnaces, and production lines of thriving industrial towns like Cleveland and Toledo, Gary and Detroit. During World War I, with the factories roaring but manpower drained by mobilization, over 65,000 blacks came to Chicago alone. Amid job discrimination and woeful overcrowding, the black ghettos stimulated and sheltered an intense subculture, many of whose values, experiences, and achievements would remain the very opposite of the middle-class prairie dweller's. Without Chicago's wailing Black Belt, or Kansas City's swinging honky-tonk section, American music could not have become the distinctive force it is today. Sadly, though, urban friction would continue to spark ethnic conflict in the big-shouldered cities of the industrial heartland.

Meanwhile, Europeans were flowing into America at a rate that would soon make their population movement the largest ever known. In the century following the Napoleonic wars, Britain and the Continent suffered through agricultural depressions, a population explosion,

and social and political turmoil. Such difficulties prompted many to ask whether a better life might not be available elsewhere. And when letters began to arrive from friends and relatives in America, glowingly describing the opportunities there, the temptation was hard to resist—especially when a check or ticket had been enclosed. Thus, the stream fed on itself, until it swelled into a tidal wave. By the time the American floodgates banged shut in the 1920s, some 35 million Europeans had reached our shores—over four times the population of the United States when the era began in 1815. During that expansive century, the old colonial stock was itself quite prolific. But the young immigrants were even more so: and the result has been that over half the blood now flowing in American veins derives from them.

Emerson's remark that "Europe extends to the Alleghenies, while America lies beyond," was prophetic. For it was the Middle West, more than any other section, whose formative years coincided with the Great Migration. Crying out for strong arms and hopeful hearts, its fields, forests, mines, factories, and towns became a mecca to millions of those who had come to the United States seeking a better life.

Like the earlier pioneers, they moved in distinct waves, each greater than the one before. Midwestern immigrant farmers occupied Ohio in the 1830s; Missouri, Illinois, and Wisconsin in the 1840s; and Michigan, Iowa, and Minnesota in the 1850s and 1860s. The government's free-homestead policy attracted many immigrants onto the dry plains in the 1870s. After 1890, the closing of the land frontier combined with the soaring needs of the factories for labor to channel most of the immigrants into the booming cities.

For each one who embarked on the arduous journey, it was a momentous decision. It meant tearing oneself forever from a social fabric into which one's family had been woven for countless generations. It meant physical risks, both on the journey and after arrival, such that within three years a third of the adults who faced them would be dead. It meant, above all, a powerful faith in the future. The qualities called out by this experience would flow indissolubly into the American character, particularly into its still-molten core in the Middle West.

If the immigrant farmer was rich in traditional agricultural experience, he was poor in knowledge of the new land and its ways. For two hundred years the ax-wielding Americans had been acquiring the specialized skills and life-style needed to convert virgin territory into primitive farms. Stretching ever westward, the seemingly endless continent of available land had given them a rather offhand attitude toward any one piece of it and taught them to be highly mobile. As on all frontiers, speculation played a role, not only in the person of the professional land jobber, but in the settlers' expectation of an increase in the value of their property—through improvements, and because the whole region was becoming more settled. Yet credit was expensive, and cash was scarce. So, when the pioneer farmers were offered a good price for their land, they tended to sell and move on. And they expected their sons to do the same as the frontier advanced.

To the European, on the other hand, a plot of good earth was sacred. He wanted to plant his family on one farm forever—passing it on to his sons and their sons, and hopefully peopling many of the adjoining lands with his cousins. He had seen too many deflationary cycles to put his faith in land speculation, and the hardships of the one great move were enough. The frontier habit of "mining" the ground—maximizing quick yields with little regard for soil maintenance—seemed to him wasteful, if not downright immoral. And he had neither the desire nor the knowledge to undertake the lonely, risky job of trying to survive in the wilderness. The answer was to join the second or third rank of those going west and to buy a cleared, partly improved plot from one of the forest-slashing frontiersmen.

This, however, required money—as much as $1000—which the immigrant did not have. Standing on the wharf at New York or Philadelphia or New Orleans, he had, typically, sold his depressed holdings merely in order to get his family this far. Before he could buy that dreamed-of piece of ground in the Garden of the World, he, and perhaps his wife, would serve their American apprenticeship—toiling in a factory, serving as domestics, hiring out as forest or farm labor, or helping dig canals or lay rails to the new West. (It was no accident that the rate of Atlantic crossings was always at a peak whenever such jobs were most available.) Finally, some months or years after his arrival, the immigrant could gather up his family, his hard-won savings and his few heirlooms, and head for the Mississippi Valley. At a time when the oratory of "manifest destiny" and "progress" resounded loudly across the burgeoning continent, the humble peasant, in moving from the Old World to the New, and then from dock to farm, might thus reckon his own progress in twelve-hour days of quiet determination.

Though organized national settlement schemes seldom worked, informal ones did. To soften the culture shock, immigrants from one

Olivet Free Will Church, Carbondale, Illinois

part of the old country often gravitated to the same area of the new. Here, the native language was preserved, special help could be given to new arrivals, and familiar customs and institutions were re-established. Institutions like the immigrant churches tended, in time, to become more conservative than those in the old country. "Like a sea that tempers the heat and cold of the surrounding land," said historian Marcus Hansen, the immigrant farmers and tradesmen played a moderate, stabilizing role. In filling up the areas vacated by the turbulent front rank of settlers, and by filtering into the middle classes, they made the Midwest country more careful, sensible, and rooted—qualities that have marked it ever since.

Among the Europeans who began settling in the Valley after 1815, the English were probably the least noticed. Scattering as individuals and families throughout the settled areas, they blended easily with the colonial stock. In general, they brought more capital with them than the Continentals, and so were able to get a head start, socially as well as economically. Neither their language nor their customs set them apart, and they felt little desire to band together to preserve an immigrant culture. If their influence was subtle, it was nonetheless important: among other contributions, they brought an intelligent appreciation of the land, its flora and its fauna; and they introduced scientific farming skills unknown to the earlier settlers.

Several of the causes of European emigration had been felt first in Britain, with the result that in the generation following the War of 1812 Englishmen poured into the Mississippi Valley via Canada. Then, about 1830, the British government took measures to keep its emigrants within the Commonwealth, and for the next forty years they chose Canada, Australia, and New Zealand over the United States. Not until the 1870s and 1880s did waves of English yeomen again flow toward the American prairies, where they counteracted the deep German influence that had, by then, been spreading across the heartland.

Though the imprint of the English has been little documented, one early British settler, Morris Birkbeck, did as much to publicize life on the Illinois frontier as anyone. A prosperous and knowledgeable Surrey farmer, Birkbeck had chafed under political restraints at home. So he and his friend, George Flower, set out to reproduce a perfected form of English country life in the West.

Charles Waldack

Riverboats at Cincinnati, late nineteenth century

In 1817, they began settling a hundred-square-mile area on the edges of the thin-soiled grasslands near the junction of the Wabash and the Ohio, and several hundred of their countrymen eventually joined them. Although the English Settlement proved only a limited success, the seven books written by Birkbeck and his followers became extremely popular in both England and America and stimulated wide interest in frontier farm life. That southern Illinois had, however, been a poor place in which to introduce the English manorial system could be inferred from passages like this:

Well begins most sentences. Plunder and truck include almost every thing. A horse is generally called a creature. Beefs are cows. Toat means to carry any thing. Strait and turn in, are words they frequently use. Woman—they always call their wives their women . . .

I was lately at an auction, of a little live stock and household furniture, belonging to a person leaving this neighborhood. The auctioneer was no less a person than a justice of the peace . . . But the most striking contrast in this sale from an English one, was, the auctioneer held a bottle of whiskey in his hand, and frequently offered a dram to the next bidder. As I made some biddings, I was several times entitled to a sip out of the bottle. And though I much dislike the taste of whiskey, I took a sip for the novelty of the thing. But I found the auctioneer had taken good care to keep his company sober, by lowering his whiskey considerably with water.

Meanwhile, impoverished Irish Catholics were beginning to land on the East Coast, and in the years to follow, well over four million of them would set foot in America. Relatively few of the Irish chose to settle on the soil. Several thousands crossed the Alleghenies as unskilled labor in the mines or on dangerous, low-paid construction jobs. Of these, some did eventually settle as farmers along the canal or rail routes they had helped build, especially in northern Illinois, where part of their pay had been in land scrip. But many more gravitated to Chicago and other new population centers, where they accepted slum conditions as the price of convivial surroundings. In the process, these cities, rising precociously along the lake shores, were taking on a polyglot quality that would become a permanent part of their character. Consider, for instance, the ethnic makeup of Cleveland as late as 1940:

The white stock of native parentage comprises only a quarter of the population; 8 per cent are Negroes and the remaining 67 per cent are either foreign-born or the offspring of foreign or mixed parentage. Once almost entirely Nordic and Celtic in make-up, Cleveland was transformed by the expanding steel industry into one of the most racially diversified communities in the United States. Forty-eight nationalities have representation here; more than 40 languages are spoken in the city. First in numbers are the Czechoslovaks, followed by the Poles, Italians, Germans, Yugoslavs, Irish and Hungarians. Where they concentrate in nationality groups, their native languages are spoken almost as commonly as English. A large section on the South Side is peopled primarily by Poles and Czechoslovaks; the Yugoslavs and Lithuanians have concentrated in an area of three square miles near the lake on the East Side. Between the Flats and West 65th Street on the west side is a densely populated section containing chiefly Germans, Irish, and Roumanians. "Little Italy" lies south of Euclid Avenue just east of University Circle. The Russians and Greeks congregate principally in the vicinity of Prospect Avenue and East 14th Street, the Jews around East 105th Street north of Euclid Avenue, and around Kinsman Road west of Shaker Heights.

Among the earliest immigrants to arrive in mid-America were the persevering Germans. Whole trainloads of them rolled into Buffalo in the 1840s and 1850s to meet the Erie packet boats bound for Midwestern ports. Thousands more chugged up the Mississippi from New Orleans. By 1860 the Germans comprised nearly a third of the foreign-born in America, and in the 1910 Census 8.3 million Americans gave Germany as their country of origin. The Middle West, their prime destination, was profoundly affected by their culture and character.

It did not take the German farmer long to earn a reputation for thrift, dependability, and hard work. While his success was seldom spectacular, he never ended in the poor house, either. No land speculator, he chose his ground with a prudent eye for soils, drainage, and accessibility to existing markets. Once he had acquired land, he held to it stubbornly; if he had to sell, he would try at all costs to sell to a relative. He had the know-how for pork and beef production and the patience needed to run a successful dairy operation. De-emphasizing home comforts, he worked long hours to improve his farm. Gradually, expertly, he diversified into such activities as bee keeping, horticulture, goose fattening, nurseries, forestry, and vine culture. As early as 1835, one German settler, who had amazed his whittling-and-spitting Missouri neighbors with his industrious ways, wrote back to his homeland: "There is scarcely a farm that is not for sale, for the American farmer has no love of home, such as the German has. I am building a smokehouse, a kitchen, a milk-house over one of the excellent springs near our house, a stable for the horses and one for the cows. My American neighbors say that I am building a town."

Dorothea Lange

Many Midwestern states enacted special concessions in order to attract the hardworking Germans, and it was not long before their orderly farmsteads and businesses had become a familiar fact of Midwestern life. One area of early German influence ran west from St. Louis along the meandering Missouri. Its high bluffs and lush forests reminded settlers of the Rhine; and the little river port of Hermann became famous for its wines and music. Today, especially at *Maifest* time, visitors to Hermann still sip the local vintages, watch costumed dancers, admire the town's historic architecture, and meander through streets named for Goethe, Schiller, Gutenberg, and Mozart. In St. Louis itself the earlier French influence was gradually displaced by the culture of the Germans, who gravitated to the southern side of town. Their heirs continue to celebrate the lively German street festivals, known as *Strassenfests.*

Just across the Mississippi, more Germans concentrated around Alton and Belleville, Illinois. Farther north, others built farms and villages near the Mississippi and Illinois rivers. Chicago, too, became a center of German influence. So did Milwaukee, whose cultural flowering in the 1850s earned it the appellation "the German Athens," and whose booming beer industry soon changed the drinking habits of America. Finding Wisconsin's landscape, climate, and social atmosphere especially hospitable, German farmers gravitated to the state's forested eastern and north-central counties and led the way in establishing Wisconsin's renowned dairy industry.

Iowa and Minnesota received their German influx not long after Wisconsin did. In Michigan the Germans spread into many agricultural counties and brought their culture to the Detroit area. In Indiana, they were strong around Fort Wayne, Richmond, and Indianapolis.

But the great early center of German influence in America was Ohio. Among the first arrivals were the "Pennsylvania Dutch" Germans. Planting their sturdy farms in the well-watered Appalachian foothills below the Western Reserve, they gave their villages such names as Berlin, Strasburg, and New Schoenbrunn. Germans were also attracted to Union, Henry, Montgomery, Auglaize, and other counties. Even more remarkable than the steady progress of the farmers were the contributions of the German townspeople, who brought to Ohio a love of culture and a well-developed knowledge of industry. In a state soon to become famous for its inventors, Germans built the first iron foundries, the first woolen mills and flour mills, the first organ factory. As intellectual and educational leaders, they published high-quality newspapers and technical journals. Among their many contributions to American life, they introduced the kindergarten and taught us many of their Christmas festivities.

Less directly, but equally importantly, the stolid Germans, along with middle-class migrants from dozens of other places, helped give Ohio that feeling of levelness so appropriate to its topography. This even-keeled quality is, in fact, fundamental to the entire Midwest. Author Bentz Plagemann caught it nicely:

> Ohio is the state of middle dreams, the state of normalcy, where it is always eight o'clock on Monday morning, and the factory whistle is blowing, and the school bell is ringing . . .
>
> You sleep well in Ohio, your brother's house. You know you are safe there. Everything is under control. The foundation of the old house is dry and sound, and the roof is good, and the flashing and drain spouts and the insulation are checked every year, and the storm windows are up if it is winter, or the screens in summer, and it is all so clean, in a favorite Ohio phrase, that you could eat off the floor.

Columbus, Cleveland, Dayton, and Toledo all had strong German elements well before the Civil War. But Cincinnati, as one visitor later observed, "did not even try to assimilate its German immigrants; instead they assimilated Cincinnati."

Here the atmosphere was—and still is—as different from the rest of safe, level Ohio as one could imagine. Being the nerve center of southern, eastern, and foreign migration, and the entrepôt of the Midwest's bustling river trade, Cincinnati evolved a worldly wise character all its own. Germans in black velvet outfits, with red vests and big silver buttons, rubbed elbows with cool-eyed riverboat gamblers, runaway slaves, white-coated sausage peddlers, upcountry farmers herding their squealing pigs through the streets, and the ultra-respectable merchants and tall-hatted bankers who ran the town. By 1859 the raffish waterfront was six miles long. Up the gangplanks stomped river roustabouts, chanting their lusty dirges as they shouldered bags of flour, barrels of whiskey, and Cincinnati's number one commodity—processed pork. At night, "The city blazed with revelry. About the bright hotel district, where were held the spectacular balls of the new and old rich, were scores of casinos, gambling halls, and bagnios." With the immigrants continuing to pour off the whistling steamboats into the overcrowded slums, friction was inevitable. Below spotless hillside streets, lined with tidy German homes, were areas where murder, mayhem, and outbreaks of cholera provided a dark underbelly to Cincinnati's soaring cultural life.

After the 1870s the railroads dealt serious blows to river commerce, and the city's growth leveled off. Yet the aging River Queen, continuing to draw on the agriculture and trade of large parts of Ohio, Kentucky, and Indiana, would retain much of her sophistication. Indeed, the interdependence of the subdued, conservative countryside and its polar opposite, the glittering city, had already become a standard feature of mid-America. In the influential McGuffey Readers, which sold well over a hundred million copies before the turn of the century, this polarity was depicted in Jeffersonian terms: the city as the den of corruption, the country as the fountain of virtue. It was typical, however—and symbolic of Jefferson himself—that the American Book Company, which published the McGuffeys, chose to reside in Cincinnati.

In Chicago, meanwhile, the flurry of canal and rail building was fueling a dramatic boom. By 1848 the Illinois and Michigan Canal had made a vital splice between an important prairie artery, the Illinois River, and the Chicago River and Lake Michigan. Eastern capital moved in to construct the Rock Island Railroad, the Illinois Central, and other lines that stitched the Windy City to the Mississippi River, and eventually spread on across Iowa to the muddy Missouri, which curved west into the nation's deep interior. Other lines stretched northwest to the rich lead mining district around Galena, south toward Cairo and St. Louis, and, eventually, northwest to Minneapolis–St. Paul and thence to the Lake Superior iron-and-lumber port of Duluth. Converging on Chicago like the spokes of a wheel, these lines here met the Michigan Central and the Michigan Southern, which, in 1851–52, had raced one another across northern Indiana to make the crucial link between the north-central Midwest and the northeastern Midwest and East.

Chicago's unique capacity to interchange rail and water cargo swelled the volume of both. By 1869, more ships were calling at its harbor than at New York, Philadelphia, Baltimore, Charleston, Mobile, and San Francisco combined. A scant four decades after being incorporated as a city, Chicago had become the world's greatest grain market, lumber market, and railway center, as well as a giant nexus of wholesaling, manufacturing, and finance. Soaring from near zero in 1830 to 30,000 in 1850, and then to 300,000 in 1870, its population had already

Old Kornthal Church, near Jonesboro in southern Illinois, was built by German Lutherans in the 1850s.

passed Cincinnati's and would shortly pass that of its only other rival, St. Louis. (In 1900 it would hit 1,500,000; in 1970, 3,400,000.) Ever since the centuries of French occupation, the trade of the entire upper Mississippi Valley had tended to drain southward on the Father of Waters. Now, however, Chicago's economic magnetism far exceeded that of New Orleans. Aided by eastern capital, the energetic upper Midwest had succeeded not only in influencing the outcome of the Civil War but in reversing the commercial polarity of the nation's heartland.

Everything came by the gross in this wholesale town at the foot of Lake Michigan. In 1871, the famous Chicago Fire was reportedly felt a hundred miles across the Lake at the Dutch settlement of Holland, Michigan. Some 17,450 buildings were leveled, including the entire "Loop," or business district. But the city's go-ahead optimism was undaunted. "Think what it would have cost us to demolish all those buildings!" enthused the Chicago *Tribune.* And indeed, out of the ashes rose a new, fancier Chicago. Fashionable brownstone and granite replaced many of the former wooden structures, and before long a new generation of designers arrived to plant the seeds of modern commercial architecture: responding to the demand for maximum well-lighted space for minimum money, they invented the skyscraper. Built of steel and glass, this simple, efficient commercial building reflected the candid functionalism and raw strength of Chicago itself. The town's brash, youthful spirit was summed up by Frank Lloyd Wright: "Here," said he, "nothing stays, everything changes."

Pleasure, too, came by the gross. Scores of saloons lined the downtown streets and alleys in the 1870s. Gamblers, whores, shady politicians, and "rogues of every description" had been endemic from the beginning, and such inheritors of the tradition as Al Capone would rise to their finest hour during Prohibition, when the hardworking, hard-playing citizenry avidly patronized some seven thousand speakeasies. Known to the horrified hinterlands as "the Gomorrah of the West," Chicago chalked up yet another "world's-greatest" during the mauve era with its famous Everleigh Club, the most lavish and expensive brothel on earth. Back-slapping friendliness, lusty steakhouses, and a permanent passion for sports added to the no-nonsense masculinity of the city. While Cincinnati's culture flowed naturally from its German ancestry, hybrid Chicago first decided it needed some, then went out and negotiated for it in big batches. Unlike the skyscrapers, earth-rooted in the direct needs of a commercial town, such first-rate institutions as the University of Chicago, the Art Institute, and many others still retain a sense of being oddly superimposed on their rough-and-ready surroundings. Typical of this highly American town-building process was the career of Walter L. Newberry. He arrived in Chicago in 1833; amassed millions from land speculation, merchandising, and finance; and on his death left half his fortune for civic projects, notably the Newberry Library. Established in the booming 1880s, the Newberry now ranks with the Morgan and the Huntington as one of the top collections in the nation.

But if the uniform and conservative small towns of the prairie had needed any more evidence of their own superior morality than the pronouncements of McGuffey's Readers and the fact of the Everleigh Club, they could easily find it in the ethnic and religious diversity of teeming Chicago. Jews, for instance, flocked in from all over Europe. Encountering considerable anti-Semitism, they went ahead and succeeded anyway, built their own clubs and apartments, and often gained acceptance on the basis of their material and philanthropic accomplishments. Every other immigrant group was here, too, creating a wild babble of languages, churches, and ethnic islands dotted all over a city that would eventually cover two hundred square miles. It was a place of incredible extremes, a glittering emblem of urbanity which conservative downstate farmers still refer to as "that cancer up there."

Around the middle of the nineteenth century, homey groups like the nativists and, later, the Evanston-based W.C.T.U. began to shout that the Germans were arriving in such large numbers as to Teutonize the whole Mississippi Valley, and to convert the pristine Garden into a beer garden. Actually, however, these Bavarians, Prussians, Swiss, and other German-speaking peoples were diffusing so widely throughout the Middle West as to dilute any such cumulative effect.

The Scandinavians, on the other hand, were concentrating in the north. Certain groups had already established narrow footholds there—the Dutch in western Michigan, for instance, and the Cornish miners in Michigan's copper-rich Keweenaw Peninsula and in the lead-rich "driftless" area of northwestern Illinois and southwestern Wisconsin. Later there would be centers of Czech and Dutch influence in Iowa and Nebraska, and Poles would settle in Milwaukee, Chicago, and Detroit. But it was the Norwegians, Swedes, and Finns who cut the widest swath across the muscular north. Although fair numbers of them arrived in the 1840s and 1850s, not until after the Civil War did veritable battalions of sturdy Norsemen break into the whispering pine forests and steel-blue lake country, then spill onto the arid grasslands farther west.

Unlike the Germans, they had come from hard, meagre lands. The overwhelming majority were impoverished peasants. On arrival, few were able to purchase a ready-made farm from their savings. Fewer still could melt easily into the towns as skilled artisans or bourgeois shopkeepers. Instead, they hired their brawn to the northern mining and forest industries, which were going full blast by the seventies and eighties. The Hiawatha country was still a frontier, and in its forests the Scandinavians, more than any other immigrant group, cleared their own farms. Many kept earning wages through the bitter-cold winter months by felling the giant evergreens and skidding the heavy logs across the snow to the shrieking mills.

Socially and physically, it was a rip-roaring atmosphere. Head-on collisions of nationalities brought stern countermeasures from the managers of the mines, which were dangerous enough places without adding the threat of human violence. In a hard-drinking mining town like Ishpeming, Michigan, the brawling Irish and rawboned Swedes established Main Street as the boundary: any Swede caught west of Main was asking for trouble. And in the forests:

> . . . though the Irish fought the Swedes every year on St. Patrick's Day and Orangeman's Day and nearly every other day, they agreed on one thing: that Finns were no bloody good. When the lumbering companies first put Finns out in the woods, the other lumberjacks refused to work with them. Since sawyers always worked in pairs and the Finns were unable to get partners, they had to work as swampers, grubbing roads out of the muck, despicable work. They had to sleep in designated corners of the huge foul-smelling bunkhouses; they had to eat at the far end of the table; and all winter nobody spoke to them except to curse them. Many changed their names, but they could not change their high cheekbones, their flat foreheads, their blond hair that somehow has a different quality from the blondness of the Scandinavian. But they were a tenacious people and they hung on grimly, keeping clannishly to themselves and working in silence.

Just as hard, in another way, were the lives of those who chose the heart-rending journey to the vast grasslands of Minnesota and Dakota. No wonder these areas had been offered virtually free to homesteaders! Sweltering in the burning heat of summer, the settlers found themselves at the mercy of droughts, tornadoes, raging prairie fires, and Indian raids. In some years swarms of grasshoppers blackened the skies, devouring a whole season's crop in minutes. The possibility that people or animals might wander off and get lost was a constant worry. The pioneers' sense of foreboding was magnified by strange, towering clouds during the day, and by howling wolves at night. Malaria, cholera, and conjunctivitis stalked the little Scandinavian colonies. Worst of all were the long winters. Shivering in the confinement of their tiny sod houses and dugouts, the settlers all grew irritable. Some even went mad. Outside, their precious oxen and cattle could easily be buried under mountainous snowbanks, and so, sometimes, were the men brave enough to go looking for them. Since wooden fuel was scarce, the women and children sat by the hour feeding bits of twisted straw into the crude stoves. And the food supply was so slim that a late spring could bring on the spectre of starvation.

Yet somehow, with their Viking stamina and deep religious faith, most of the Norwegian and Swedish families managed to survive those terrible first years. Before too long, their farms in the Red River Valley and elsewhere were yielding grain on a scale unknown in the old country. Their children would hear the chug of locomotives and watch the rise of white spires over churches where the "gospel according to Martin Luther" was proclaimed in Old-World tongues. In later years these immigrants would never tire of reciting the dates of each family's arrival, how much had been accomplished the first year, the next and the next. Faith and tenacity had paid dividends, and the earliest efforts, like the oldest trunks, would seem to hold the greatest value.

Thus did the immigrants' upward mobility serve to underline the Midwestern view of life as a strenuous race, in which progress was to be won by steadfast virtue and constant energy. As the century hurried on, this ethic would be etched in the mind of every schoolchild who read McGuffey or Horatio Alger. And many years later, after the country chapels had been engulfed by suburbia, the son of a $50,000-a-year executive might astonish a comfortable European visitor by rushing out, before breakfast, to deliver newspapers.

Of the three main Scandinavian groups, the Norwegians arrived first, and stuck together the most tenaciously. In 1860 more than half of America's Norwegians lived in Wisconsin. In time, these settlements sent many other Norwegian home seekers out to Iowa and Minnesota and the Dakotas. Today, perhaps a million and a half of their descendants live north of a line from Chicago to Sioux City, Iowa. On the Great Lakes, Norwegians have predominated as ships' captains. Their folk art has always been noteworthy; one of the best places in the world to see it, together with an exceptional collection of pioneer artifacts, is at the Norwegian-American Historical Museum in Decorah, Iowa.

The Swedes arrived a little later, and in greater numbers. They spread themselves more thinly than the Norwegians, and Americanized more quickly. Down to the present day, the Swedes have shown themselves more ready to marry beyond the in-group, and to leave the farm for the town. Yet they were great farmers in the beginning, clearing or planting an estimated twelve million acres before 1925. Although small groups settled early in Wisconsin and Iowa, it was the black prairie soil of northern Illinois that, in the 1850s, drew impressive numbers of Swedish farmers to a belt running west and southwest from Chicago to the Mississippi. Towns like Galesburg, Geneva, Moline, Rock Island, Rockford, and Swedona all had strong

Precious articles in the trunks of Norwegian immigrants included a small oak loom (above) *for making garters, skirt braidings and other fancywork; a pine ale tankard* (left) *for carrying beer from the farm's brewing house to bowls on the table; and a birch spoon* (right) *for dipping porridge from the communal bowl.*

Swedish elements before the Civil War. Bishop Hill, Illinois, was the site of an interesting Swedish communal-farming experiment. Like other prairie utopias, this one ended in dissension; but its stout buildings and quaint, primitive paintings are still there to be seen.

The Finns followed the same pattern as the Norwegians and Swedes in selecting those northern parts of the Midwest that most resembled their homeland. Though the total Finnish stock in America is only about a fifth that of the Swedes, their contribution has been distinctive. Historian Carl Wittke wrote that "The hay barn, so typical of Finnish farms, is a pentagonal structure, with its sides sloping inward toward the floor, which is several feet above the ground. Between the logs that make up the floor and sides, a space of several inches is left in order to keep the hay dry and to expedite the curing process. The roof is steep and sloping, and overhangs the sides." And the Finnish bathhouses, or saunas, are still prominent in the north country. They look like small log cabins out behind the main house. A hundred years ago the sauna was often the first building to be raised—the entire family living in it until the larger home could be completed. Later, because it was so warm and clean, the bathhouse doubled as a maternity ward. The Saturday night sauna is a tradition that is staunchly preserved on Finnish farms. When you see smoke wisping out of the little chimney, you can guess that the whole family, and maybe some friends, are inside—for this is a social as well as a hygienic occasion. As a

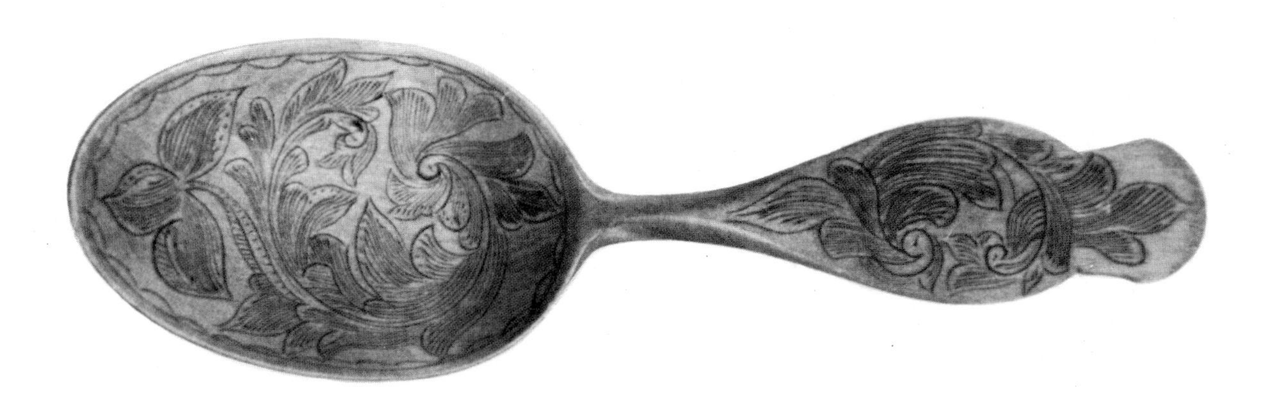

finale, the sauna takers may or may not do as their strapping forefathers did—flail one another with branches to get the blood flowing, then rush out into the subzero night, yelling with pain and glee as they tumble through the crusted snowbanks.

Besides the Swedes at Bishop Hill, and Morris Birkbeck's English Settlement farther south, several other idealistic groups chose the wide-open Midwest of the nineteenth century in which to hatch communal experiments. To Union Village, near Cincinnati, came a group of the plain, orderly folk known as Shakers. Like their eastern brethren, they built richly productive farms, but eventually dwindled in numbers because of their commitment to chastity.

The Mormons, by contrast, were actively dedicated to increasing their population through both birth and recruitment. Despite virulent opposition, they tried to settle first in Ohio, then in Missouri, and finally in Illinois. Here, beside the Mississippi, they built the prosperous town of Nauvoo, whose population leapt to 15,000 by 1844. But internal and external political problems soon proved the settlement's undoing. When anti-Mormon mobs threatened the community and murdered its leader, Joseph Smith, the Saints were forced to pull up stakes again and head west, under Brigham Young, to their final Zion of Salt Lake.

In 1818, an anti-Lutheran group of Germans established the wilderness village of Zoar in northeastern Ohio. A "sober, quiet, orderly, industrious, and thrifty people, entirely unintellectual, and satisfied with the barest necessities for life," the Zoarites plodded steadily ahead until, by 1874, their woolen factories, flour mills, and other useful properties were estimated to be worth around $3 million. The younger generation, however, lacked commitment to the enterprise, and grew so indolent and quarrelsome that the community was finally dissolved in 1898. Fortunately, quite a number of its interesting old buildings and artifacts have been rescued from oblivion by the Ohio Historical Society and are now open to the public.

Also worth a short visit are the original structures of two utopian experiments that flourished successively on the Wabash River in southwestern Indiana. The first of these, a commune of German religious dissenters led by George Rapp, lasted from 1814 to 1824. Believing that the "premillennial advent" of Christ was close at hand, the Harmonists, as they called themselves, pooled their resources and shared

J. W. McMan

equally in the results of everyone's labors. After a few years of apparent prosperity, they decided to move back to Pennsylvania, where the movement crumbled after a revolt against Rapp's coercive rule. The Wabash properties had been sold to a British idealist named Robert Owen, who re-named the settlement New Harmony. He and William Maclure, a Philadelphia educator, announced that they intended to create a center to promote "universal happiness through universal education." Backing the communal venture with their own funds, and publicizing it heavily, they succeeded in attracting to New Harmony an odd assortment of genuine scientists, ne'er-do-wells, visionaries, and other hopefuls. Some of the New Harmony ideas would later take root across the land: here, America's first free public school system, free library, kindergarten, and geological survey were established. But the scheme's vague communism was totally impractical. "Factories were mismanaged, cattle and sheep were neglected, fences were being used for firewood," recalled one participant: "the drones became the masters of the hive." Not surprisingly, Owen's utopia-on-the-Wabash collapsed within two years of its inception.

Longest lived of the communal experiments are the Amana Colonies in east-central Iowa. In 1854-55, a Lutheran splinter group of German, Swiss, and Alsatian families, calling themselves the Community of True Inspiration, bought 25,000 acres of prairie soil and began an experiment in cooperative living that would last until the 1930s. Divided into five German-style villages, the Amana Colonies stressed plainness, piety, fellowship, and enterprise. The hardworking Amanans became famous for the craftsmanship of their handmade furniture and for their woolens, smoked meats, and baked goods—products for which they are known to this day throughout the Midwest. And with the villages transformed into corporations owned by the workers, their top-quality Amana refrigerators and appliances have earned a high national reputation. Situated not far off Interstate 80, the Colonies offer today's visitor a genuine sampling of old-world *Gemütlichkeit.* There are tours of the woolen mills, winery, and crafts and antique stores; and there are big, German-style meals that include the delicious Amana-smoked pork chops, Amana-cured ham, and Amana-smoked sausage.

Thus were the many streams of humanity braiding into one wide, turbulent river. While old boundaries were already blurring in the East, and though cracks had begun to appear in the social glaciers of Europe, the Middle West was the first region whose very seeds had been carried on a tide of diversity.

Toting their roughhewn democracy over the Alleghenies, the backwoodsmen had planted a spirit of individualism on successive frontiers. Behind this outer margin of ground breakers, opportunity seekers of every stripe rushed in to claim and settle the land. Jostling one another for a place in the bountiful Garden, these migrants were so imbued with the hope of progress that many would continue to change their location. Not even the New Englanders, planning their orderly villages, or the Scandinavians, staking out their adjoining farms, could prevent others from hurrying in—or their own sons and daughters from departing. Nor could any settler foresee the widespread upheavals to be brought to the land by continuing revolutions in technology and commerce.

So the upper Mississippi Valley became a vast mixing bowl. No

Pioneer farms near Lone Rock, Wisconsin, about 1875

one group could expect to predominate for long, even on the county or township level. Therefore, few Midwestern communities acquired that singleness of character that had marked the older sections of America. Rather, the spirit of pluralism, first tried in polyglot Pennsylvania, and later codified in the Constitution, became, here, an everyday fact of life. Which seemed proof enough of Lord James Bryce's assertion that the Midwest was the most American part of America.

Within the mixing bowl, all had their own customs, their own faiths and hopes, their own special reasons for moving. Yet, whether they came from Rhode Island or Virginia or Würtemburg, all were seeking a better life. For many, this included social or religious or political freedoms. As Santayana noted, however, the American is "an idealist working on matter," and the overriding motive of these nineteenth-century pilgrims was the hope of material advancement. Amid the churning diversity, it was this drive for self-betterment that became the great common denominator.

Like the century itself, the character of the Midwesterners could be summed up in a single term: get-up-and-go. Committed to change, they valued the future over the past, the workable over the theoretical, the new frame church over the ancient cathedral. They were not the contented, the fortunate, the secure. Nor were they the totally impoverished masses, who lacked not only the means of moving, but the very belief that one could lift oneself. Asking neither privilege nor patronage, most were small capitalists at heart, preaching self-reliance and willing to take measured risks. The very decision to commit one's destiny to the nascent, unknown Mississippi Valley had taken courage enough.

And they were moral. Life was not a state of being, but a process of becoming. You were judged not by what you were, but by what you achieved. The start must be fair, as it was supposed to be in America, and the track must be fast, as it was on an unsettled continent. Then anyone could overtake anyone else—and should. Otherwise, why were you here? To be an American, and especially a westering American, was not an accident of birth, but an act of will. It proved you had the gumption to lift yourself by the bootstraps, that you were a self-made man, that you had get-up-and-go. Which meant that your visible progress and your degree of Americanism were reliable yardsticks of virtue—an eminently middle-class view that brought strong pressures to conform. Thus, while diversity was adding richness, assimilation was subtracting it.

If these social processes were as American as Thanksgiving, they were at their most vivid in the Middle West. For, like so many inland peoples, Midwesterners saw life in simple terms. To the colonial farmers who first breached the Appalachian barrier, and to the generations who followed, the widening net of laws, taxes, gray-shaded moralities, and institutional power emanating from the East seemed a betrayal of the American promise. But the pure promise might be re-seeded in the undefiled ground beyond the mountains, in isolation from that dependence that Jefferson had felt "begets subservience and venality" and "suffocates the germ of virtue." The simplicity of the hard struggle to subdue the wilderness would be matched by an equally clear view of the difference between good and bad. Clear-countenanced Midwestern farm boys and girls would learn to beware of city slickers, and the motif of virtue-in-simplicity would run deep in American mythology, from Hiawatha to Marlboro Country. So, too, in other ways, would the theme of regeneration, through a commitment to begin again on fundamentals.

For all the turbulence of its seeding, the inland Garden would retain its image as the pure heart of America.

Chapter Three

The Furrow

THE RUSH TO AMERICA and across America was accompanied by another migration which would cut even deeper into our national life: the move from farm to town. In under two centuries our society would change from 90 per cent rural to 90 per cent urban. This transition did not begin in America, nor would it end here. But only in America did it occur while the national character was still liquid and jelling. Only here would it be canonized by tales of progress from log cabin to White House, enshrined in the rural nostalgia of Henry Ford, the paintings of Norman Rockwell, the Bell Telephone "keep-in-touch" photos. While many societies seek a golden age in a partly factual, partly idealized past, only in the land of the generation gap would that past be found within a single life span. And only in this most mobile of societies would a sense of the past be so strongly equated with a sense of place.

The Middle West country has served as a major spawning ground. Typically, its farm families have been large. Yet the corn and wheat belts have led the world in ever-increasing productivity—meaning more machinery, larger fields, fewer hands. And so, steadily and inevitably, many have moved away from the farms, and from the small towns that depend on the farmers' business. Going on for well over a century, the process is an economically rational one—and yet it has left a residue of human poignancy.

Less well documented have been the stresses and benefits of the continuing infusion of country-born youths into our urban society. Unlike the blacks and poor whites leaving that other major spawning ground, the rural South, many of the sons and daughters of middle America grew up well-fed, self-confident, disciplined, educated, and strongly imbued with the work ethic. Despite the many hard times known by all farmers, those in the humid prairie states have fared better than most, so that many of the children leaving the land were able to take along some form of capital, such as shared equity in the family farm. Such a pattern, unique among rural migrants, meant that they and their children often flowed smoothly into the dominant middle class. Thus our evolving urban character has been steadily infused, not only with the ethics of achievement, but also, more subtly, with such rural traits as informality, social equality, middle-brow culture, and the habit of seeing the world in moral terms.

No wonder, then, that such canny purveyors of mass feeling as Hallmark and Ma Bell should select the golden harvests and small towns of mid-America to sum up what we were—or wish we had been and still were. Nostalgia, of course, is never entirely accurate. But it is always partly so. In the gray and glut of urbanity, we crave vividness: and the impressions of childhood are nothing if not vivid.

Fortunately, concrete glimpses of Midwestern farm life have been left us by the sons and daughters of each agricultural era.

William Nowlin, for instance, gives an unforgettable account of a boyhood spent on a pioneer farm in the woods of Michigan. In 1833, when he was twelve, his family did what so many others were doing: abandoned their stony, twenty-five-acre farm sixty miles north of New York City to strike for the hazards and rewards of life in the West. Their early experiences were the classic ones:

> Father immediately commenced cutting logs for a house. In one week he had them ready, and men came from Dearbornville to help him raise them. He then cut black ash trees, peeled off the bark to roof his house, and, after having passed two weeks under Mr. Pardee's hospitable roof, we moved into a house of our own, had a farm of our own and owed no one. Father brought his axe from New York State; it weighed seven pounds; he gave

me a smaller one. He laid the trees right and left until we could see the sun from ten o'clock in the morning till between one and two in the afternoon, when it mostly disappeared back of Mr. Pardee's woods.

Father found it was necessary for him to have a team, so we went to Detroit and bought a yoke of oxen; also, at the same time, a cow . . . we planted late corn, potatoes and garden stuff. The corn grew very high but didn't ear well. The land was indeed very rich, but shaded too much.

The next thing, after planting some seeds, was clearing a road . . . We blazed the section line trees over, cleared out the old logs and brush, then felled trees lengthwise towards each other, sometimes two together, to walk on over the water; we called it our log-way. We found the country was so very wet, at times, that it was impossible to go with oxen and sled, which were our only means of conveyance, summer or winter. When we could not go in this style we were obliged to carry all that it was necessary to have taken, on our shoulders, from Dearbornville.

We had many annoyances, and mosquitoes were not the least, but they did us some good. We had no fences to keep our cattle, and the mosquitoes drove the oxen and cow up to the smoke which we kept near the house in order to keep those little pests away. The cattle soon learned, as well as we, that smoke was a very powerful repellant of those little warriors. Many times, in walking those logs and going through the woods there would be a perfect cloud of mosquitoes around me. Sometimes I would run to get away from them, then stop and look behind me and there would be a great flock for two rods back (besides those that were around me) all coming toward me as fast as their wings could bring them . . .

> We found wild animals and game very numerous. Sometimes the deer came where father had cut down trees, and browsed the tops. Occasionally, in the morning, after a little snow, their tracks would be as thick as sheep-tracks in a yard, almost up to the house. The wolves, also, were very common; we could often hear them at night, first at one point, then answers from another and another direction, until the woods rang with their unearthly yells . . .

Like most woodland pioneers, the Nowlins, while expanding their farm little by little, continued to obtain much of their food from the forest. They made maple sugar, they learned to find wild honey and berries in season, and they ate the meat of bear, deer, wild turkeys, and fish. Naturally enough, young William developed a deep affection for trees, and, above all, for hunting.

> Sometimes I would rise early in the morning and go out of the door just at daylight. I could hear the notes of the little songsters, just waking, singing their first songs of the morning. I would listen to see if I could hear the gobbling of the wild turkeys . . . The old gobblers commonly selected the largest trees, in the thickest woods, with limbs high up, for their roosts and as soon as it came daylight, in the east, they would be up strutting and gobbling . . .
>
> . . . a small instrument that I almost always carried in my vest pocket . . . was made from the hollow bone of a turkey's wing. I called it a turkey call. By holding the end of my hand and sucking it right, it would make a noise, or squeak, very similar to the turkey's voice . . . I would . . . take the hollow bone out of my pocket and call. I have seen them come up on the run, sometimes one, at other times more. While lying in ambush once I shot two, at the same time, with one rifle bullet and got them both.

At this stage farming was highly experimental, since no one had any experience with the new conditions. The earth was so entangled with forest roots that corn often had to be planted with an ax. As for fertility, the Nowlins discovered what would soon prove true of Michigan generally: that even within a small area, the soil could be highly variable. Wheat succeeded—even though seed was expensive and the field vulnerable to trampling by wild animals and a neighbor's unfenced oxen. Because the soil's sandiness reminded the father of Long Island, where melons were grown, he tried planting watermelons, and they flourished. Apples, too, did well, and on a wilderness diet they tasted marvelously good.

Lessons of industry and frugality were brought home in a very direct way:

One time father wanted to clear off a piece of ground for buckwheat by the first of July. He had not much time in which to do it. We had learned that buckwheat would catch and grow very stout on new and stumpy ground. Sometimes it filled very full and loaded heavy. It was easily gathered and easily thrashed, and helped us very much for our winter's bread. One night after supper, father sat down and smoked his pipe; it was quite dark when he got up, took his ax in his hand and went out. We all knew where he had gone. It was to put up his log heaps, as he had some burning. Mother said, "We will go and help pick up and burn." When we started, looking towards the woods, we could see him dimly through the darkness. As we neared him we could see his bare arms with the handspike in his hands rolling up the logs. The fire would shoot up bright, and his countenance appeared to be a pale red, while thousands of sparks flew above his head and disappeared in the air. In a minute there was an awkward boy at his side with a handspike, taking hold and doing the best he could to help, and there was mother by the light of the fires, who a short time before in her native home, was an invalid and her life despaired of, now, with some of her children, picking up chips and sticks and burning them out of the way.

We were well rewarded for our labor. The buckwheat came up and in a little time it was all in bloom. It put on its snow white blossoms, and

The Nowlin family's bark-covered house near Dearborn, Michigan, in 1834

the wind that caressed it, and caused it to wave, bore away on its wings to the woods the fragrance of the buckwheat field.

The little industrious bee came there with its comrades and extracted its load of sweet, then flew back to its native home in the forest. There it deposited its load, stored it away carefully against the time of need. Nature taught the bee that a long, cold winter was coming and that it was best to work and improve the time, and the little fellow has left us a very bright example to follow.

Yet the family's progress was far from assured. Like many another farmer after him, the elder Nowlin, though short of cash, was anxious to expand his operation. He was proud of the deeds to his land—his had been signed by Andrew Jackson, whom he much admired, and the deed to his wife's eighty acres had been signed by Martin Van Buren. But in 1836, despite the forebodings of his wife and son, he decided to mortgage the property in order to raise cash and buy more livestock. Disaster soon overtook the family as, one by one, the new livestock died.

. . . one of the small children asked mother what a mortgage was, she replied that it was something that would take our home away from us, if not paid . . .

We still had wheat but sometimes had to almost do without groceries. We always had something to eat but sometimes our living was very poor. Sometimes we had potatoes and milk and sometimes thickened milk. This was made by dampening flour, rolling it into fine lumps and putting them into boiling milk with a little salt, and stirring it until it boiled again. This was much more palatable than potatoes and milk . . .

Mother had been used to better days and to treating her guests well, and her early life in Michigan did not take all of her spirit away. She was a little proud as well as I, but I have learned that pride, hard times and poverty are very poor companions. It was no consolation to think that the neighbors, most of them, were as bad off as we were. This made the thing still worse . . .

The mortgage was like a cancer eating up our substance, gnawing day and night . . .

But the forest remained abundant, and the father earned some cash by helping build an army arsenal. Little by little, the family was able to recover. In 1841 the mortgage was finally paid off. Gradually, now, the Nowlins could expand and improve their farm. And they built a new house:

On the crane hung two or three hooks, and on these, over the fire, mother did most of her cooking. As we had no oven, mother had what we called a bake kettle; this was a flat, low kettle, with a cast cover, the rim of which turned up an inch or two, to hold coals. In this kettle, she baked our bread. The way she did it; she would heat the lid, put her loaf of bread in the kettle, take the shovel and pull out some coals on the hearth, set the kettle on them, put the lid on and shovel some coals on to it. Then she would watch it, turn it round a few times, and the bread was done, and it came on the table steaming. When we all gathered around the family board we did the bread good justice. We were favored with what we called "Michigan appetites." Sometimes when we had finished our meal there were but few fragments left, of anything except the loaf, which was four or five inches through, a foot and a half across, and four and a half feet in circumference . . .

Now I have in my mind's eye a view of my mother's front room. Ah! there is the door on the south with its wooden latch and leather string. East of the door is a window, and under it stands a wooden bench, with a water pail on it; at the side of the window hangs the tin dipper. In the corner beyond this stands the ladder, the top resting on one side of an opening through which we entered the chamber. In the centre of the east end burned the cheerful fire, at the left stood a kettle, pot and bread-kettle, a frying pan (with its handle four feet long) and griddle hung over them. Under the north window stood a table with its scantling legs, crossed, and its whitewood board top, as white as hands and ashes could scour it. Farther on, in the north-west corner stood mother's bed, with a white sheet stretched on a frame made for that purpose, over it, and another at the back and head. On the foot and front of the frame were pinned calico curtains with roses and rosebuds and little birds, some perched on a green vine that ran through the print, others on the wing, flying to and from their straw colored nests. These curtains hung, oh, how gracefully, around that bed! They were pinned back a little at the front, revealing a blue and white coverlet, of rare workmanship. In the next and last corner stood the family cupboard. The top shelves were filled with dishes, which mother brought from the state of New York. They were mostly blue and white, red and white and there were some on the top shelf which the children called their "golden edged dishes."

. . . In hooks attached to a beam overhead hung two guns which were very frequently used. A splint broom and five or six splint bottomed chairs constituted nearly all the furniture of this room . . .

While isolation has always been part of farm life, in pioneer days it was extreme. The arrival of a new neighbor was a memorable event. It not only reduced loneliness, but, in a commonplace phrase of the day, "tended to build up the country." Often neighbors would walk considerable distances to borrow fire from one another. Occasional contacts with Indians sparked fear and wonder on both sides, and Nowlin also tells a touching story of a no-questions-asked encounter with a runaway slave on his way to Canada. He tells, too, how one neighbor, who had been a mechanic, built a cart and how the other farmers all borrowed it to carry their grain to the mill. In nearby Dearbornville, trade was frequently handled on a barter basis. Later, as commerce expanded, and more settlers moved in, goods became cheaper and more plentiful. And the arrival of the railroad was all-important. Piercing the silence of the woods, its screaming whistle frightened men and animals alike.

Such intrusions of man-made civilization into the innocent landscape were already becoming a favored theme of American fiction—a romantic device that critic Leo Marx has called the "machine-in-the-Garden" motif. Loss of the forest-bound purity of Cooper's Leatherstockings, of the untrammeled independence of Mark Twain's early river pilots, and of the virgin beauty of nature herself would bring sincere grief to the hearts of many. Our age would inherit the yearning for lost innocence in a variety of forms, including the conservation movement. But for millions of farmers like William Nowlin and his successors, man's triumphs over nature were a source of pride—and relief. As Nowlin says of one of his neighbors:

> He was a man of strong mind and an iron will. He cleared up his land, rescued it from the wilderness, acquired, in fact, a good fortune. When he died, at the good old age of eighty-one years, he left his family in excellent circumstances. He died in the year one thousand eight hundred and fifty-nine.

Nowlin's modest volume was published in the nation's centennial year, and for many an old settler who read it, the author's picture of his aging father must have struck a chord:

> So he went at it, and built him a good, substantial plain, brick farm-house in 1854. Not so palatial as some might admire, but a good substantial house; a brick basement under the whole of it, with two stories above. He set it right facing the "Hard scrabble road" and right in front of his door yard was the junction of the three roads. He lived on the corners and, by looking south, he could see to the place where he first settled in Michigan, from his own door. He built across the front side of his house a double stoop or piazza running the whole length of the front. There he could sit, in the cool of the day, and rest himself, accompanied by some of his family. Two of my sisters yet lived at home; the rest of the family had gone for themselves. While sitting there he could see people passing and repassing, coming and

going in every direction. What a contrast it was to our early life in Michigan. Now he could sit on his veranda in the twilight, when it was pleasant, and when the shadows of evening were spread over the face of nature, he could peer away into the distance to the south and southwest, for a mile and more, and see lights in different places glistening and shining like stars through the darkness. They were the lights of lamps and candles, burning in his distant neighbors' dwellings and shining through their windows. He could go to his north window and see lights all along, from his house to Dearbornville, for he was in plain sight of the village. Now he lived in what might be styled, if not an old country, a thickly inhabited part of the country.

By the 1830s, however, at the time the Nowlin family was moving to Michigan, farm life in Ohio was considerably more advanced. Writing in the nineties, Martin Welker, a retired Ohio judge, recalled the crowded cheerfulness of "work socials." The young people, especially, were drawn together by apple parings, maple sugar making, log rollings, and wood choppings. But the perennial favorites were the corn huskings:

The farmer would pull the corn with husks on from the stalk in the field, haul it to the barn or pile it outside under some cover. Then huskers would be invited, and sometimes girls would be invited and participate. The corn pile would be divided, and captains chosen, and huskers divided equally for the work, and the merry contest would begin, and victory would make the winning leader, of the side that finished first, a hero for the time. When girls were present one law was always enforced; that was, that he who should find a red ear should be allowed to kiss the girl next to him. Sometimes it was said, some rascal would be guilty of the fraud of carrying red ears from home in his pocket to win the kisses.

With Midwestern agriculture still at the subsistence stage, Judge Welker remembered his less frolicsome boyhood tasks with equal clarity:

The plowing was generally done with what was called the bar-shear plow with wooden mold-board, with a boy alongside with a paddle to keep the dirt from clogging on the mold-board; and afterward it was again stirred with the one-horse shovel plow. Occasionally a plow with an iron or steel mold-board was used by the more advanced farmers.

Wheat and rye and oats, and all seeds, were sown broadcast by hand, and were covered by the triangular wooden or iron toothed harrow, and were dug in with the mattock around the stumps and trees. Corn was planted by hand, covered with the hoe, and cultivated with the shovel plow and the hoe. Hoeing corn was the special work of the boys, and sometimes of the girls; and a boy or girl would ride the horse hitched to the plow when the corn was high . . .

All grains were thrashed with the wooden flail, and cleaned with a sheet, two men so swinging the sheet as to blow the chaff from the grain, as it was slowly poured out of the half bushel by another man, after which the hand riddle was used to clean the wheat for use. It was about a winter's job for a lone farmer to thrash out and clean the crop of a ten-acre field. Men made it a specialty to so thrash during the winter for an agreed price per bushel, going around the neighborhood . . .

The harvest time was then, as it has always been and still is, a great event as well as a busy time on the farm. Usually quite a number of hands would be employed to reap in the wheat or rye field, who with sickle and regular step, each one upon his allotted land, would literally march through the golden grain, with a leader in front, enlivened by song or joke, until the end of the round was reached, where water, and whiskey and shade, would rest the jolly reapers. With sickle on shoulder, the reaper would bind back his sheaves. And woe to the reaper who did not stand the day's work and had to "give out" and lie in the fence corner, and, in the parlance of the day, whose "hide was hung on the fence."

. . . The old men and boys, and often girls, carried water to the harvest or hay field in the coffee pot or jug, and generally the bottle of whiskey was to be found in the shade of a tree or fence corner. The favorite amusement was to see who could get the most blackberries out of the bottle in one drink. The one able to stand the most whiskey usually got the most berries. To the workers on the farm, the blast of the dinner horn was a welcome sound, and particularly so to the hungry boys.

And if men were the producers, women were the processors and manufacturers—of food, children, candles, soap, and clothing:

The raw materials available for the farmer's clothing were supplied by a flock of sheep on almost every farm, and a flax patch yearly sown to furnish flax for linen and tow cloth . . .

The men sheared the sheep, after having washed them completely. The wool was carded on hand cards by the women, and made into rolls for spinning. They spun the wool on the big and little wheel, mostly on the big one, made it into skeins on the reel, and colored the yarn as desired; and with the yarn they made flannel, being all wool, for the women and girls. Of the spun wool the women wove also the elegant and almost everlasting coverlet, which was the pride of every good housewife . . .

The flax was spun by women, and so was the tow, on the little wheel, the one making linen, and the other rough cloth. With the linen thread thus spun, they made beautiful table cloths, yet to be found in many a country home . . .

The women, as a general thing did the milking and buttermaking, using the old dasher churn. Except in a Yankee family no man or boy could be induced to milk the cows, it being regarded as woman's work . . .

Usually the women did most of the gardening, and did the necessary cultivation of all sorts of vegetables raised for the table, as well as the flowers for the door yard. They also cared for the fruit, and dried apples, peaches and smaller fruits, besides attending to the raising of chickens, turkeys, geese and ducks for home use and market . . .

Before the advent of the washboard and the washing machine, the washing of clothes was done by our mothers by rubbing with the hands, or beating them with a stick on a bench made of a puncheon, and wringing them with the hands. The clothes were dried upon a grape vine, where they were fastened with thorns for pins. The flat-iron was then nearly as now, with the exception that never more than one was owned by a family, and neighbors borrowed from each other on ironing day . . .

The women and girls, for everyday wear in the winter time, wore flannel dresses, plain, striped, or cross-barred, as fancy might dictate, with quilted or red flannel petticoats. In the summer they generally wore gingham, calico and lawn for dresses, with dimity skirts, and sun bonnets when out of doors.

Most of the women and girls had an extra suit or two for dress occasions of alpaca, merino, or other fine goods, with fashionable bonnets, shawls and wraps of various kinds.

The average girl was considered well provided for when her mother furnished her with a good bed and bedding, a side saddle, a cow, six knives and forks, the same number of plates, cups and saucers, teaspoons and tablespoons, a tea-kettle, dutch oven, and a wash tub, in addition to her wedding and Sunday dresses. Generally the bride wore a neat cap made out of light stuff, and well trimmed with ribbons, and the groom wore his best new suit made for the occasion.

Bridal tours were not then taken to any extent, and usually housekeeping immediately commenced. The night of the wedding the couple generally had a grand serenade, the music being made by cow-bells, horse fiddles, and horns, not very harmonious, but loud in tones. The next day after the wedding there would usually be what was called an "Infair," at the home of the groom, where most of the wedding guests would meet and have a great family dinner . . .

Within the fabric of family and neighbors, every thread of life was interwoven with every other. The union of home and field, the meshing of the cycles of human life with those of nature, and the necessary concern of each for each other would forever distinguish farm life from town life.

Yet deep changes were coming. American farming was rapidly emerging from the subsistence level. When commercial agriculture first began to appear in the Midwest in the 1830s and 1840s, it was already well advanced in New York and Pennsylvania. But within a few years the cash crop yields of the prairie states would far surpass those of the East. The shift was a momentous one. It signaled a steady lessening of the farmer's isolation, his ever-greater involvement in the world of commerce, and the demise of that self-sufficiency so prized by the backwoodsmen. To be sure, the family farm system would remain intact down to the present day—but not because of agrarian ideology. Free of the feudal inhibitions of his eastern and European ancestors, the Midwestern family farmer has not only proved uniquely innovative and adaptable but has consistently demonstrated that his homestead is the most rational and efficient unit of agricultural production in the world.

Typically, the Ohioan who had grown up wearing linsey-woolsey grown in his father's fields would decide to replace flax with corn. He would fatten hogs on that corn and sell the hogs to a Cincinnati meat packer. The processed pork would then be shipped to the South, which would pay for it, in effect, by sending the farmer cotton to wear. If this kind of progress increased the farmer's financial risk and his vulnerability to economic forces beyond his control, it also gave him hope of being able to accumulate capital with which to buy more land and machinery. Which could mean, in time, that his children would inherit a valuable farm—even though many of them might move away to town.

In this atmosphere of gradually increasing specialization, it did not take Midwestern farmers long to learn what their best crops were.

So universal was the demand for wheat, and so well did it keep, that a bushel of wheat became a kind of currency, a stable arbiter of value that varied mainly with respect to the nearness of transportation. Since costs were lower and yields higher in the West than in the East, western wheat enjoyed a competitive advantage. And a cash-poor pioneer needed little capital to get started, since wheat could

Dorothea Lange

be raised with simple tools and a primitive barn. Enormous labor was needed for brief periods, but in the family-farm, good-neighbor system this was generally available. Later, as fields grew larger, the farmer would have to hire migratory labor, which was unreliable as well as expensive. By the prosperous 1850s, however, this situation was beginning to be remedied by such crucial inventions as the McCormick reaper. Cyrus McCormick's main factory, established in Chicago in 1848, would eventually spawn the giant International Harvester Company, and his heirs would continue to occupy high rungs on the Illinois business and social ladders. In the same way, the family concern established by plow manufacturer John Deere at Moline, Illinois, would mushroom into today's highly sophisticated Deere & Company, the largest maker of agricultural equipment in the world. Such enterprises as these would symbolize that close meshing of basic agriculture and basic industry that forms the foundation of the heartland's century and a quarter of spectacular, well-balanced economic growth.

But in the early years, wheat, as a crop, still had plenty of drawbacks. The land had to be very carefully cleaned and prepared. After a few seasons, parasites, plant diseases, and soil depletion would take their toll. The farmers learned to combat these problems by cleaning the seed well, and by planting later in the fall or earlier in the spring. Most important, they learned to rotate their crops—this in itself a sign that the frontier period in which the land was used, conquered, and "skimmed" was giving way to the more enlightened era in which it was conserved.

The great variable was still transportation. Wheat farmers sometimes faced monumental obstacles in trying to get their crop to market:

> With a bushel of wheat weighing 60 pounds, the load that could be carried was not large. Oats and possibly hay for a number of days had to be carried; otherwise the draft animals had to live off the land on the way and, if through developed areas, at considerable expense. The experience of three men who hauled thirty bushels of wheat to Chicago from Lake County, Indiana, with seven yoke of oxen illustrates the difficulty of providing for forage on the way. Twice the oxen broke into cultivated fields of pumpkins, corn, and cabbages, causing damage that called for compensation. As a result, the nine-day trip involved greater expenses than the return from the sale of the wheat . . .

Little wonder, therefore, that early wheat farming centered along the navigable lakes and rivers—or that the spreading railroad networks gave it a sharp boost by lowering shipping costs from fifteen cents per ton-mile to a cent and a half.

Another remedy was local processing. Gristmills dotted the back country, usually on little waterways that turned the stones which ground the wheat or corn into flour. For this the farmers paid a toll or royalty of from 10 to 20 per cent of their grain. Many millers also purchased grain directly, for resale as flour. Thus they became important figures in the local economy. The remarkable numbers of old gristmills that have survived give today's visitors a fascinating glimpse of the early days of farming.

During this period, local distilleries and breweries also appeared in virtually every county. Ohio, with its strong southern and German influences, had nearly five hundred of them by 1840. While most of the output of the smaller enterprises was consumed locally, certain cities processed grain into beverages in a big way. In 1850, for example, Cincinnati shipped over fourteen million gallons of whiskey down the Ohio River.

By the 1850s, with the railroads pushing onto the prairies, wheat boomed as a cash crop. In those ten years the U.S. output soared by 72 per cent, a figure wholly accounted for by the dramatic expansion of Midwestern plantings. Strong export demand was spurred by the Crimean War—a pattern that continued well into the sixties, keeping prices high, contributing to the nation's balance of payments, and further stimulating the westward expansion.

Like the pioneers, wheat followed the setting sun. The eastern states were the first to start abandoning the crop when low-cost western wheat flooded the market, mainly via the Erie Canal. And before long, Ohio herself began to relive the eastern experience: declining yields, rising land prices and other costs, and unbeatable competition from the huge tracts of virgin soil being opened up farther west.

By the time Illinois sent its most famous son to Washington, the Middle West had already transformed American agriculture.

If wheat was the star, corn was old reliable. Since it flourished even under primitive conditions, and since a few seeds would plant many acres, it was usually the pioneers' first crop, especially in the earlier-settled areas toward the south. Southerners and Yankees alike had carefully brought bags of their respective corn seeds from home, and it was more than symbolic that the two strains soon cross-pollinated to produce a vigorous new Midwestern variety.

Wrote one central Illinois pioneer in 1835: "The principal crop is corn, and to the Illinois farmer this is everything. It feeds him and clothes him and pays his store account sometimes without any money, or but little, passing through his hands, as the merchant receives his corn and pork and produce in general, in exchange for goods."

In time, corn would surpass wheat as a cash crop. By the 1880s it was already giving its name to a whole region. Half a century after that, Thomas Wolfe would exult at the sight of this ubiquitous plant. As recounted by his biographer: "Autumn and harvest time had come and, as always, he went into ecstasy about America. 'Corn,' he exclaimed several times in a low voice, looking at the fields of it, which were now in shock. 'Corn, the most American thing in America.' "

Indeed, its New World heritage was venerable. In 1954, scientists proved corn's American origins by drilling two hundred feet below Mexico City, where they found fossil pollen grains dating back some eighty thousand years—far earlier than the arrival of man on this continent. Corn has a unique ability to store energy from the sun. It was this ability that enabled the early Indians to emerge from a scanty, nomadic existence and to create the remarkable cultures of the Mayas, the Incas, and the Aztecs, as well as that of the mysterious

Mound Builders of the Mississippi Valley. Aptly, corn has often been called the New World's "great civilizer."

Not until Columbus and his followers carried seeds back to Europe did corn spread through the rest of the world. And it was from the native Indian that the early white colonists learned the techniques of raising and utilizing this hardy plant. In 1621 William Bradford, governor of Plymouth Colony, summed up his people's gratitude in heartfelt terms: "And sure it was God's good providence that we found this corne, for else we know not how we should have done."

The earliest varieties were tiny. Some prehistoric cobs of wild corn found in southern Mexico are only as long as the diameter of a penny and contain less foodstuff than a single kernel of modern strains. But between 2300 and 900 B.C. this corn hybridized with some closely related plants, setting off a chain reaction of further hybridizations that is still going on. It is this unmatched capacity for continual improvement that has made corn so valuable and given it the greatest diversity of any plant ever cultivated. As early as the Paris Exposition of 1867—long before man himself learned to control the quality called "hybrid vigor"—the American exhibit proudly displayed 115 types of corn. Today's farmer can select from a seemingly unlimited number of seed types, ranging from high-sugar "sweet" corns for direct human consumption, to popcorn varieties, to the brightly colored ears used for decoration, to the most important type, "dent" corn, which is fed to livestock and thereby transformed into meat.

It was during the era when the settlers, like the Indians, were still consuming most of their corn directly that the southern influence was strongest in the Midwest. Thus, the names of corn foods eaten by generations of Midwestern country people carry a southern twang—corn pone or bread, hominy, mush, corn griddle cakes.

But a meat-based menu, the rise of commercial agriculture, and the development of sophisticated processing would gradually give corn a more indirect role in our diet. It is no accident that the nations with the highest per-capita meat consumption have traditionally been those with vast grazing lands and relatively sparse populations—such as Argentina, Uruguay, Paraguay, Australia, and New Zealand. During much of the nineteenth century, the United States also fit this description. Although a swelling populace soon changed the picture, America's meat production and consumption were able to remain high because of her unique ability to grow the corn on which her hogs, cattle, sheep, and chickens thrive.

Yet, while some 80 per cent of the corn grown in the United States is now fed to animals, an astonishing variety of other foods and non-foods are in some way derived from it: margarine, mayonnaise, salad and cooking oils, starch, chewing gum, soups, sweets of many kinds, breakfast cereals, alcohol, paper, wallboard, charcoal, solvents, adhesives, and many more. This amazing plant seems nearly as vital to our civilization as it once was to the Toltecs and Incas.

In the years before the Civil War, however, few could have envisioned so spectacular a role for corn. It was still the downhome crop. If corn was universal wherever there was farming, this was not because there was much of a market for it, but because it was a sure thing for the family's subsistence. Not only was the price of corn lower than for wheat, but corn was bulkier, and therefore less worth shipping. And its growing season was longer than that for wheat. On the other hand, its harvest time was much less urgent. Ideally corn should be harvested in the fall; but it could be left on the stalk as late as the following spring without too much loss. And its yield per acre was higher—a factor that would become increasingly important as land values climbed.

Wonder stories about Midwestern corn began appearing in agricultural journals, and in the letters of awestruck pioneers:

> . . . as I strolled through it, I could but laugh heartily, for it seemed as though I was in a world of corn. I could see nothing else except the sun which heated the black soil so hot that I could scarcely bear my hand on it.

> Only conceive in your mind a vast plain as far as the eye can reach, waiveing as the sea, groaning under from 60 to 70 bushels of corn to the acre, and you can have some idea of the corn crop of Illinois . . .

> . . . can you hear corn grow in hot weather? An affirmative answer, nobly felt, advises you to go at night so deep into a cornfield that you are surrounded by corn higher than your head . . . "There is a whisper, a faint crackling, coming from no where and everywhere at once. It might be the ghost of a sound, imagined perhaps. But listen again!
>
> "It is the minute stretching of a billion corn leaves, stalks, husks, kernels. It is the dark chemistry of earth, working upward through roots, drawing up through the standing plants, transmitting the essences of soil into life. It is the sound of growth, a sound perhaps heard by insects and other lowly creatures as a veritable roar of creation."

On the rich bottomlands adjoining the Ohio and Mississippi, corn was, in fact, already yielding as much as 100 to 125 bushels to the acre. And though it was hard to ship overland, corn could be marketed in the form of whiskey, starch, and other products—or, of course, as pork or beef. Yet the early western farmers were too preoccupied with other urgent concerns to pay much attention to their few livestock. Their energies went into clearing, fencing, putting up barns and houses and corn cribs, and draining wet soils, rather than worrying about keeping their stock inside during the winter, or improving breeding practices, or growing a surplus of high-quality feed. But the situation was changing, and one sure sign of this was that between 1840 and 1860 the number of cattle in the nation approximately doubled.

In the South, however, the rapid spread of specialized plantation agriculture actually caused a decline in beef production during this crucial period. And in the increasingly urban East, whose population was racing ahead, the number of beef cattle stayed about even. Since the plains were not yet open to settlement, it was clear that the soaring demands of the East and South could be met only by the prairie states, and by Texas.

But how, before the railroads, could Midwestern cattle be moved to eastern markets? The answer was simple: they could walk. Roving the back country, professional drovers would buy a steer here, and a couple more there, until they had a herd of perhaps 120 cattle. Then began the great drive to New York or Philadelphia. The problems were many: the fording of rivers, the necessity of selling off the laggards, the constant need to find food and water and bedding for the herd, the cost of paying helpers. Worst of all was that each animal lost from 150 to 250 pounds during the long journey.

As a partial remedy, farmers along the main routes began to establish feeding and resting stations. Elsewhere, the drovers lingered in rich, open prairie country, fattening their beef. Ohio's Scioto Valley became one of the favored spots. Here the drover might supplement the grazing with a period of feeding on corn. And so, although the journeys seem incredible today, it was out of them that the idea of the modern feedlot seems to have evolved.

As the region's center of gravity moved steadily westward, cattle feeders in Indiana and Illinois began competing with those in the Scioto. Increasingly, during the 1840s, the Illinois stockmen could sell their beef to the growing Chicago and St. Louis markets, as well as to the more distant East. A little later Iowa, too, joined the trend, benefiting from the surging demand of western migrants who hurried across the

Missouri River on their frenzied trek to the California gold fields.

In this way, the abundance of prairie grass and cheap corn in the younger Midwestern states was creating a new and distinctively western enterprise: the large-scale feeder-cattle operation. To succeed at it, the owner needed plenty of credit, acreage, and merchandising acumen—which made him quite a different sort of man from the buckskinned forest-slashers, the painstaking Germans and Scandinavians, and the impoverished William Nowlins:

> There came to the fore a score or more of prairie cattle kings, each with herds of 1,000 or 2,000 cattle grazing in fenced pastures of thousands of acres and cared for by small armies of laborers. Isaac Funk, Jacob Strawn, Benjamin F. Harris, John T. Alexander, and Michael Sullivant, whose family was also heavily involved in the feeder-cattle business in Ohio, were leaders in Illinois. Alexander fattened and shipped to the New York cattle market between 1857 and 1860 from 10,000 to 15,000 cattle. On his acres, Jacob Strawn, one of the most successful of these feeder-cattle men of the Illinois prairies, fed 1,600 to 2,000 cattle and 700 hogs. He had 2,900 acres in corn divided into 40-acre plots each tended by a laborer, who was paid eight cents a bushel for the corn he raised. All the corn was fed on the place. Steers for feeding were brought in from southern Illinois, Missouri, and Iowa. His gross sales of stock were $100,000 in 1854. Perhaps the size of his operations justified Strawn's being called "The Napoleon of Cattle."

Accompanying the westward move of livestock raising were continuous geographical shifts in the meat packing industry. Until just before the Civil War, slaughtering was mainly done during the winter months to prevent spoilage. Cincinnati, with its southward-looking river commerce, remained mid-America's leading abattoir. But in 1857, Chicago introduced "ice packing," which made year-round slaughtering feasible. The advent of the railroads, the emergence of the northerly "Corn Belt," a swelling foreign demand for Midwestern beef, and the Civil War all combined to fuel a dramatic growth of the Chicago slaughterhouses. The Windy City quickly passed Cincinnati to become the nation's number one meat packer, a position it would hold for many years. Opened in 1865, the Chicago Union Stockyards established new standards of efficiency. These were soon duplicated in such other important centers as Kansas City, St. Louis, Cincinnati, Indianapolis, Omaha, St. Paul, Sioux City, and St. Joseph. The advent of refrigerated railroad cars after 1879 gave a further boost to the Midwestern beef and pork business and transformed Chicago's Swift, Armour, Wilson, and other firms into nationwide giants.

After World War I, with the rapid improvement of roads, trucks, and, particularly, refrigerated trucks, the pattern began to shift again. Little by little, the meat packers began moving out into the country. Like the railroads, the great urban slaughtering centers slowly declined. Eventually, the famous stockyards of Chicago and Kansas City disappeared altogether. By 1962, Illinois had dropped from first to fifth among meat packing states. Nebraska had risen to second, and highly rural Iowa was the new leader.

If commercial glamour made the cattle crop analogous to the wheat crop, it was the lowly porker who, like corn, remained the old standby of the downhome farmer. The hog had many things going for him. He converted food into meat more efficiently than the cow. He matured earlier and reproduced much more prolifically, which also meant that his breeding could be advanced faster. And he needed far less capital investment than beef. Thus the hog would come to be called "the mortgage lifter." His main drawbacks were that he was harder to drive to market on hoof and that he was susceptible to diseases, such as hog cholera, which occasionally devastated Midwestern farms until the development of vaccine after the turn of the century.

The early hogs were as rough and self-sufficient as the pioneers who rounded them up. Roaming wild in the woods, swamps, and streets, they were "long and slim, long-legged and long snouted, slab-sided, large boned, gaunt bodied, flat eared, with arched back and bristles erect from head to tail." They fed on wild nuts, roots, grass, and garbage, and earned breed names that were, to say the least, graphic: razorbacks, land pikes, alligators, thistle-diggers, stump-suckers, hazel splitters, wind-splitters, and prairie sharks. With western hyperbole, one orator claimed that, "provided by nature with snouts not less than a yard long . . . they could lift the top rail off of a ten rail fence," and that "A lean-sucked sow . . . could outrun Rarus, and had to be hunted down in the timber with fast horses."

But the backwoods hog would vanish as rapidly as his human counterpart. Before and after the Civil War, with corn production booming, breeders hurried to bring in eastern and imported swine. Among the many combinations that resulted, the three main blood lines bore the respectable appellations of Duroc Jersey, Poland China, and Chester White. So favorable were conditions for them in the Corn Belt that a legend claimed that if you bent a pigtail into a U-shape and stuck the two ends into the prairie soil, you would get two piglets. A less debatable formula was the corn-hog ratio: a farmer must project the likely market prices of both, then figure whether the value of the ten or twelve bushels of corn needed to put one hundred pounds of gain on a pig was more or less than the resultant increase in the animal's value. In making such decisions, nineteenth century farmers discounted their family's labor—as many still do—which is one of the reasons why corporate farming has never made much headway in the Middle West.

At first, partly because of the difficulty of getting hogs to market before the railroads, and partly because easterners preferred beef, much of the Midwestern pork was consumed at home. Even before the Civil War, however, Cincinnati and other centers were packing great quantities of pork into hooped, white-oak barrels weighing over 200 pounds. Loaded onto flatboats and keelboats and steamboats, these were shipped south, either for consumption on the plantations, or for transshipment to the West Indies, the east coast, or Europe. With more vehemence than feeling, one orator exulted, "The hog eats the corn, and Europe eats the hog. Corn thus becomes incarnate; for what is a hog but fifteen or twenty bushels of corn on four legs?" Earlier, an Indianapolis man had exclaimed, "Hogs, and hens grow almost spontaneous here." Soon it was an Ohio editor's turn to tell his readers: "The ringing crack of the whip and the whoop of the driver in our streets reminds us that the Hog season is again upon us." Hogs, like cattle, were driven across country to the auction barns and stockyards, and even across the ice of the frozen Mississippi. The railroads, of course, made marketing far easier, and after the Civil War, swine production continued to be profitable. The result was that between 1850 and 1900, Illinois' production of hogs rose from under two million to almost six million, while Iowa's soared from well under half a million to nearly ten million.

And yet the corn-hog ratio also taught the family farmers the hazards of a steeply fluctuating market. When the price of corn was high, it made more sense to sell it than to feed it out. But when the farmers all did this, the price of corn plummeted, and the price of hogs shot up. So the farmers rushed to feed more hogs—causing the same thing to happen in reverse. It was extremely difficult for the inelastic small producer to plan around these "corn-hog cycles." With the situation aggravated by high freight charges, he was often forced to sell his hogs well ahead of their maturity, or even to burn his nearly worthless corn as fuel. To cushion the shock waves, he might try to keep his crops diversified; but this ran counter to the efficiencies of scale. Such vulnerability to market swings was a grim new fact of

John Vachon

Midwestern farm life. The majority were bound to guess wrong. Even today, with all our economic wizards and government planners, no one has come up with a basic solution to this kind of farm problem.

Despite the increasing benefits and problems of producing for a commercial market, the typical Midwestern farm remained surprisingly self-sufficient. In his book, *An America That Was,* Albert Britt fondly recalls growing up on a farm in western Illinois during the eighties and nineties. Though cash was often scarce, the Britts always ate well. At the center of their diet were the pork, beef, and poultry grown on their own farm. The garden was well stocked with sweet corn, carrots, radishes, beets, parsnips, onions, squash, sweet potatoes, beans, peas, lettuce, asparagus, tomatoes, rhubarb, strawberries, and turnips. And the family was proud of its orchards, which included several varieties of apples, Concord grapes, and plums. Sorghum was carried to the local mill for squeezing into syrup. When the boys were not hunting or fishing, the nearby woods might tempt them with blackberries, crab apples, wild grapes, plums, hickory nuts, walnuts, hazel nuts, and butternuts. The few foods not available from the farm itself were obtained from a grocer in nearby Galesburg, who was glad to barter them for the Britts' surplus potatoes, apples, eggs, and butter, and who "settled up" their accounts once a year.

To Albert, the youngest of six, fell some tasks that he loved—a trip to the local gristmill, the delivery of letters to neighbors—and some other jobs, too:

> There was one season of the year when my contact with potatoes was intimate and grievous. That was in the early spring when the cellar bins in which they were stored began to show signs of sprouting. Then it was made clear that there was a job waiting, to rub the sprouts off before the tubers began to soften and decay. Cellars are dark and gloomy places at best, and our potato bin was always in the darkest and gloomiest corner. Fate usually decreed that the day of my solitary confinement with the potatoes was also the day selected by my brothers for fishing or hunting crows' nests . . . Wearing the look of one of the more bad-tempered martyrs, I crept down into the depths and resigned myself to my hard lot.
>
> Gathering eggs was a daily contest between secretive poultry and the boy charged with the collecting . . . Setting hens are notoriously bad tempered and the prying hand that tried to evict Biddy would be received with a volley of hard pecks . . . The output of eggs had seen sinking unaccountably and I was put on notice that the trend must be reversed. The dilemma was unescapable. More eggs or else! Before I could arrange my defense or construct an alibi an outlaw or two emerged from their hideouts brazenly convoying broods of fluffy chicks. They had achieved the ultimate hennish triumph, a hidden nest and a growing family, but I was sunk.

From such light chores, the boy was proud to graduate into the real man's work of plowing, driving the horses hitched to a hay stacker, and helping with the threshing. Neighbors still traded work on large jobs needing extra men and horses, but now they kept careful records of who owed how many days to whom. Since the horse-powered threshing machine was too big an investment for any single farmer in the Britts' area, threshing was done on a contract basis, with every available hand pressed into service to complete the crew of seventeen or more men.

Thrashing scene, North Dakota, late 1800s

Laboring in the steaming kitchens, the women and older girls worked as hard as the men, for the huge dinners were the high point of the threshers' day. Manners were at a minimum, and the men were seated in shifts. Cries for more fried chicken or pork or mashed potatoes-and-gravy comprised the main conversation. If the American habit of fast eating did not originate at threshing time, it was certainly reinforced here. Three or more kinds of pie and cake topped off this gigantic refueling operation, before the threshers scraped back their chairs and went lumbering off to the fields.

Women's work, of course, still involved extensive canning, fruit drying, baking, butter-making, soap-making, candle-making, washing by hand, ironing, sewing, and knitting. Britt sums it up: "My memory holds no picture of my mother sitting with folded hands . . . Except in cold weather the kitchen was the family center. There we cooked, ate, lived, and had our being." Neighborhood quilting bees were common, producing designs with names like Log Cabin, Bear's Paw, Rising Sun, Sunburst, Wedding Ring, and Old Maid's Puzzle—as well as country miles' worth of gossip.

The male equivalent was the crossroads store. On Saturday evenings in winter the regulars would cluster around the overheated stove, chattering about near-to-hand subjects, playing checkers, smoking, digesting the contents of the cheese wheel and cracker barrel, and infrequently making a small purchase—harness oil, perhaps, or tobacco, or a rake. And some summer afternoons, when farm work happened to be at a low ebb, the clang of pitched horseshoes might be heard coming from a level spot behind the store.

It was characteristic, not only of the 1890s, but of country life generally, that male and female roles were sharply distinguished. Women seldom rode horses, never swam or showed their legs, rarely worked in the field (except in the vegetable garden), and talked only about "womanish" subjects. It seems odd that given the obvious fecundity of plants, animals, and families, prudishness should hold the sway that it did. Blunt farmers daily involved in livestock breeding could never mention the subject in mixed company. Even a word like "bull" was barely allowable. "Rooster" was all right but not "stud" or "boar" or "bitch." Of course human pregnancy was shrouded in guilt and secrecy.

And the range of emotional responses was carefully limited:

> Open expressions of affection were not common. Within the family circle kissing was for babies or the brief period of courtship. Our life was as sparing

of praise as of money. Undoubtedly parents liked to hear their children praised, but the common response was deprecatory. Compliments were likely to make a child "big-headed." Also there was a lingering fear that praise of children to their faces was likely to attract the jealous attention of a bad-tempered God. One of my teachers incautiously in my presence told Mother that I was doing good work in school. The prompt reply was calculated to put me in my place: "He ought to. He's lazy enough at home."

We had little skill in expressing gratitude or conveying compliments. If a young man had so far lost his head as to praise a young lady's hat or gown, both of them would have suffered torments of embarrassment. Doubtless there were exceptions, but I do not recall them. We had no skill in graceful phrases and well turned compliments and we were wise to avoid them.

Such training would be hard on some spirited souls, and was scarcely geared to the arts of high civilization. Yet it would also spare us some of that swagger and braggadocio attributed to the Texan and far westerner. Whatever else they might become—Britt himself became a college president—Midwesterners with upbringings like his would seldom pretend to be more than they were, or promise more than they thought they could deliver.

In Europe and New England, farm families had often tended to live in villages, going and coming every day from the fields, and building up ancient customs and relationships. But in the relatively extensive agriculture of the Midwest, and under the homestead system, each family lived separately on its own farm. If this pattern bred isolation, and sometimes loneliness, especially among pioneer wives, it also lent a special warmth to neighborly contacts. The Midwest would never need the high walls and hedges of England and Massachusetts.

The homestead pattern also underscored the integration of the farm family as an economic whole. The welfare of all depended on everyone's playing his expected part. To keep mental or emotional separatism from threatening such an enterprise, young hearts and minds must be carefully yoked to family responsibilities. Robust energy was a major asset. Physical work was accorded higher status than in older, more class-conscious societies. Mental agility might be helpful when applied to machinery or real estate, but it was useless in the abstract—dangerous, even, should it lead to the questioning of fundamentals. Emotional subtlety, though indispensable to the civilizations that corn makes possible, would not bind up the sheaves, or hold the family together. Seen in this light, the idea that agriculture is a particularly moral pursuit was no wispy theory, but a necessary part of the farm's system of social and economic controls.

Then as now, a farmer's values must be related to production, rather than consumption. Thrift, industry, sobriety, simplicity of living, social conservatism, and deferral of gratification would all enhance his farm and his image of himself. Not so the virtues attached to leisure—contemplation, aesthetic pleasure, social worldliness, or conspicuous consumption. Today's city dweller defines himself by activities and tastes that have less and less to do with his work. The farmer defines himself by his farm. When he can accumulate some capital, it goes into the farm, and perhaps to the local church. To leave his family in good circumstances, to leave his farm better than he found it, to make it possible for his sons to carry it on—these are among his deepest desires. So if his vistas sometimes seem to the urbanite to be horizon-bound, this is because he views the seasons of life from a different perspective, one that to him seems longer, and truer.

Sorghum growing near Osceola, Wisconsin, in 1895

Chapter Four

The Stalk

Of the cornucopia of natural and human resources that were transforming the Midwest into the nation's agricultural heartland, one of the most precious gifts was also one of the simplest: grass. For countless millennia, grass had carpeted a third of the continent. Yet generations of pioneers had hesitated to move too far from the edges of the life-sustaining woods and rivers. Now, as their axles began to creak into the flat and rolling ocean of tall grass, the settlers were filled with high hopes—and deep misgivings:

> The youth cried in his happiness at "finding the newest, strangest, most delightful, sternest, most wonderful thing in the world—the Iowa prairie." At this, the somewhat tarnished lady in the wagon beside him burst out, "I don't wonder that you cry. Gosh! It scares me to death."

Even before being cleared for farms, heavily wooded Michigan, Ohio, and Kentucky had had their mosaic of prairie parks. Known variously as "openings," "plains," or "barrens," they were soon recognized as mere eastern outliers of the larger, "true prairie." This sidewise triangle of tall grass had its apex in northwestern Indiana and its feet in southeastern Kansas and northeastern North Dakota. Thus it blanketed northern Illinois, all of Iowa, most of southern and western Minnesota, and the eastern edge of the plains states. Ancient glaciers had mantled the prairie with extraordinarily deep and fertile soils. Generous rainfall spurred showy forbs and breathtaking fields of wildflowers and would support corn and other cash grains. Farther west, the short-grass country would soon beckon the wide-ranging cowboy and the expansive wheat farmer.

The first settlers were not the only ones who responded diversely to the virgin grassland. "One of the most marvelous sights of my whole life," exclaimed one experienced traveler. Yet Charles Dickens merely shrugged. "The effect on me was disappointment . . . It was lonely and wild, but oppressive in its barren monotony. I . . . should often glance towards the distant and frequently-receding line of the horizon, and wish it gained and passed." Probably the most common comparison was to the sea:

> I do not know anything that struck me more forcibly than the sensation of solitude . . . I was perfectly alone, and could see nothing in any direction but sky and grass. Leaving the wood appeared like embarking alone upon the ocean; and, upon again approaching the wood, I felt as if returning to the land. Sometimes again, when I perceived a small stunted solitary tree that had been planted by some fortuitous circumstances, I could hardly help supposing it to be the mast of a vessel. No doubt the great stillness added very much to this strange illusion. Not a living thing could I see or hear, except the occasional rising of some prairie fowl, or perhaps a large hawk or eagle wheeling about over my head.

Among the more perceptive commentators was Harriet Martineau, an English writer who toured America in the 1830s. Of her journey across the Illinois prairies she wrote:

> The feeling is quite bewildering. A man walking near looks like a Goliath a mile off. I mistook a covered wagon without horses, at a distance of fifty yards, for a white house near the horizon . . .
>
> I never saw insulation, (not desolation,) to compare with the situation of a settler on a wide prairie. A single house in the middle of Salisbury Plain would be desolate. A single house on a prairie has clumps of trees near it, rich fields about it; and flowers, strawberries, and running water at hand. But when I saw a settler's child tripping out of home-bounds, I had a feeling that it would never get back again. It looked like putting out into Lake Michigan in a canoe . . .
>
> . . . the rest of the party went in to dry their feet, after having stood long in the wet grass. I remained outside, watching the light showers, shifting in the partial sunlight from clump to level, and from reach to reach of the

brimming and winding river. The nine miles of prairie, which we had traversed in dim moonlight last night, were now exquisitely beautiful, as the sun shone fitfully upon them.

Finally, a modern naturalist's account of the blooming of Iowa's primordial prairie:

> In the early springtime before the grasses could sprout, millions of pasqueflowers tinted the mat of dead grasses of the previous summer. In May the grasses would begin to push up through decaying vegetation of previous years and would be accompanied by a succession of flowering broad-leafed plants, each of which would set its seed and become dominant as the grasses pushed higher and higher. The flowers included scarlet lilies, shooting star, phlox, rosinweed, oxeye, daisies, Indian dye flower, cowslips, gentians and many others. In late summer the asters reached up six or seven feet to compete with the tallest grasses.

Did soil differences create the prairie triangle? Certainly the soils under the forests are different from those under the meadows. Yet acclimated trees will thrive in the humid prairies. It has also been shown that as the forest invades the prairie, it readily converts the soils to its own lighter, shallower type. So soil differences alone did not cause the great grasslands of mid-America. And while various theories have been advanced, there still seems to be no comprehensive understanding of how the true prairies were first formed.

Experts do agree, however, that once the tall grasses were established, it was fire that maintained them and that preserved the prairie soil. Flames swept the prairies again and again for many thousands of years. Whipped along on the wind, the conflagration often traveled faster than a man could run and licked as high as thirty feet into the air. A slow-growing sapling or woody shrub would be fatally damaged. But timothy, bluestem, and other forbs and flowers would spring back in a single season. This was why settlers along the prairie margins often found that the heavy forest growth ended in an abrupt wall behind a protective stream or swamp. Crackling across wide Midwestern skies, lightning touched off many of these fiery housecleanings. Others were set by Indians—either accidentally, or in warfare, or in pursuit of wild game.

The game was, in fact, wondrously abundant. Lewis and Clark mentioned many forms, and John James Audubon described the fauna at length in his *Missouri River Journals* of 1843. A century and a half earlier, Louis Hennepin, a French priest whom La Salle had sent to explore the upper Mississippi, was captured by a band of Sioux and later described the cunning ways in which these prairie tribesmen killed and utilized their prey:

When they see a herd, they gather in great numbers, and set fire to the grass every where around these animals, except some passage which they leave on purpose, and where they take post with their bows and arrows. The buffalo, seeking to escape the fire, are thus compelled to pass near these Indians, who sometimes kill as many as a hundred and twenty in a day, all which they distribute according to the wants of the families; and these Indians all triumphant over the massacre of so many animals, come to notify their women, who at once proceed to bring in the meat. Some of them at times take on their backs three hundred pounds weight, and also throw their children on top of the load . . .

The meat of these animals is very succulent. They are very fat in autumn, because all the summer they are up to their necks in the grass. These vast countries are so full of prairies, that it seems this is the element and the country of the buffalo . . .

The paths by which they have passed are beaten like our great roads in Europe, and no grass grows there . . .

The Indian women spin on the distaff the wool of these cattle [buffalo], out of which they make bags to carry the meat, boucanned and sometimes dried in the sun, which these women keep frequently for three or four months of the year, and although they have no salt, they dry it so well that the meat undergoes no corruption, four months after they have thus dressed this meat, one would say on eating it that the animals had just been killed, and we drank the broth with them instead of water . . .

They paint it [the skin] with different colors, trim it with white and red porcupine quills, and make robes of it to parade in their feasts. In winter they use them to cover themselves especially at night. Their robes which are full of curly wool have a very pleasing appearance.

When the Indians have killed any cows, the little calves follow the hunters, and go and lick their hands or fingers, these Indians sometimes take them to their children and after they have played with them, they knock them on the head and eat them. They preserve the hoofs of all these little animals, dry them and fasten them to rods, and in their dances they shake and rattle them, according to the various postures and motions of the singers and dancers . . .

Many other kinds of animals are found in these vast plains . . . stags, deer, beaver and otter are common there, geese, swans, turtles, poules d'inde, parrots, partridges, and many other birds . . .

Two centuries after Hennepin's adventures, the Sioux had fled westward. Yet strange encounters still took place between remnant Indian families and the white settlers. Some farmers of today can remember their grandfathers' talking about these curious, usually harmless confrontations.

The excitement of the prairie-taming years emerges from the autobiography of Herbert Quick. Having grown up on a pioneer farm in Iowa, Quick remembered the prairie fires with a special vividness:

> The sky shut down over the prairie like a bowl of blue with its lower edges unbroken. The grass was vivid green in spring, grew more neutral in tint as summer advanced, and turned brown in autumn, even before frost; and then to a light russet or gray, varying according to moisture and soil. Every year this heavy coating burned off in the great fires, which brought sometimes loss and even danger and death, but unfailing excitement and joy to the boys. No country with scanty rainfall ever had such prairie fires. The grass grew from a foot or so in height on the dryer knolls to a stature which would hide a tall man walking through in the swales. I have been wet with dew to my waist while riding a horse through it in summer. Sometimes when the autumn was dry or the snow held off late, conflagration would sweep from river to river in the fall. More often it came in the spring . . .
>
> To the prairie pioneer the fires were a danger, a risk, a splendid spectacle

and a necessity. They made the pastures better. They burned off the dead grass so that we could make good hay. We mowed the grass on any lands near us with no thought of trespass, and we pastured it freely. Our farmsteads lay surrounded by the grass and our stacks of hay stood out on the prairie over which swept the flames. Our grain stacks stood in the fields of inflammable stubble. So we plowed fire breaks about all of them . . .

When night came, the whole sky and countryside were lighted up. One could lie in bed in a curtainless room and read by its light. Where it had passed over a hill, the flames went out of sight to reappear roaring up the farther slope . . . Before it was the gloom of lurid smoke and behind a waste of ashes. The next day, over this waste would pass little whirlwinds which would lift columns of ashes in inverted cones to a height far out of sight, at the base of which the ground squirrels, the prairie chickens, the plovers and other denizens of the prairie were eagerly running about to find whatever there was of interest in the swept and garnished landscape.

Surprisingly, the farming methods of the mid-nineteenth century were actually a boon to the prairie chicken, just as those of modern times have been to the pheasant. The grassy patches left beside hedgerows and in the zigzag angles of split-rail "snake fences" made good nesting sites. The cutting down of forests widened the prairie chickens' habitat; and the farmers' hay, oats, and other small grains also helped the birds. But gradually the old, crooked fences and hedges were replaced by straight metal ones, or by no fences at all. Farming became more specialized and intensive, the land more valuable. Even today, virgin grassland is still being broken. At the same time, fire prevention is allowing trees and shrubs to encroach on the unbroken patches.

Thus, the prairie chicken's habitat has shrunk drastically—and so have his numbers. In Illinois, which counted millions of the birds during the Civil War, only about 450 were left by 1971. In Minnesota, where hunters shot nearly half a million prairie chickens in 1925 alone, the survivors now number around 4000. Farther west—in remote parts of Canada, the Dakotas, Nebraska, Kansas, Oklahoma, and Texas—as many as a million prairie chickens may still be left. But, as one expert warns, "it's not the number of birds that makes a species threatened. It is the disappearing habitat. And the prairie chicken's lands are disappearing precipitously."

Alarmed conservationists have responded by establishing sanctuaries in various Midwestern states. Regional chapters of the Audubon Society may be able to direct visitors to these sites. The colorful bird's most exotic ritual is the males' spring courting dance, in which, to win mating rights, the cocks stomp about, showing plumage, making flutter-jumps at one another, and "booming"—emitting a deep *ooo-loo-woo* that can be heard for miles.

Similar efforts are being made to regenerate the nearly vanished buffalo. In the 70,374-acre Theodore Roosevelt Memorial National Park in western North Dakota, for example, visitors can observe buffalo herds, as well as prairie dog colonies and antelope. Nebraska's Fort Niobrara National Wildlife Refuge has buffalo, too, along with elk and Texas longhorn cattle. Tracts of the virgin prairie itself have also been saved, especially in Iowa, whose State Prairie Preserves have successfully developed techniques of controlled burning. Some prairie grasses are now being used to seed highway landscaping. And at the Nebraska National Forest, near Halsey, there are many miles of original, rolling grasslands, containing innumerable varieties of whispering grasses, bright flowers, darting birds, and scurrying prairie rodents.

No such hope exists for the passenger pigeon. Like the chattering Midwestern parakeet, he is totally extinct. In pioneer times, great swarms of passenger pigeons were one of the characteristic features of the mid-American landscape. One fascinated observer watched a column of passenger pigeons a mile wide pass overhead for four hours, from which he calculated that this flock alone was 240 miles long, and contained more than two billion birds. On another occasion, he thought he heard a tornado approaching; a friend reassured him, "It is only the pigeons." Other reports stressed the threat to farming: "Sometimes they would be gone for years, and then they would come back when the nuts were plopping. They would clean up the woods of everything edible and turn their attention to the farmer's corn. In an hour they would ruin him." Naturally enough, the farmer was no friend to the passenger pigeon. Wrote a ten-year-old to his uncle:

> You aught to of been here to see the pigeon we been having. Mother says there was more the first year they came here. I don't see how there could of been. Bird and I shot till our guns was all hot. We been eating pigeon pie till we are sick of it. People came from all around lots we never saw before. Some boys that did not have any gun but pretended they did would pick up my pigeons. Uncle Am said there was plenty for everybody but he is always so easy goin. Old Milerand drove in his hogs the third day to get fat on the dead birds.

Defended by fire, moistened by freshets, enriched by grasses and animal droppings, the sticky prairie earth had slept undisturbed for numberless centuries. Then a flashing steel blade came to slice it open—rousing its fertility and inciting later vivid accounts:

> The tough wirelike roots of the bluestems and prairie clovers twanged with a thousand ringing sounds as each step of the horses pulled the sharp blade forward through the sod of ten thousand years. As the soil was turned, a black ribbon reinforced with the living foundation of the prairie thudded into the trench made by the preceding round of the plow. Bee nests were upturned, mice scurried from their ruined homes, and raucous gulls swarmed behind, picking up worms, insects, and other small creatures evicted from the sanctuary of their grassland homes.

So tough was the sod that huge, ungainly breaking plows, requiring up to six yokes of oxen, had to be used. Later on, lighter and more efficient cast steel plows were marketed by John Deere, James Oliver, and others. But either way, the equipment was too expensive for most prairie pioneers. Instead, they hired the ground broken by custom crews, who charged from two to four dollars an acre for the grueling work—much more than the original price of the land.

This was but the first of many indications that prairie farming was going to require more capital than older systems of frontier agriculture. Many of the meadows were poorly drained or dotted with soggy bottomlands that restricted cultivation, as well as breeding typhoid, mosquitoes, and malaria (then called "ague"). Yet field drainage with tiles or by other methods was so costly that it was generally delayed for many years. Thus, the rolling areas were farmed first, and much of the low-lying prime ground—termed "duck ponds"—was not tilled until after 1900. On the treeless grasslands, fencing was another expensive problem, as was transportation. Near Madison, Wisconsin, so many travelers got lost in the ten-foot-high grass that the residents finally put up tall stone pyramids to guide them on their way.

But in the decade before the Civil War, and for some years thereafter, the most startling change in farming implements was the rapid improvement of harvesters, binders, seed drills, and other implements. Such advances were made possible not only by the industrial revolution, rail delivery, and the growing commercialism of agriculture, but also by the prairies themselves. Their smooth contours, their vastness, and their lack of stones and stumps were perfect for labor-saving machinery. Here, again, the Midwestern farmer could feel excited by the hope of greatly increasing his yield—yet dismayed by the attendant increase in his financial risk.

His wife, meanwhile, was dismayed by his need to plow every available penny back into the farm. Whether she lived in an Illinois frame house, built of boards from the Wisconsin forests, or in a dingy sod hut on the edge of the endless plains, she could scarcely insist that hanging new curtains or adding a room was more important than getting the reaper repaired. Yet babies often arrived almost yearly. The most universal memory of prairie wives, both during and long after the pioneer period, was of washing diapers every day for twenty or thirty years. The farther west the frontier family planted itself, the larger the farms grew, the farther apart the houses stood, and the more meager the social life became. The ague and other sicknesses were common, and the doctor frequently arrived too late. Wives, as well as children, died young.

Given the long, wavelike roll of the frontier across the continent, it would be surprising if the memory of such experiences had not created strong drives to overcome them. Indeed, foreigners tell us that we Americans over-venerate our togetherness rituals, our medicines, our money, our wives and children, our plumbing and our appliances.

Yet the farm women of the Midwest still possess that no-nonsense bustle and energy that were essential to survival in pioneer times, and that continue to mark the region as a whole. No one person can be typical, but here is how one attractive farm wife and mother, Mrs. Barbara Searle, describes her life: "This morning I was baking bread, also making some candles. I still do a lot of canning. I make eight or ten kinds of pickles, I freeze apple sauce from our trees, and I can tomatoes and brandied peaches. I pick a hundred and twenty to a hundred and thirty quarts of strawberries and freeze some, give some away, make a lot of jam. Also raspberries. Then we have a large garden, cucumbers, tomatoes, and so forth. For my anniversary, one year, I got a garden tractor. That meant I could plow the garden in an hour instead of hoeing all day.

"You know, I hear this silly women's lib song on the radio, 'I can do anything a man can do,' and I know very well the one that's singing it wouldn't know how to put the wings to the disc down, like I did this spring when we were real busy in the fields. I did most of the discing, all of the harrowing, and some of the plowing. Now, when we start picking, I'll haul in corn weekdays. I like it. The air smells nice, the ground smells nice, and there's no telephone.

"In the spring and fall we put in fourteen hours a day, six days a week. But not on Sunday. My father-in-law never did, and this is

the way our son has been raised too. Oh, you know, I might work on UNICEF at the church, and like tomorrow for the hay ride I'll make donuts and hot chocolate, things like that. I'll mix up the donuts and the girls will finish them. But I don't count that as work on Sunday."

Of the many new factors involved in prairie farming, none had summed up the old settlers' mixed feelings better than the uncertainties of land ownership.

The ideal, of course, was magnificent: millions of acres of choice public land which the federal government was anxious to transfer to hardworking yeoman farmers. In such hands the prairies would become a cradle of plenty, of grassroots churches and schools, of fireside virtue, and of a slaveless, classless society sprung to life in the freedom-loving West. While land tenure had long since been discarded as a qualification for voting, it remained, for native-born and immigrant alike, a powerful symbol of democratic citizenship and personal worth. It remains so today in the mind of many a Midwestern countryman.

Since Jefferson's time, America had believed that her unpeopled western lands operated as a safety valve. "When employment fails or wages are inadequate," enthused Horace Greeley, "they may pack up and strike westward to enter upon the possession and culture of their own lands on the banks of the Wisconsin, the Des Moines, or the Platte, which have been patiently awaiting their advent since creation." To further that happy advent, Washington was prepared to dispose of its lands in a variety of ways. But it was at this point that the ideal gave way, rather abruptly, to the real.

In the 1850s, the basic system called for an official survey of each district, followed by a land auction, after which any unsold lands could be purchased for $1.25 an acre. But by the time the auctions were held, squatters had usually been living on much of the ground for years, and improving it. To protect their own direct and speculative interests, they formed "claim clubs," which used extra-legal persuaders—such as the threat of tar-and-feathering—to make sure no one outbid them. Actually, the money-men were less interested in bidding against the squatters and settlers than in lending them the cash to buy the land—in exchange for tough mortgages and high interest rates. Even more resented by the local citizens were the outside speculators. In practice, however, they were often hard to tell from the other actors in the speculative drama swirling across the prairies and undermining the simple intent of the government's one-man, one-farm program.

Complications mounted. Another way in which Washington distributed its grasslands was by direct grants to former soldiers. Eventually, almost anyone who had served in the armed forces could get free title to 160 acres of western real estate. Plenty of veterans claimed their quarter sections of prairie turf—but very few ever set foot on them. Instead, they sold out quickly to speculators, who roamed the East, shrewdly working their way through the military rolls.

To stimulate needed improvements, the government also granted huge parcels of land to the states and to key concerns such as the railroads. In one way or another, much of this prime ground found its way onto the open market, too, and at prices far higher than many naive settlers, lured on by the states' and railroads' own propaganda, had thought they would need to pay. One booster, urging others to join the hopeful thousands already streaming toward Iowa, crooned, "It is not the Garden of America, but of the World!" Indeed, his enthusiasm seems justified, for Iowa contained fully one fourth of the highest grade topsoil in the United States, and still does. Despite the homestead laws, however, three fourths of this state's rich grassland was available to the actual users only at excessive premiums, through professional land jobbers. In 1860, a scant four years after his glowing evocation of the safety-valve theory, Horace Greeley was forced to note sadly that the two hundred million dollars received by the Treasury in land sales had "cost the settlers and improvers of those lands

Five or Six Hundred Millions, in the shape of usury, extra price, Sheriff's fees, costs of foreclosing mortgages, etc." Latter-day students of the question would show, in fact, that the widely held safety-valve theory had been mostly wishful thinking: quite logically, the prairies and plains were populated not by impoverished eastern factory workers but by seasoned farmers from the South, Europe, and the older Middle Western states.

Yet the agrarian ideal was far from dead. Under a principle known as "Pre-emption," the government showed itself willing to grant squatter-farmers special rights. Then, pressures mounted for the extension of that concept into a new, liberalized land law. Finally, in 1862, President Lincoln signed the Homestead Act. This provided that any adult citizen who had not fought against the Union could obtain title to a quarter section of public land, free, provided he lived on it, cultivated it for five years, and paid a small recording fee. Alternatively, he could buy his 160 acres for $1.25 an acre after living on it only six months.

Here was new political vision and a further spur to westward expansion. In practice the Homestead Act, too, had its defects. For one thing, most of the best prairie ground had already been sold by the time Congress got around to voting the law. For another, it did not stop much of the best land from passing through the hands of various institutions, who slowed growth by either holding it off the market entirely or demanding lofty prices. Eventually, too, the 160-acre limit proved impractical, as the agricultural frontier rolled onto the Great Plains, where larger farms were a necessity. Nonetheless, the Homestead Act worked fairly well for its first twenty years. It was during this period that pioneer farmers, many of them immigrants, were breaking the last prairie sod in northwestern Iowa, southwestern Minnesota, southeastern Dakota, and eastern Nebraska and Kansas. One indication of the bill's success was that some 57 per cent of these farms were acquired directly by the users under its legal terms of residence and cultivation.

In sum, then, the government had managed, rather stumblingly, to transfer the richest stretch of farmland in the world into private hands. Between 1860 and 1910, well over half a billion acres of new, arable land were broken in the United States—an area greater than all of Western Europe and Great Britain combined. In a bustling half-century, the number of American farms more than tripled; and more farmers were settled on the land than in the previous three centuries.

As the legislators intended, the emergent pattern was that of the small to midsized family farm. The homestead laws, and the Civil War, had succeeded in keeping plantation agriculture and slavery out of the West.

But the laws had been circumvented, too—their idealism marred by all-too-human distortions, as the middlemen intervened between the land and the settler. It was no accident that the crafty banker, about to foreclose on both the farm and its virtuous daughter, became the stock villain of nineteenth century melodrama. Yet the financial intermediaries also rendered valuable services to the needy frontier: through infusions of capital, by broadening the tax base, in advertising and community leadership, and by holding onto undeveloped pastures and woodlands which benefited the farmers in a variety of ways.

Still, the recognition that land was big business was a sure sign that the Jeffersonian dream was fading. The harshest statistics were those relating to farm tenancy. As early as 1880, 31 per cent of the farms in Illinois, and 24 per cent of those in Iowa, were owned by absentee landlords. And ironically, tenancy increased most quickly where the soil was most productive. In twenty-five counties of the central Illinois prairie, it stood at over 35 per cent; by 1900 the tenancy in one Iowa county had reached a disheartening 50 per cent. The

"agricultural ladder" was another phenomenon scarcely in accord with the classless utopia foreseen by the boosters. Its rungs extended from the seasonal laborer or hired hand at the bottom to the owner-operator at the top. In an agricultural version of the Horatio Alger stories, the chest-thumping county histories popular in the last decades of the century were crowded with accounts of successful farmers who had ascended this ladder. What the authors of course failed to mention was that many others had also slipped to lower rungs, or jumped off entirely and headed for town. In fact, it was quite difficult for the average tenant or laborer to climb the agricultural ladder, because land prices were rising faster than savings. So, in this sense, the mushrooming cities were acting as a safety-valve for the farms, rather than vice-versa.

Speculation in western real estate was nothing new. But the prairie experience helped to make "doing a land office business" a permanent entry in the American lexicon and to convince Corn Belt settlers that remorseless competition had become a permanent fact of farm life. Undoubtedly, this commercial spirit has helped to spur a fabulous physical output—as well as to devaluate alternative philosophies of living. The easygoing southern uplander may have found the prairies first, but it was the sharp-eyed Yankee and work-loving German whose life-styles soon prevailed, at least in the economic sector.

And yet the prairie farmer was no easterner either: he was a son of those ax-wielders who had breached the Appalachians in order to free themselves from eastern entanglements. He believed in the sanctity of the family farm. He believed that goodness meant simplicity. He saw himself as a producer, not a capitalist, and to him the distinction was a moral one. He resented the army of middlemen, their pockets stuffed with drafts drawn on New York banks—just as, a hundred years later, he would resent the profiteers who bought his grain at bargain prices, then resold it to the Soviet Union. The brokers who staked the turf with pointed pens, the railroads who conspired to charge exorbitant rates, and the food processing monopolies who manipulated grain prices would reinforce his long-standing suspicion of those nefarious "others" who have often seemed to Midwesterners to be threatening their inland sanctum. And so, like the pioneers before him, the prairie farmer would continue to seek purity through insulation—whether that meant forbidding branch banking in his state, or refusing to hear the unholy thoughts of a distant intelligentsia, or avoiding internationalism and a hundred other "isms."

Doing a land-office business in Kansas, 1874

Toward the end of the nineteenth century, Corn Belt farmers endured many hard years. They made painful adjustments to a new and chronic disequilibrium between supply and demand—the underlying source of their troubles—and to the commercial, financial, and industrial revolutions—the real culprits in defeating the agrarian ideal. But nothing is as basic to the farmer as his land. Over the long term it would prove his most precious asset, his best hedge against inflation, his worthiest legacy. In the prairies its very value made land hard to acquire at all; and then the communicable fever of speculation tempted farmers to leverage it so heavily as to risk losing everything. Historian Ray Allen Billington may have overstated the case, but his remarks are cogent:

> Thus the Middle West that emerged from its pioneer period bore little resemblance to the Garden of the World pictured by propagandists a generation before. With its unrivaled riches still only partially tapped, with almost half its population unable to buy excessively priced lands and reduced to the menial status of tenants or farm laborers, and with the more energetic renters fleeing still farther westward in hope of finding a purchasable farm, the region was saddled with a heritage of debt and dissatisfaction rather than one of prosperity and hope. Little wonder that its settlers, viewing this vast gulf between dream and reality, have felt justified in demanding a larger share of the national income through political action, from the days of the Grange and Populism to those of farm parity and soil banks.

Indeed, the farmers were beginning to fight back with agrarian gusto. "There are three great crops raised in Nebraska," snapped one of their partisan newspapers in 1890. "One is a crop of corn, one is a crop of freight rates, and one is a crop of interest. One is produced by the farmers who by sweating and toil farm the land. The other two are produced by men who sit in their offices and behind their bank counters and farm the farmers." In a nation of political power blocs, in which the relative number of farmers has declined steadily, organizations like the Grange, the Farmers Union, and the Farm Bureau have struggled to defend agricultural interests down to the present day. Like individual farmers, however, such groups have often disagreed with one another on basic policy objectives. Surer progress seems to have been achieved by marketing and purchasing cooperatives, to which some three fourths of the farmers in the Midwest now belong.

In the 1890s, it was a sign of the times that William Jennings Bryan, in his colorful but unsuccessful race for the Presidency, felt called on to champion the virtuous small farmer against the mounting power of the urban-industrial complex. "The great cities rest upon our broad and fertile prairies," he thundered in his famous Cross of Gold speech. "Burn down your cities and leave our farms, and your cities will spring up again as if by magic; but destroy our farms, and the grass will grow in the streets of every city in the country." And Herbert Quick summed up the farmer's economic woes in characteristic tones:

> The farmer is often accused by the city dweller of being a confirmed calamity howler. He is. He is such because almost every calamity which comes on the land hits him sooner or later. Whenever any other industry shifts from under an economic change it shifts it in part to the farmer, and the farmer is unable to shift it in his turn; while most other shiftees can, by adding to prices or wages, get from under the load. The farmer is so placed that there is nothing beyond him but the wall. He is crushed against it. There is nothing under him but the earth. He is pressed into it. He is the end of the line in the economic game of crack the whip, and he is cracked off. He has been cracked off into city life by the million.

Perfectly true—and yet the farmers have also *stayed* on the land by the million. This is, in fact, part of the creative tension of the Midwest country. As prime destination, mixing bowl, transfer stop, entrepôt, and point of departure during a century and a half of unprecedented mobility and progress, the region has long been habituated to change and movement. On the other hand, the men and women who have marked the land most deeply did *not* move, but, despite the hell-and-high-water that often lapped at their doors, hung on. Land, after all, is among the least liquid of assets—unless you count character itself.

Hence the deep prairie paradox: a heritage not merely of fear but of hope, of deep conservatism as well as rife speculation, of calamity-howling and unshakable faith. Quick expresses this polarity in a kind of unintended parable about the frequent arguments of two of his farmer neighbors, one a Yankee, the other a German:

> He [Crippen] put his foot up on the hub of Riemann's wagon after it came to a halt, and began descanting on the awful condition of the farmers. I can imagine about what he said. Everything had gone to the devil. The wheat wouldn't pay for cutting. The grain there was in the rotten straw wouldn't make bread. So far from being No. 1 or No. 2, or even No. 3, it would grade as "rejected" only. It wouldn't pay wages for hauling it to town. We all might as well quit and let our farms go for the mortgages. Any one who was fool enough to move into such a hell of a country as Iowa deserved to starve. Well, we'd starve all right!
>
> Riemann sat listening to this flood of pessimism and felt it surging against the dike of spiritual quiet which he had built about his soul. This Yankee neighbor was destroying his preparation for religious comfort. His glance strayed from the horses' ears and fixed itself sternly on the face of Crippen the tempter. From sternness it passed to rage. He pulled up on the lines as a signal for his horses to start, and spake.
>
> "Why, damn your lousy Yankee soul," said he; "don't you know that our Lord yet lives?"

Since the 1870s, Midwestern farming has changed so greatly that Messrs. Crippen and Riemann would have a hard time recognizing it. One thing they would recognize, though, is their own weave of pessimism and serenity. Much of the characteristically soft humor of the countryside, as well as its dead-serious talk, is based on this contrast.

Not long ago, Jim Reschke and his brother Bud, both in their fifties, were driving around their 470-acre farm in the rich prairie soil of western Illinois. It had been raining for days. As their pickup zipped by their fifteen hundred head of cattle and hogs, and past field after field of ripe corn, Bud glanced nervously at the sky. He shook his head. "Gettin' kinda pressed because of this weather," he said. "Can't get the machines in the field to pick the corn. Last year we had an ideal crop, but this year's going to be bad."

Suddenly Jim looked over. "Say, you know what? The American farmer is a big bragger."

Charles O'Rear

Bud smiled, recognizing the story. "To his neighbor."

Jim nodded. "To his neighbor. One'll ask the other, 'How many pigs you get to the litter?' And the other one'll say, 'Oh, not too good. Only average about nine.' But, see, nine is fantastic! He's counted 'em some funny way or something. But at first we didn't know that. Some of the stories we'd hear around here when we first came would make us feel awful bad!" The brothers chuckled. "Now here's another thing. Farmers are big gripers. Everybody knows that. But they're really big optimists!"

"Why?"

" 'Cause they have to believe prices will go up. Now isn't that right?" Jim grinned ironically.

Bud remained sober. "You have to relate farm prices to the price of the land. There's ground around here selling for twelve or fifteen hundred dollars an acre, and there's just no way you can justify that with corn at a dollar-ten a bushel."

"But if it's not economical, how come you keep working it?"

For a long moment the only sound was the windshield wipers' flapping. Finally Jim said, "We're paid in another depth."

Bud, who was driving, shrugged. "The monetary part? Most people wouldn't think of putting in the number of hours we do for what we get out of it in terms of money. If we put our investment out at interest we'd come out a lot better. We stay in farming because we truly love it. It gives you a sense of independence and accomplishment you can get nowhere else."

Later, at dinner, Jim said, "Agriculture and agribusiness and the food producing industry are subsidizing our whole country. If Americans had to pay the per cent of their incomes that others do for their food, that is, not fifteen per cent but forty per cent, you'd see other things like our medical bills be cut. But the way things are, about three more kicks and all us farmers will quit."

Bud shook his head and pounded his heavy fist on the table. "We wouldn't quit! We're individuals, we're not organized, so we suffer by that. We belong to organizations that don't tie us in knots. But our independence is far-reaching. Farmers all say they're broke. Yet they have a crib full of corn and so forth. So half of them don't realize their true wealth, which is not in cash. When we have something of quality, we like to keep it. And yet—we've stretched God's good grace on this ground. This is where our foolish folly will come out. We'll be forced to overproduce beyond the natural capacity of the ground."

"I disagree," said Bud. "The fertilizers we have now are better for the ground than what we were doing twenty years ago."

The conversation continued in this fervid way until the meal was over. Then, all joined in unison:

> "Oh give thanks unto the Lord
> For He is good
> And His mercy endureth forever."

Dolores, Bud's wife, stood up to clear the table. Silent during all the man-talk, she spoke up at last: "That part of the prayer always gives me a lift."

For all the permutations of faith and despair that the farmer uses in trying to cope with his unique situation, the basic cause of his marketing woes is quite simple: a persistent imbalance between supply and demand. Since eating habits are slow to change, and since the capacity of the human stomach has its limits, demand for basic grain foods cannot easily adjust to variations in supply. And since production is in the hands of millions of strong individualists, deeply committed to their way of life, and virtually unable to adjust or diversify their output, supply cannot adapt to short-term variations in demand. Expecting a wheat farmer to grow less wheat because others are growing

more is as unrealistic as expecting the American family to suddenly eat more bread that season. On the contrary, if wheat prices drop, a farmer may well try to increase production in order to meet his fixed costs—causing prices to slide even more. In this situation, in which supply and demand cannot respond sensitively to each other, unpredictable factors like the weather, or foreign demand, can cause prices to rise and fall with a sharpness that often seems unfair to both producer and consumer.

The farmer's problem is compounded by the fact that his prosperity is a function not of farm prices alone but of the relationship between his receipts and his expenses. Although he sells at wholesale, he must buy at retail, and he has no control over either price. And though most of the economy is closely intermeshed through small compensating adjustments, the farm sector often finds itself far out of phase with the rest, exaggerating the steep swings in the farmer's fortunes. A desire to smooth out these swings has led to the concept of "parity"—an effort to stabilize the farmer's purchasing power by artificially maintaining farm prices at a certain ratio to his costs. But in practice, parity policies have not made producers or consumers very happy.

From the end of the Civil War until the end of the nineteenth century, farm output was increasing faster than the population. Enormous new tracts of land were being opened in the Middle and Far West. As human power gave way to animal power, great advances were made in farm productivity, as well as in storage and shipment. The result was that agricultural production more than doubled within thirty years. To be sure, the population was increasing—but not that fast. And to counter the inflation created during the Civil War, the government followed a policy of deflation and currency contraction. The combined result was a long, steep slide in farm prices. From 1867 to 1894, the gold-equivalent price of wheat sank from $1.45 a bushel to $0.67; its currency-equivalent decline was far worse. Farmers struggling to pay off borrowings made at earlier levels were devastated. Tenancy rose sharply, as we have seen, and by 1890 half the farms in the newer Midwestern states were mortgaged.

Anguished cries from the Populists, the Grangers, and others finally helped persuade Washington to resume a modest expansion of the money supply. More important in lifting the heavy cloud of gloom from the farms was that population growth caught up with agricultural growth. The frontier had ended, the supply of new land that could be tilled by traditional methods had run out, and the number of farmers

Russell Lee

soon peaked at eleven million. Since manufacturing had passed agriculture in the total value of its products, the newer immigrants headed not for the farms, but for the cities, where the jobs were. Just after 1900 this swelling influx reached a million a year, and within another generation the new urbanites would decisively outnumber the rural populace.

Thus, the farmer's situation had reversed itself: the demand for his products was now rising faster than his output. Consequently, in the first ten years of the new century, agricultural prices leapt 50 per cent, and the value of an average acre of farm land doubled. Since non-agricultural prices were rising much more slowly, the farmer's purchasing power continued to widen until World War I.

Then it took another upward leap. By curtailing European farm output, the war created a powerful new demand for American foodstuffs. Wheat exports, as an example, jumped from $88 million to $298 million in six years. Farmers responded by expanding their long-term productive capacity. Seventy-seven million new acres were brought under cultivation. Productivity raced ahead as the gasoline tractor jerked agriculture into the motor-driven age. Power machinery not only multiplied the area one man could work in a day, but also released millions of acres that had been used to grow horse and mule feed. And once again, with farm prices at record levels, and with the post–Civil War experience largely gone from living memory, the farmers began to speculate. Borrowing heavily against their land and machinery, they drove the price of an acre of prime ground to above $500.

Inevitably, the bubble burst. First, European farms resumed normal production, so export demand fell off. Then, for a number of reasons, domestic demand slackened. Though the farmer was locked into a system of high-cost production, farm prices suddenly plummeted. By July 1921 they had dropped a staggering 85 per cent from their highs of the previous year. Yet supply remained at lofty levels as scientific methods and mechanization spurred productivity to ever greater heights. And even after the broad economic slump of 1920–23 had ended, the farmer found himself facing the same ironies as his predecessor of half a century earlier: within a wider, high-priced boom, a continuing depression on the land. Tenancy resumed its relentless climb. Mortgages mounted ominously. Soon the whole face of the Middle West country—that Garden of agrarian virtue and contentment—was pocked by a terminal illness: foreclosure.

Some rebelled. Declaring "farmers' holidays," they tried to cut supply and force up prices by manning country roads with pitchforks—blocking shipments and dumping milk in the gutters. Such news caused staid old J. P. Morgan, relaxing on a liner in the mid-Atlantic, to cable his Wall Street headquarters: WHAT IS HAPPENING IN IOWA. For some farmers, the irony of that belated recognition almost made the illegality worth it. Others revived the spirit of the old claim club: attending sheriffs' sales en masse, they intimidated would-be buyers, purchased the land for a penny, and turned it back debt-free to the farmer who had lost it. But these were the sporadic, last-ditch efforts of desperate men. Few farmers favored radical government intervention, and their organizations were, as ever, deeply divided on what should be done.

J. W. McManigal

Yet the farm lobby was crying out for federal action, and as the idea gained acceptance, Congress twice passed parity bills. Presidents Coolidge and Hoover vetoed these. However, another program, calling for the government to buy up huge farm surpluses, went into effect in 1929. But at that point the stock market broke and the entire economy collapsed. In the next four years farm prices sank another 50 per cent. The hopeless farm plan was abandoned.

An elevator in South Dakota put up a sign: SHELLED CORN TWO CENTS A BUSHEL: CORN ON THE COB, THREE CENTS LESS. Wheat dropped as low as $.20 a bushel. Families who for thirty years had sunk every penny and every working hour into their farms were suddenly told by a land bank agent to get their personal belongings together and be off the property within twenty-four hours.

Irony of ironies, the only one who now seemed determined to save our individualistic yeoman spoke with eastern cultivation and socialistic overtones. Roosevelt quickly unleashed some heavy weapons which many a Midwestern countryman would call "regimentation" and forever resent. Yet many others, saved from ruin, would be eternally grateful for the forty cents a bushel the government paid them for the corn they had been burning in the kitchen stove.

One series of New Deal measures tried to halt foreclosures, give farmers better access to credit, and help them repossess their land. These it did—but in the process, private lenders fled the field, so that by 1941 various federal agencies held over 40 per cent of all farm mortgages. Electrification and similar measures helped improve the quality of rural life, especially in poorer areas. Roosevelt also moved to persuade farmers to cut back on production. Under parity formulas, growers received billions of dollars for leaving acreage unplanted. Hungry city dwellers failed to see the logic of this. And partly because of excellent weather, partly because of strong production overseas, partly because of continued gains in agricultural efficiency—and partly because of the stubborn resistance of the farmers themselves—parity didn't work very well. Bumper crops and low prices prevailed until World War II.

At that point—just as in 1914—the fortunes of the American farmer suddenly raced ahead once again. But the prairie paradox would remain. For a hundred years the Midwestern farmer had faced a perplexing disparity between his efforts and his rewards, and this was not about to end. So he would continue to move along a tightrope between hope and fear, between the disparate roles of independent businessman and injured yeoman, between wanting to be left alone and demanding to be helped. As in the days of the Populists, this duality of outlook would show up in sharp disputes within his own ranks. Says one: "Franklin D. helped the farmer with corn and hog money—I don't know what some would have done without it." His neighbor snaps back: "Those durn handouts just stuck in our craw." If the New Deal pulled many back from the brink of disaster, it also opened the door to a permanent government role in agriculture. Against which our fiercely independent farmers would continue to struggle with the passion of that old Iowa prairie boy, Herbert Quick:

> But in spite of the sun which beat down upon our heads, of the bleeding hands which could not be favored in the maniacal struggle with the grain, in spite of the impossibility of the thing, we did it; and we made a sort of adventure of it. For the grain was ours, you see. Human effort grows ineffective just in the proportion that men are taken from tasks which they do for themselves and are put to work for others.

But the bare, often harsh economic realities scarcely do justice to the inner tone of Midwestern country life. Even on the most commercial of farms, nature forces the farmer to think beyond the merely commercial. Each day he sees, as Sir Francis Bacon did, that "Nature, to be commanded, must be obeyed." The eternal twining of his purposes with nature's makes for painful decisions:

> I am now at the quivering stage of uncertainty through which every farmer passes just before he takes the plunge and cuts his hay anyhow. The worth of the crop depends upon his judgment and the weather. I have a very fine field of soy beans. The leaves are beginning to turn at the bottom of the vines, but the beans have not filled out. If I cut them too soon the leaves will turn dark, parch and drop off, and the beans will be worthless. If I wait, the spell of bad weather we always have around the equinox may delay the harvesting too long. Meanwhile, the bean beetle is within three miles of this place, consuming everything as it comes. And every man who has this kind of hay is cutting it regardless of whether it is mature or not. I know exactly how a speculator feels when he is in doubt about whether to sell or hold on the risk of losing everything in order to make a greater profit. Every year of my life on this farm I have passed through these tremors of uncertainty and anxiety. I expected to have the hay cut yesterday, but the night before there was lightning in the north, not flashes but real forked lightning—a sure sign of rain in this section. Today the wind is from the

east, the sky overcast—no rain yet, but the weather too threatening to risk haying.

That such a description is as applicable today as it might have been in 1900—or in 1924, when it was written—is proof enough that, in the ancient art of husbandry, continuity is as inevitable as change. Other features of farm life are equally enduring: the time, space, and privacy to appreciate simple things; commonality of interests with one's neighbors; the centripetal tug of local institutions and the family; the openness and clarity of a life spent under vast skies.

Recollections of Midwestern farm life are as full of these qualities as they are of surprise at the changes wrought by every era. At the turn of the century the swelling clangor of the cities made the quiet isolation of rural life seem as anachronistic as it still does. To contemporaries, the arrival of RFD, the Tin Lizzie, the Sears catalogue, and the telephone—like TV and superhighways—seemed certain to doom such differences. Indicative of the long reach of the mail-order business were the personal replies it drew from country people. At their Chicago nerve centers, jaded Montgomery Ward clerks slit open envelopes to find orders like this:

> I suppose you wonder why we haven't ordered anything from you since the fall. Well, the cow kicked my arm and broke it and besides my wife was sick, and there was the doctor bill. But now, thank God, that is paid, and we are all well again, and we have a fine new baby boy, and please send plush bonnet number 29d8077.

Even as such threads were beginning to stitch the farm family into a wider "consumption community," country life kept to its own forms. A boy growing up on a typical farm in the early 1900s would probably not leave his immediate neighborhood more than three or four times a year, when he made the five- or ten-mile trek to the local town. The exception was that rare treat, the county fair.

Family life centered in the kitchen, as it still does in the rural Midwest. Unless they were lucky enough to have a windmill to lift the ground water, the wife carried water in from a well with the help of her children. She cooked for her family and for the hired hands on a wood or coal stove, and another cast-iron stove heated the house through the severe Midwestern winters. Other rooms were literally called "the other room," or "the front room." The parlor was carefully set aside for weddings, funerals, and the daughters' courting. Over

J. W. McManigal

its horsehair furniture hung crayon enlargements of family photos. On the table there might be a piece of embroidery, or even a stereoscope. A wooden or galvanized washtub doubled as a bathtub on Saturdays. The house was lighted with kerosene lamps. On the front porch, carved posts and scrollwork proved this was a civilized house and not a barn. The Bible was read each day. Church socials were the main recreation, but the smooth-worn floorboards of the roomy cow and horse barn were ideal for country dances. Since "swapping meals" made little sense to the farmer, he seldom invited his neighbors to dinner. In terms of income, this was, as we have seen, the golden age of grain farming. Yet the horse still set the pace, and the farm was still diversified. Its self-reliance extended not only to food but to all sorts of services, repairs, and light manufacturing—such as twining rope, hewing beams with a hewing ax, or making lye soap.

It was during this same period, near the turn of the century, that the age-old sounds of feeding and nurturing caught the ear of Sherwood Anderson:

> In the farmhouses and in the houses on the side streets in the villages, life awoke at dawn. Back of each of the houses there was a barn for the horses and cows, and sheds for the pigs and chickens. At daylight a chorus of neighs, squeals, and cries broke the silence. Boys and men came out of the houses. They stood in the open spaces before the barns and stretched their bodies like sleepy animals . . . The men and boys went to a pump beside the house and washed their faces and hands in the cold water. In

the kitchens there was the smell and the sound of the cooking of food. The women also were astir. The men went into the barns to feed the animals and then hurried to the houses to be themselves fed. A continual grunting sound came from the sheds where pigs were eating corn, and over the houses a contented silence brooded . . .

All day long on the wide western prairies when the gray fall days have come, you may see the men and the horses working their way slowly through the fields. Like tiny insects they crawl across the immense landscapes. After them in the late fall and in the winter when the prairies are covered with snow, come the cattle. They are brought from the far West in cattle cars and after they have nibbled the corn blades all day, are taken to barns and stuffed to bursting with corn. When they are fat they are taken to the great killing-pens in Chicago, the giant city of the prairies. In the still fall nights, as you stand on prairie roads or in the barnyard back of one of the farm houses, you may hear the rustling of the dry corn blades and then the crash of the heavy bodies of the beasts going forward as they nibble and trample the corn.

But it was the next period—the years from 1920 to 1945—that have become the "old days" for the many who can still recall them. For the farmer this was a time of economic uncertainty. Yet, across the span of later changes, those who spent their youth in the rural Midwest remember that formative period with a special warmth. Harvey Jacobs, for instance, recalls his Indiana boyhood in *We Came Rejoicing,* a memoir fondly crowded with such down-home events as pie suppers and maple sugaring, hog-sticking and lard making, spelling bees and decisions-for-Christ. Jacobs tells of folks getting a new magazine called *The Saturday Evening Post,* and of how his relatives joined hands to help one another remodel their houses and tool sheds to make room for those revolutionary inventions, the radio and the tractor. Two or three nights a week the neighbors would cluster around his mother's piano, singing songs like "We'll build a sweet little nest somewhere in the West, and let the rest of the world go by."

Though this was the transition era from the cracker barrel to packaged goods, the vitality of the pot-bellied-stove general store was still undiminished. Harvey's storekeeper, old Mr. Perton, unlocked the door of his establishment at five-thirty every morning, and he was there until ten at night. Perton's had a competitor, too: the huckster. Ubiquitous in rural America, hucksters had begun as gypsies with packs on their backs, cadging meals and hayloft lodgings. Later they had graduated to horsedrawn wagons, well stocked by the local merchants. But now the familiar huckster had become motorized. And, like the mail-order clerk, he inherited the merchant's role of good listener, advisor, and disseminator, plucking and planting newsy tidbits on his weekly rounds:

"What are most people doing?" my father asked. "Are they replanting or taking a chance that a stand is left?"

"Some are and some aren't," he replied. "Most of the boys across the ridge are planting over. They seemed to be nipped a little harder over there. To the south, it's about half and half." He walked on across the field, dropping to his knees to examine the sprouts from time to time. We walked on out to the end of the row with him and bought a nickel's worth of horehound candy . . .

With serious shaking of the head, he reported the news as he looped the cord around the legs of the chickens we were trading for groceries. He suspended them, clucking and flopping, upside down from the scales at the rear of the wagon. After a long time, during which the recital of events went right on, the chickens became quiet enough for him to read the scales. "Yes sir, the folks over on Indian Creek say they have—28 pounds and a quarter—never seen the water so low for this time of year."

With cooperative harvesting, threshing, and the accompanying dinners still indispensable, male and female roles were drawn as sharply as ever. Earlier, a Wisconsin housewife had made her girls a checklist which remained typical:

(1) Pump two pails of water from the cistern. Put them on the bench on the back porch with four wash basins and four bars of soap on saucers. See that fresh towels are on the nails and a comb on the shelf.

J. W. McManigal

(2) In the dining room, set two tables for eighteen people, with knife, fork, spoon, glass, plate, and coffee cup at each place. On each table, put pepper and salt shakers, sugar bowl and spoon, cream pitcher, tooth picks. Put chair at each place.

(3) Chop the cabbages.

(4) Husk the corn.

(5) As soon as men start coming to dinner, put the bread, butter, jelly and pickles on the table. Fill the two big pitchers on each table with milk and water.

(6) When the men are at the table, help pass the bowls and platters of food and bring empty ones to the kitchen for refills.

(7) Put the dessert plates with the apple pie and cheese on the dinner plates as soon as the men have finished with their meat and potatoes.

And young Harvey Jacobs, to whom harvesting was a drama, was so inspired by his male responsibilities that he lined them into blank verse:

There's a binder to be cleaned and trucked
And a sickle to be sharpened;
Is there too much play in the pitmans?
No, it will go another season if we keep it oiled.
Oil the bundlecarrier—
Sun the canvases;
And don't forget the threader and knotter—
They can delay us and madden us.
Ready the hitches—
Load the twine,
Tell the shockers it's $3 a day and dinner;
Harvey, you will carry water.

Millstone, Lincoln's New Salem, Illinois

Among the many early gristmills still standing throughout the Midwest is the Motor Mill on the Turkey River near Elkader, Iowa.

Flour bag stencil at Schech's Mill, near Caledonia, Minnesota

When the Depression struck, the boy watched hundreds of destitute men aimlessly riding the rails on those same trains by which the farmers still set their clocks. The local bank closed; yet its president, who was also the local doctor, eventually managed to repay his depositors every penny. If they were luckier than most, Jacobs himself felt fortunate in another way:

> Especially during the depression years, when our cash went for taxes, interest on the mortgage, and fertilizer, we guarded our food supply. No matter how poor we became, we knew we could eat—and well. We had traded wheat for flour at threshing time; we had canned tomatoes, peaches, and green beans during summer; we had stored potatoes and turnips in the basement. With maple syrup in the cupboards, we might not even need to buy much sugar. Meat, however, was the main course, and I acquired an outlook toward menus which stands today: A meal is hardly worth sitting down to unless it offers meat and gravy.

But it was the innovations that stood out most sharply against the level horizons of country life. Jacobs recalls the gradual but dramatic changeover from one-row cultivating with horses, when he had to uncover each little corn shoot with a forked stick, to hydraulically operated plows that cleanly cultivated four or more rows at once. In another chapter, he relives his open-mouthed wonder at watching the first airplane any of them had ever seen land in a neighbor's hayfield —and his excitement at getting a brief ride in it.

Technical changes brought social changes, too, such as the transition from the one-room schoolhouse to the consolidated school system. Bit by bit, the isolation of rural life was lessening, as the farm began to be joined to the wider world. Such changes could be painful, and country-born conservatives remained dubious about the modern trend. Yet they welcomed its benefits. On Saturday nights, farm families chugged to town in their Fords to see the movies. In summer, they could watch Hollywood's one-reelers in the coolness of the barricaded street in front of the hardware store.

Directives from Washington were another matter. Jacobs describes a play, produced by the local Farmers' Institute, ridiculing Secretary of Agriculture Henry Wallace and featuring live pigs set loose onstage. By 1940 the Sears catalogue had announced—prematurely, perhaps —that its dresses were "inspired by Schiaparelli," and that the "traditional lapse between the acceptance of new fashions in metropolitan centers and on farms apparently no longer exists." Naturally, it would be up to the local preacher to set such goings-on in the proper light:

"Where do our styles come from? Well, perhaps ours come from Sears and Roebuck—in Chicago. Where does Chicago get them? From New York, they tell me. And where does New York get them? I'm told they come from Paris. Where does Paris get its fashions, ladies and gentlemen? I'll tell you where Paris gets them"—and the pastor's voice rose to an angry crescendo—"Paris gets them straight from hell!"

Jacobs' sunny directness of style does full justice to the regional character: the folkways of the Corn Belt have never been colored by the nuance and indirection one finds farther south. Yet it was an Englishman, Graham Hutton, who, in 1946, published what is still one of the best all-around books on the area: *Midwest at Noon.* Hutton's graciousness of tone and his melding of the near and far perspectives emerge from passages like this:

I recall many winter evenings with Midwest farmers—in Illinois, Wisconsin, Iowa, Ohio, Minnesota—when, neighbors having been advised (or, perhaps I ought to say, warned), about twenty would foregather in one farmhouse just to talk. The visiting wives would get someone to look after their children and come over to the host's farm to help the hostess with the baking and preparations. They would bring jars of this or that, or a pie, or a cake. . . . At six we would see the headlights of cars steadily eating up the straight, white, snow-deep roads and finally snaking along the driveway up to the farm. Muffled, their occupants would come in, greeting each other only by first names: "Ned," "Matt," "Charlie," "Mis' Clarke." There would be an intense, hushed, and entirely propitious bustling in the kitchen in the rear. The summons would come, and we would sit down, nine or ten a side, host and hostess at either end, and the other ladies "in waiting," to a dinner which fairly sang of Midwest hospitality: fresh mushroom soup; two kinds of chicken or pork; lima and string beans, baked potatoes, corn biscuits, preserve of baby strawberries and butter with the biscuits; salad of lettuce with fresh cranberry and pomegranate jello thereon; ice cream and maple syrup or three kinds of pie; and coffee. (I know they did not eat like that ordinarily. But I also know they could do it regularly for the enjoyment of their friends and for an evening in their own home.) In the offing, over the banisters, curious and wide-eyed youngsters, regularly shooed off to bed and as regularly returning, would give the false impression of Christmas eve. Afterward the ladies washed dishes—none would dream of leaving that pile for the hostess next morning—and then we would talk, and the ladies would join us.

The heroic mythology of nineteenth century agrarianism appeared in this poster promoting the Grangers, a farmer's organization.

Of all the talk and discussion I had in the Midwest, I think I relished that in the farmhouses most; and not only because of the preliminaries. It was direct, elemental, simple, often oversimplified, but extremely rational and open-minded . . .

I have already noted the unparalleled neighborliness and mutual help of the rural community in the Midwest; but it is worth noting that there are severe and recognized limits to this. Kindness in "trouble" and mutual aid—"trouble" is a capacious portmanteau word in the region—are general and dependable. But the same farmer who will help out on a sick neighbor's farm will not give him an ounce of seed, or yield an inch while bargaining, if he feels that the context is one of trade or business and not of human need . . .

But the Midwest farmer knows he is your equal. He does not shout it in your ear and blazon it upon his forehead. He takes it for granted, but quietly.

If the near-and-far view could be acquired by an Englishman who had come to reside in the Midwest, so might the double perspective be taken by his counterpart: an Iowa farm boy who had gone east and abroad to join the literary mainstream. In *We Have All Gone Away,* Curtis Harnack looks back on the loamy world of his youth with an

GIFT FOR THE GRANGERS.
"I PAY FOR ALL."
FAITH, HOPE,
CHARITY, FIDELITY.
P
H
HARVEST DANCE.
RUTH & BOAZ.
HALE POWERS & CO. FRATERNITY & FINE ART PUBLISHERS, CIN.
Entered according to Act of Congress in the year 1873 by Strobridge & Co. in the Office of the Librarian of Congress at Washington.
STROBRIDGE & CO., LITH. CINCINNATI, O.

eye for fine-grained detail—and a perspective lengthened by his postwar adulthood:

Barns were masculine, sensibly clean-lined, massive, smelling of grains, sweat, animals, and excrement, a composite odor no female endeavor could cope with and most sensible farmers' wives didn't try. The barn couldn't be clean enough for human habitation; no toilet training, no rules of deportment held. Even the hungry flies specked the light bulbs so thickly they had an amber glow, as if shining through tobacco juice. For all these reasons a child felt free there . . .

. . . warmth in winter from animal heat . . . the glow from the dim, cobwebbed windows of the milking section when I stood in snowbanks outside—then going into the barn, catching the lactic smells of mother and babyhood, feeling the calmness of this extraction . . .

When the cranking became harder, I knew the paddle was spinning in whipped cream—that I must now strenuously press forward to beat the reluctant liquid, master it, whack the living daylights out of it, shatter the heavy mountainous piles that suddenly welled up, almost to the top, struggling to be stronger than me—until suddenly it all gave up and splattered into butter-islands, bits and hunks here and there . . .

We were never far from the pleasure a plant took in growing, an animal in living. At night I'd stare heavenward at the curds of stars called the Milky Way. In a galaxy of such infinite milkiness, we were alive and attentive here at the nourishing breast of the world.

Richly associative are Harnack's memories of the many bedrooms, the attic, the basement, and those typically Midwestern porches that ringed his farmhouse. And his descriptions of people are uniquely valuable: the wilderness-taming German grandfather whose fierce, loving shadow lay heavy over the lives of his descendants; Miss Flock, the pathetically ineffective schoolmarm; Uncle Jack, the wholly practical farmer, eternally captivated by any new machine or downtown improvement, and instinctively opposing any boyish or feminine softness for older things; Aunt Bertha, in her ruffled cap, grinding out raw pork and stuffing it into sausage skins for canning; Barney, the Dutch hired man, "a sort of guest here on his way to becoming an American," who later graduated into marriage, a house of his own, a high-paying job in an Oregon defense plant, and—most proudly—full citizenship; a sad, older uncle, unsuccessfully trying to re-establish meaning in his life by returning to the farm; and the three aunts, regular visitors who were forever spinning those complex webs that bind large farm families:

For Lizzie these visits sometimes seemed inspections. Should one of the aunts reach down to pull a stray weed, she was insulted. If they offered to help with the supper dishes, perhaps it was a criticism that the job hadn't been done yet. She feared the housekeeping might not seem up to the gleaming family standard when these "girls" had lived here. She tried her best to make her food as tasty as anything her sisters-in-law could produce. We children must be as well behaved as little automatons, particularly in church. (Although a late communicant in the Lutheran fold, she'd show she could be as pious as anyone.) "How're the crops coming along?" to brother Jack from his sister, Bertha, might mean, Lizzie felt: *We're the landlords over part of this farm and how well are you working our acres?* My paternal grandfather's estate remained unsettled for years. Jack paid cash rent to his sisters in the name of his mother, although it wasn't clear how much was owed and to whom—this place was in every sense the family farm. Lizzie bridled under the sloppy arrangement, feeling Jack was being taken advantage of by everyone; and yet she knew nothing would be done about it. And *she* was the newcomer.

Finally, and surpassingly, Harnack's theme is that of his Thomas Wolfe-like title. The father having died early, the mother and Aunt Lizzie, who together shared the housekeeping, had lived out the American dream of motivating their seven children to have "better, different lives" than their own. Ultimately, this would mean that all but one of the seven children would move away to the coasts. Even the one, Cousin Lois, would become a supervisor in a city school system, before marrying a farmer and settling into a modern rural life very different from that of her childhood. In older agrarian societies, so wide a scattering of the clan within a single generation might seem remarkable. In the kinetic, progress-minded Corn Belt, however, it is far from unusual. Speaking of his mother, Harnack concludes by describing her dream of continuing the prairie family's steady march toward those ever-receding horizons of the future:

> She divested herself of her four offspring in order to save us; *that* was why we were all to go away. Almost mystically, she had a sense of launching us into the mainstream of future American life, for we would die if we remained where we were born . . .
>
> The land here might nourish our bodies, build stamina and spirit, but in our progress through the years, it too would have to be left behind for what it could never do for us. The mindlessness of Nature would erode our ambitions to hurl ourselves into life and make our marks. Only in a man-made environment—the city—could one forget the humdrum futility of the years in passage. The illusion that there was a lot to *do* in life besides merely *being* in life could only be sustained in an urban setting. In this way our

generation, using the mulched dead matter of agrarian life like projectile fuel for our thrust into the future, became part of that enormous vitality springing out of rural America.

For over a century, prairie sons and daughters like the Harnacks have been infusing this most middle-class of nations with their ambitions and moralities. Today, with farm birthrates down to the national average, and with the rural population a less significant factor than it once was, this "spread" effect has undoubtedly diminished. But in other ways, as we shall see, the prairie wellsprings are more copious than ever. Incised in the sticky sod, the hopes and disillusions of the pioneers yield an extraordinary vigor among those who choose, staunchly, to remain.

SWEET CIDER
Zucchini .25¢ LB.
Egg Plant .20¢ LB.
Red Beets 2 lbs. 35¢
LAGRANGE SWEETS
LOUISIANA YAMS
"Hot"
Parsnips 29¢ lb.
Turnips 29¢ lb.
Carrots 2 for 25¢
10 LBS. NET WT.
GROWN AND PACKED BY
SELECTED TOMATOES

Reinard A. Wulkow

Chapter Five

The Yield

ABUNDANCE, said historian David Potter, is the key to the American character. And even in a generation weaned on computers and moon shots, one can add that the nation's abundance is summed up in her spectacular ability to produce grain. On the world stage, some of the advanced countries may well surpass the United States in the production of various goods and services. But there are no signs that anyone is about to "catch up" to us in agriculture: the family farms of the Midwest have remained nuclear to what we are, and to what we will become.

As Potter points out, abundance derives not from natural resources alone, but, more importantly, from human resourcefulness. It was the mental climate—the technologies, the incentives, and other intangibles—that enabled the young nation to exploit its physical treasures more successfully than the Amerindians or, say, the contemporaneous Brazilians or Chinese. In his definition of the term "region," geographer Vidal de la Blache gave full recognition to man's input:

> A region is a reservoir of energy whose origin lies in nature but whose development depends on man. It is man, who, by molding the land to his own purposes, brings out its individuality. He establishes a connection between its separate features. He substitutes for the incoherent effect of local

circumstances a systematic concourse of forces. It is thus that a region defines and differentiates itself . . .

De la Blache was writing in 1903—an age less well informed about ecological coherence than ours and less unctuous about it. A generation later, Sherwood Anderson could still, without self-consciousness, echo man's old fears of the inland emptiness: "Hills are at their best when white farm houses cling to their sides. Nature untouched by man is too difficult of approach. You become terrorized." If de la Blache's definition seems more applicable to a region like the eastern seaboard than to one like the Sahara, it is also an apter description of the intensively cultivated Corn Belt than of neighboring regions.

Flying at low altitude into Ohio from Pennsylvania or West Virginia, you can look down on the ancient Appalachians, deeply dissected by rivers and valleys, and see that the hand of man has touched this region but lightly. Then, as the hills flatten out, the small irregular parcels—part-time or subsistence farms—give way to larger, more commercial operations. Across this broad transition zone there is a one-to-one correlation between the flatness of the terrain and the amount of human investment in it. As you continue west, more and more of the fields' edges seem drawn with a ruler, until the flatlands become a patchwork quilt. The farther west, the better the soils, and the larger the plots. Mixed farming is replaced by ever-larger corn and soybean operations. These reach a climax in Iowa, where well over 90 per cent of the state's land area is occupied by large family farms. Beyond the winding Missouri, the cornfields give way to even vaster expanses of wheat. Finally, as the ground tilts higher toward the open rangelands and Rockies, man's impress visibly lightens once again.

Or if you fly northward across the Corn Belt—from the hilly margins below the Ohio River to the more northern latitudes, with their thin soils, short growing seasons, and conifers—you can watch the same rise and fall of this human gradient. You will be passing across the heart of the "cyclonic" zone. Throughout the world, wrote geographer Ellsworth Huntington, the highest levels of physical, mental, and cultural output occur in a relatively few middle-latitude strips. Having strongly pronounced seasons, these zones are called "cyclonic" because restless air masses bring frequent, but not disastrously large, shifts in temperature and precipitation. Citing convincing statistics, Huntington showed that these areas are not only well endowed with agricultural and manufacturing resources, but most significantly, that their climate

acts as a direct and positive stimulus to human life and achievement. He located the cyclonic zones as follows:

> Lands with this climatic influence form two irregular belts. The southern belt includes only the southern part of South America and a small bit of southeastern Australia together with New Zealand. The northern belt crosses North America and Eurasia at their widest parts. In the western hemisphere it includes most of the United States and southern Canada, and in the eastern, most of Europe. Its central and most important portion consists of two main parts: (1) northwestern Europe from southern Scandinavia through Germany, the British Isles, and France to the northern edge of Spain . . . and (2) the northeastern quarter of the United States as far south as Virginia and as far west as Nebraska.

But if the energy of the Corn Belt derives from its land and climate, it also springs, as we have seen, from its history—from the character of the people who hurried toward its fertile soil and planted themselves there. They were not, in the main, the easygoing, forest-bound back-

C. J. Uban

G. L. Hightshoe

J. B. Sinatra

R. Spangler

woodsmen; nor were they the Irishmen or southern Europeans who arrived, for the most part, after America's factories had replaced her land as the great magnet of immigration. Rather, the Midwestern settlers were a combination of colonial and northern European farmers—particularly Germans, English, and Scandinavians—blending rather well with one another, while never entirely "melting," and transmitting to their children the values of the energized, "rising" classes.

The confluence of all these forces created an area that has often been called "the American heartland." If the term has sentimental overtones, it also carries a harder meaning. The Random House Dictionary defines "heartland" as "that part of a region considered essential to the viability and survival of the whole, specifically, a central land area, relatively invulnerable to attack, and capable of economic and political self-sufficiency."

But to the Midwest, as to everywhere else, the past few years have brought great changes. The old isolationism is gone. Physically or ideologically, no inland sanctum is any longer "invulnerable to attack." There are, today, more absentee landlords, more expansion, more custom planting and crop spraying and harvesting. Thus the social, economic, and political integration of the farmer has broadened immeasurably. Where once he managed his whole enterprise out of his hip pocket, now he spends many hours a week over a desk, calculator, filing cabinets, and the other appurtenances of modern business. Writes sociologist Roy Buck: "He keeps informed by infinite commodity publications and reports. His calendar is filled with notices of meetings, field days, committees, and appointments with income tax advisors and credit managers. He has trouble keeping up with market reports, weather predictions, spray schedules, and breeding charts . . . Religious, educational, and civic groups beckon him toward both membership and leadership responsibility." The grain producers who are unable or unwilling to adapt to this way of life, or who do not have descendants to carry it on, are the ones whose lands are eventually bought up by the ever-larger, ever-fewer, and ever-more-highly-capitalized units. The "get-big-or-get-out" trend remains controversial—but inexorable. Typically, Iowa's 1972 farm income rose to about $1.5 billion, a record, while she was losing about two thousand, or 1.4 per cent, of her farmsteads.

But the seventies have been unusually good years; and Iowa, the only state lying entirely within the original prairies, is among the richest of the rich. The broader statistics tell a more sobering tale. Between 1940 and 1960, 17.5 million Americans moved off the farm—a migration greater than the total foreign influx during the peak years, 1896 to 1915. Then, from 1960 to 1970, another six million moved away, leaving fewer than ten million on the land. And the economic picture has scarcely been one of steady progress. The fifties were especially bad. From 1947 to 1965, while output was rising enormously, net farm income dropped from over $17 billion to about $14 billion, and inflation eroded the farmer's purchasing power still further. Here, again, was the old prairie dilemma: rapidly rising production in the face of static demand and rising costs. Hence, falling prices, and an ever-diminishing absolute income to the producer. By 1967 some dairymen were again dumping milk in protest. Another sent the *New York Times* this letter:

To the Editor:

My mother used to tell of the farm in Minnesota, where they had to tie the dog up on Sunday nights so that he would be around on Monday morning to operate the treadmill that ran the churn. That dog, it seems, had more sense than the average dairy farmer.

The farmer works ten hours a day, seven days a week, to maintain and enlarge a property to which he is never out of debt, the taxes, constantly increasing, costing him the value of the property every ten years or so.

The oxen and team of horses that used to supply the power are now replaced by gasoline-driven machinery and the farmer is a slave to big industry. In order to get increased production, he must cover his acres with a yearly spread of manufactured fertilizers and poisonous pesticides. These cost as much as his land is worth . . .

Nearly 90 per cent of the farmer's production must now go to pay the interest on his investment, and so more thousands of dollars must pay for several silos, and the loading and unloading equipment, granaries, haylofts, combines, balers, choppers, seeders, grinders and conveyors. The pitchfork hangs up beside the broom and the pail.

Besides the state milk inspector, the dairyman is also under the lash of the creamery's bulk truck driver, who shows up whenever he feels like it, usually twice a week, weighs, tests for butterfat and temperature and, if he feels so inclined, takes the milk.

The weather determines whether he breaks even. Three out of four years he owes the bank. His barns burn or the tractor tips over on him or disease wipes out his herd, but he never just sells out and retires. He doesn't know, as the treadmill dog did, what freedom is.

He sides with his masters when some of his fellow farmers rebel, and when their half-hearted attempts fail he is glad that he stayed home on the treadmill.

P. F. MacDonald

The government, of course, has tried to ameliorate this situation by buying up surpluses, enacting price supports, establishing set-aside programs, and such. But the individualists it ought to aid—and whose votes it wanted—reacted as always. Summing up the feelings of many, one southerner wrote his Congressman:

My friend over in Terebone Parish received a $1,000 check from the government this year for not raising hogs . . .

What I want to know is, in your opinion, what is the best kind of farm not to raise hogs on and the best kind of hogs not to raise.

Abundance, it would seem, has its ironies. Meanwhile, millions live on the edge of starvation. The Corn and Wheat belts' extremely high levels of energy input—not only of fertilizer and gasoline and cash, but of motivation and education and management—make their complex systems of energy transformation virtually impossible to apply to less developed lands. And the starving millions, as short of fertilizer as they are of cash and knowledge, have nothing to send us for our golden kernels.

If America has been softened by affluence and security and consumption-related values, the Midwestern farmer has not. For one thing, he is not all that affluent or secure. For another, values and ideas travel with people, and in the Middle West country the direction of flow has been out, not in. As for the media, the locals judge the programs by local standards, rather than looking at themselves through network eyes. If you decide to differ from local norms, and from the view that life is a race with definite ground rules, no one is stopping you from moving away. Midwestern life, like the weather—and the commodities market—is a harsh teacher.

The level landscape seethes with get-up-and-go. At harvest time, wives and sisters literally run across the half-stubbled fields bearing pitchers of lemonade—or word of an essential phone call—to the perspiring men. In the old days, there was a big bell outside many farmhouses. It could be used as a dinner bell, or to call the men in an emergency, or to pass a fire alarm around the neighborhood. In the case of newlyweds, it became the vehicle for much kidding: the merest mention of the bell carried the implication that the young wife might be using it more than was absolutely necessary. These days, the telephone, radio, and wristwatch have largely replaced the old farm bells—yet many have been retained as sources of nostalgia and humor.

Machinery has also acted as a sex equalizer: freed by appliances from all-day chores in the house, some wives now spend hours behind the wheel of a tractor, doing tasks only a man's brawn could have handled a generation ago. Some help with the bookkeeping, too; and many play a leading role in spinning the social and educational threads that have helped to reduce the isolation of farm life. Nonetheless, homes and minds remain uncluttered. If our civilization breeds contradictions between some kinds of morality and some kinds of expediency, they aren't the kinds the countryside concerns itself with. Productivity requires that the 4 H's—head, heart, hands, and health—be unified. They are. And productivity abounds.

But, as noted, grain yields are not equivalent to income yields, or to satisfaction yields. Midwestern farmers are willing to invest their considerable resources, not just for the modest return-on-capital they may achieve in the best of years, but to preserve a way of life they love and believe in. In our great grain regions, neither corporate nor any other form of collectively organized agriculture has been able to make serious inroads against such stiff competition. One corn-and-hog man figures his time is worth about $400 an hour during the fourteen-hour days of picking season—that is, if he'd do it at all for wages. Another, asked why a corporation might not achieve greater economies of scale by amalgamating several large family farms into one super-farm, asks in turn what they'd have to pay a man to get up in the middle of the night to go look for an animal lost in a blizzard, or bloody his arms reaching into a pregnant heifer's uterus to turn the calf around so it can be born—the same man you could later trust to make on-the-spot marketing decisions as dozens of thousand-pound steers, worth forty cents a pound, were being guided through a gate. And what neither farmer may mention is that part of his value-received is the ability to do what he is doing right now—stop work and chat. However precious his time may be, it does not come in the tick-tock units the rest of the world uses to measure input/output. For the family farmer's time is not only uniquely elastic: it is *his*. And in these wide prairies, one of the unstated rules is that when a human being is there, you recognize him. In town, this may mean yelling across the street to somebody, or lightly tapping the car horn. On country roads, it is often a finger wagged over the steering wheel. Out in the field, it could mean shutting off a thirty-thousand-dollar combine and climbing down from the enclosed cab to greet you—though that would be a pretty tough decision.

Whatever the circumstances, this peasant-capitalist—this recalcitrant Yankee-German-Scandinavian with some warm Scotch-Irish and southern blood thrown in—is no interchangeable part. He would be a hard person for any smoothly ticking management system to try to "coordinate." Of all the factors in our complex farming equation, he is the least replaceable.

Energy, yes. But lacking the natural drama of a Grand Canyon, or the exposed egoism of the Chicago skyline, the Midwest countryside does not easily offer up its riches to a casual visitor. Perhaps this is one of the reasons why its residents often ask not where you are from, but how long you have been here. The surface seems as bland as the faded spines of books on library shelves—until you start to read.

Take that thirty-thousand-dollar combine, or its versatile and ubiquitous older brother, the tractor. Various brands come in various colors—the Deeres in green and yellow, the International Harvesters in red and white, and so forth. Each machine is an astonishing conglomerate of the physical and social sciences, of market research and mass production, of the Midwest's iron and coal resources and imports, of the vast network of lakes and rivers on which these resources are moved, of lonely inventors like Deere himself, of giant oil companies like Standard of Indiana, of rubber makers in Akron, and of a hundred other streams, all feeding through the one funnel called a tractor and into that ancient capsule of energy called corn. So, when, hurrying along the Interstate, you notice dust pluming from a distant row, or tractor headlights jiggling along like fireflies at dusk, you are really witnessing more than meets the eye. This is equally true of a simple object like a corrugated grain bin. Or those intermittent clusters of silos, pointing their silver shapes skyward like missiles packed with payloads of yellow energy.

Indeed, the machine has become very much a part of the Garden.

While some go on viewing man's drive to dominate nature as a kind of Fall, the farmer pays homage, instead, to the drudgery saved, the muscle leveraged, the yield advantaged. Anyone who wrestles with nature every day from sunup to sundown is bound to view it differently from the way a tourist does. You won't see the farmer taking pleasure walks on country roads, or lugging home weathered slabs of barn siding to hang in his living room. In a field of grazing animals he will be looking not for bucolic inspiration but for clues to meat development and carcass composition. And where a camera buff finds joy in a clump of wildflowers, the farmer views it as nature's counterattack on the straightedged orderliness of his fence lines.

Proud of his increasing mastery over nature, the Corn Belt countryman makes owning the most up-to-date machinery as strong an ethic as soil conservation. So much so that any farmer who doesn't do both is considered backward and incompetent. Talk to the local banker, whose business it is to know, and you'll soon find out who is on which rung of this modern agricultural ladder.

Or talk to the county assessor, and you'll learn how visible a farmer's holdings are. In a state like Illinois, which levies a tax on personal property, this is a sore point: the farmers complain, with some justification, that a corporation or well-off person up in Chicago's populous Cook County, which holds the political strings, can more easily conceal or devalue its holdings than a family whose assets can literally be totaled up from the road. Yet the farmers also fear that if the property tax were abolished, it would be replaced by a form of income tax even more burdensome. In all this, to be sure, there is an element of old-fashioned rural suspiciousness. Summing up the situation, one seasoned country banker smiles and says, "The farmer is discriminated against—but not as much as he thinks he is."

Ex-Midwesterners who return after ten or twenty years say the landscape looks bigger now, more opened-up, more "western." This is because there are fewer fences. Which, again, derives from the productivity spiral: bigger machines needing bigger fields, and bigger fields needing bigger machines. The trend, as we have seen, got its impetus shortly after the Middle West was opened to settlement. In the Old World, labor had been plentiful, but land scarce. Here, the reverse was true. Even when more settlers flooded in, driving up land prices, the steady drain-off to the newly opened factories and cities helped maintain a low man-land ratio. However fervently the immigrant might have wished to plant his family forever on one holy plot, the frontier taught America a different way of thinking: that the plot was elastic in extent and speculative in value. Thus, while output per unit of land remained basic, another, industrial-age statistic overtook it: output per man. This important shift in emphasis inhered in the transition from feudalism to capitalism, as well as in man's steadily rising power over the land itself. So in those disappearing fences, as with the jiggling tractor, there is indeed more than meets the eye.

In the ever-larger fields, where there would once have been whole crews at work, now you see the farmer or his son, laboring alone. The resident hired man, like the old-fashioned threshing dinner, has largely disappeared. Thus, while the farmer's circle of off-farm contacts has been widening, his work itself has grown more isolated. And while the pickup and automobile greatly increase the range of his visiting, they have, correspondingly, taken some of the old intensity out of local and extended-family relationships. Abandoned farmhouses bear mute testimony to the declining number of farms and families, as do those notices of farm auctions and property sales that crowd the pages of local papers. In parts of the Wheat Belt, some farmers have even broken away from the homestead pattern by moving to small towns, from which they commute to their fields. Such are the social changes wrought by the presence of the machine in the Garden.

Nonetheless, these changes tend to be of degree, rather than of kind. The custom of mutual aid lives on in new forms—as you will gratefully discover if your car breaks down in the middle of the wide prairies. Leaving on a trip, many Midwesterners still allow time in case they need to help someone in trouble. When a family suffers serious illness or other crisis, it is not unusual for the women of the church group to come over at intervals and change the sheets, fill up the refrigerator, and clean the house. The price, of course, is the steamroller effect: the leveling out of individual differences, the go-ahead assumption that we're all in this together. Which, again, is very middle-class, and very American. Cleanness and good order are such absolutes that no one thinks to wonder if someone else might actually *prefer* to leave a few weeds around the gatepost, or their own all-too-human clutter inside the house or mind.

The men may also help out—*com*bining a field, or patching a leaky roof, or shoveling snow off the driveway. And farm work is still regularly traded in normal periods, as well.

Mobility means not only that families disperse far and wide, but, often, that they suddenly converge again in times of trouble or celebration. In the summer of 1973, the Conger family of Iowa set something of a record by drawing over a hundred of its members from twenty-one states and Canada to a weekend reunion at the small community of Janesville. Midwesterners love to get together in other places, too. The many thousands of ex-Midwesterners residing in Southern California have made its enormous "Iowa picnics" and other state get-togethers famous. The cars and tractors may be getting sleeker, but those are still Midwesterners and "exMids" driving them.

And driving up the price of ground. The relatively prosperous years of the early seventies fueled a land-buying binge that pushed the price of some first-class prairie real estate as high as $2500 an acre. In the rarefied climate of inflation, good weather, and full capacity induced by high domestic and foreign demand, loans taken at these levels appeared to be discounting farm prosperity for years to come. Wishing well for the farmers, one also wishes they would read their own history. Not since the precarious boom of the early 1920s had land prices risen as fast as they did in 1973 and 1974.

A new wrinkle was that a few foreign investors, particularly Japanese and Germans, had begun buying top grade prairie farmland in Iowa and elsewhere. Meanwhile, millions of acres of semi-arid ground were coming under the plow for the first time. Much of this was with poor erosion control, even while more and more advanced methods of preventing topsoil loss were being applied in the older Corn Belt. One thinks back, again, to the dustbowl.

A final problem has been that, with the boundaries between town and country increasingly blurred, more and more farm ground is getting covered by housing developments, factories, and shopping centers. This adds a premium to the prices of nearby land. States and localities try to fight back with zoning regulations. While ostensibly designed to preserve the farmer's way of life, these, like other bureaucratic measures, go against his instincts.

Today, the costs, risks, and sheer availability of a viable farm are such that it has become difficult for a qualified young man to get into Corn Belt agriculture, even as a tenant, unless, as the saying goes, he "inherits one or marries one." By 1974, the U.S.D.A. put the average capital investment in a Midwestern farm at about $610,000. Mindful of the problem, the older generation tries to plan ahead, using incorporation and other techniques to reduce the family tax burden. At the same time, and paradoxically, a back-to-the-land movement seems to be bubbling up from coast to coast. The motives, apparently, have less to do with economics than with the search for a more wholesome, satisfying life. Ralph Reynolds, a respected Midwestern farm editor, writes:

> Probably never in history has an advanced society known such an itch for agriculture. North America, settled by seekers of land, has witnessed many a land rush, but those . . . new farmers are a different breed. Many come highly educated, some are well-heeled, most left high-paying and promising jobs or professions behind . . .
>
> One of the appeals of agriculture is that people see it as the last stand of the truly independent man. . .
>
> They've found a lot of work and action—as one puts it, "I move at a faster pace here than I ever did in the city"—but they know a kind of peace and satisfaction, too. "I don't hear horns honking," one drop-out says simply, "and I can look up and see the sky."
>
> A recent study contrasting mental well-being of rural vs. city people indicates that the new farmers have a point. Researchers in three states found that rural people suffered less anxiety than city people, were not as nervous, had better appetites, and generally showed only about half as much psychiatric impairment as city people.

Some think the back-to-the-land movement will turn out to be ephemeral. Whether or not it does, it appears unlikely to alter prairie agriculture to any great extent. Nonetheless, it is symptomatic of a tide of discontent in our urban society—of a desire to turn away from the technocracy, back toward earlier values and a simpler life.

Down-to-earth: that is Midwestern. Feet on the ground. Not head in the clouds. Not flighty, or fancy, or foolhardy: these are strong pejoratives. Nature is always there, kindly and brutal, checking excess and teaching peasant wisdom. When controllable, she inspires effort; when uncontrollable, she teaches resignation.

Wander alone in a summer cornfield, lost in the tall stalks. Above you, an unseen presence trembles the leaves. Stand beneath one of the few elms spared by the recent bark blights, on the only bit of grass spared by the plow. Those four white dominoes are pioneer graves. Birds soar, wheel. Rows of corn stride off to the horizon. Can you really hear it grow?

But the farmer doesn't talk in a fanciful way. He prefers to cloak his intuitions in the metaphors of expediency. "Church drain spouts look nice and new!" "That cemetery could stand mowing!" Bring it to earth, bale it, banish the loose ends, store it up behind Sunday clapboard for measured parceling. Talk to him any day of the week about Jesus and the Bible: those subjects will not embarrass him, those are well grounded. God's presence may even be a daily, hourly reality to him. But try broadening the inquiry, and he'll end up feeling genuinely sorry for you. As he does for a local preacher who tried the same thing and had to be replaced.

Ride with an Iowa farmer in spring, 1974. Under sunny skies, his corn planter goes *click-click-click,* every eight inches squirting out an exact combination of hybrid seed, fertilizer, weed killer, and bug killer. The farmer is optimistic. He has amassed nearly a thousand acres and a million dollars in assets, including the cattle to which he will feed the corn. Last year he grossed around $300,000 and netted $25,000. This year he expects to do better.

But he is wrong. Summer brings temperatures that soar above 100 degrees—and no rain. In the worst drought since the thirties, the thirsty corn furls its long leaves, withers, dies. The farmer's reward for a year of back-breaking toil and heavy risk: a net loss of $30,000. Statewide, Iowa's farmers lose around a billion. The havoc will take years to repair. Once again, nature's whipsaw moods have taught the settler how toughness is mingled with kindness—death with life. As the Bible warned him.

The contest continues daily. If man makes a better bug killer, nature makes a better bug. Man draws a straight line across the land; nature softens it with wind, water, snow. If nature invades the shoulders of a road with voracious grasses, the farmer, wasting nothing, harvests it for his stock. He keeps his tractor radio tuned to the weather reports: if they bring tornado warnings, he must hurriedly batten down the hatches and bundle his family into the basement. In autumn, he trudges over stubbled fields, gun in hand, searching out pheasant and grouse. Meanwhile, his wife tends her bird feeders. She may mark the seasons in the comings and goings of the sparrow and starling, the cardinal and snowbird, the hummingbird and whippoorwill. In her book, *Rural Free,* Rachel Peden records these and other impressions of her life on a Hoosier farm:

It is a comfort to hear the bobwhite calling from the road's corner down near the red lilies. Almost a month after wheat cutting, the bobwhite's song is as summer-filled as it was a month before the wheat ripened. For this comfort, bobwhite, I shall remember to put extra amounts of cracked corn for you down under the maple trees this winter, when you will walk through snow to reach it, leaving your pronged snowshoe tracks in the deep white drift.

"In these hectic times," exclaimed Dick, throwing down the newspaper to come to the table, "the only time a farmer really knows what he's doing is when he's hauling manure."

The day was cold and windy, the sky heavy and gray. We had to keep the kitchen light burning all day. When I hung wet clothes on the line, I wore scarf, gloves, and winter coat. The sheets raged, arguing with the wind for a while, then subsided in frozen dignity. From the maple in the front yard a broken rope swing dangled emptily.

"I'll tell you how you can tell the farm women from the others at a meeting," said Dick after he had been to a meeting of the County Extension Committee. "You look around, and you can tell 'em by the scratches and bruises on their shins. You can see 'em, you know, right through their stockings."

I know.

"My, ain't it greened up nice since the rain!"

. . . the neighbor's six-year-old boy comes through the yard, driving the tractor.

He stepped into the intersection of streets and yelled at the departing merchant: "Cort, oh Cort!"

Nobody showed any surprise. Cort, formerly a farmer, came back, unlocked his store, turned on the light, and made neighborly conversation while Dick selected a cap and a pair of gloves.

Cort's store is a leisurely place that sells a great many things, and nobody is urged to buy anything. There was an assortment of men's and boys' clothing, dry goods, hardware, kitchen equipment. A stack of milk buckets, tin pans, and small tools were displayed carelessly in the window. There were the red and black plaid caps that are standard equipment for the farm men and boys; the soft, warm brown gloves; the stiff canvas gloves; blue denim overall jackets; assorted boots and overshoes . . .

Cort smiled, talked, offered caps. His dark, shrewd eyes were friendly and unopinionated . . .

Dick, having selected a cap, did not look into the mirror. He put it on and looked into his wife's face. "Oh!" she exclaimed, "I think you look just beautiful!" His daughter nodded, and Dick smiled at Cort. "I'll take this one," he said.

In the doorway of the barn a wheelbarrow, freshly filled with silage, was standing. Steam was rising up from it into the cold air, like steam from a gigantic kettle of soup just taken off the stove. At this time of winter, silage still has a pleasant pickledy smell, with a suggestion of sorghum. Cattle like it. The cows in the barn could smell the steam and were bawling in happy anticipation.

There is no better place than the blackberry patch for that hour of solitude every farm woman craves now and then.

If Mrs. Peden's writings serve to refute the notion that Midwestern life is as flat as its topography, the same principle—that variety is in the eyes of the beholder, for grains may hold universes—can also be applied to a wider canvas of the farm country.

Take the topography itself. Even Iowa, that "flat" prairie state, is far from uniform. Its weathered surface is divisible, overall, into two large parts and two smaller parts. The north-central/northwest third of the state is nearly level, with only modest ripples. Agriculturally, this is the most productive part. Fields and roads follow the mile-square grid pattern of the old surveys, on which the homestead concept was based.

By contrast, the southern half of Iowa is gently rolling, but with slopes that often rise to steepness. Intermittently limited by dryness, drainage problems, or bedrock, farming varies from poor to good. Some fields and roads follow the geometric grid; others are are bent by the topography into organic twists and turns.

In the northeastern corner of the state lies an unglaciated diagonal wedge, variously called "Little Switzerland," because of its steep hills and cliffs, and "Little Scandinavia," because of its original settlers. The area is contiguous with southeastern Minnesota, southwestern Wisconsin, and northwestern Illinois. Farming is spotty, the roads crooked.

Finally, in southwestern Iowa, the level Missouri floodplain runs north-south between the Missouri River and high loess bluffs. In this fertile slice, the farms are big, rich, and intensive; and the roads, like the fields, follow man-made section lines.

Traveling by car across the state, you can see countless local variations on these themes and work out their relationships to the general scheme. There is, for instance, the matter of trees. On the dark prairie soils of the level north-central/northwest region, trees occur naturally only along the streams. But man has also planted some others to protect himself from the sun and wind. On the farmsteads, therefore, the location of the tree clumps in relation to the buildings often reveals the direction of the prevailing winds. As you move westward from central Iowa, the denseness of these windbreaks gradually increases—as does the force of the winds blowing off the Great Plains.

But if you go eastward to "Little Scandinavia," you find forests clinging thickly to hillsides that are too steep and rocky to cultivate. The northern slopes, which retain their snow cover longer, generally grow trees that prefer cooler and wetter conditions. Through the centuries, such conditions helped protect this northeastern corner of the state from prairie fires. It is the only part of Iowa where such northern varieties as balsam fir and white pine can be found. Yet farmers have also cleared many of the flat hilltops and other relatively level places. To prevent erosion of the thin, forest-formed soil, they "strip-crop"—plow along contours, then plant alternating strips of hay, corn, and oats. As in southern Wisconsin, this kind of agriculture is highly conducive to dairying and gives Little Scandinavia's fields a dramatic, swirling look.

Very different is the Mississippi floodplain to the south. Here giant irrigation machines "walk" around the fields, creating perfect circles of cultivation which can be plainly seen from the air. Nearby Davenport, Rock Island, Moline, and other urban markets have spurred the floodplain farmers to do a bustling trade in truck-farm items such as fresh vegetables, potatoes, and melons.

Very different, again, are the geologically ancient lands toward Iowa's southeastern corner, where deep, well-filled gullies course through soils developed under both prairie and forest cover—a combination that makes the farming highly variable.

Farther west, about halfway across the southern part of the state, the soils turn heavy and the slopes difficult. Typically, the farms are widely separated by open grazing lands. And in some places the land's own contours have been erased forever by the brackish, water-filled pits and "spoil banks" left by the strip mining of coal. Here, and farther north, there are ghosts of Iowa's "coal boom" of the late 1800s and early 1900s—remnant towns like Fraser, Coal Valley, Moingona, and Ridgeport.

Superimposed on the varied landscape are the complex effects of simple things. Water, for instance—not merely in its spectacular yearly blessings and devastations, but also in its quieter roles—trickling into the tile drain, the farm pond, the grassy watercourse; lying sullen in slough, backwater, or prairie pothole; splashing through the meandering stream, or rippling across the old swimming pond. Each appearance of water adds a factor to the delicate equation of farm management. And each adds its tint to the prairie canvas.

Likewise, the paths of early settlement still color the land in varied hues. Up around Remsen, a village in northwestern Iowa, most of the farmers and townspeople are of Luxembourgian descent. They have earned a reputation for living simply, wasting nothing, and gradually prospering. Hearty drinkers, they relish a locally made Luxembourgian sausage called "treipen." And the state's 320 Amish children—their numbers are larger in Indiana and Ohio—are carefully exempted from the state school attendance laws. Iowa, whose citizens care deeply about their religious prerogatives, has sometimes found itself working out unique forms of church-state separation. The flavor of the problem is evident in the following exchange in the House of Representatives on a bill, later defeated, to allow alcohol to be sold on Sundays:

> "I refer to the Christian principles on which this nation was founded," said Representative Horace Daggett of Kent. "On behalf of the non-drinkers, the church-going people and in honor of Our Lord and Saviour, I ask this bill be voted down."
>
> "At the Last Supper, I wonder what Our Lord had. Pepsi Cola?" snapped back Representative Richard Norpel of Bellevue. "Did He have RC at the feast of Cana when He changed water to wine?"

On this, as on sex and many another subject, probably the most typical view, not only in Iowa, but throughout the Middle West, is one of "tolerance within prescribed limits." And while it is easy to multiply the examples of varied national origins—the Dutch at Pella, the Germans at Amana, the Czechs at Spillville—it is also important to place these in the wider context of assimilation. As Grace Flandrau writes of her own, highly ethnic Minnesota:

> In my childhood, Anglo-Saxon Minnesotans tended to regard the foreign-born and their progeny, especially those on the farms, as beings from a different planet. And indeed, there was some difference in dress and appearance. Now all that is changed. Everybody wears the same kind of clothes and looks the same in them . . .
>
> It is true that for a national festival they may put on the old costumes, dance the old dances to the old tunes. But it is not a part of their daily living. When the girls, for instance, are being themselves, it is in their smart ready-made dresses, with their beauty-parlor hairdos. In the blue jeans with which they lead their 4-H calves or panda-faced lambs into the judging

ring. When they preside over their classrooms or dance in their strapless evening gowns at their university or high-school proms. Americans, and in a hundred ways, making the most of it.

Those blue jeans and ready-mades are significant. For it is this relative thinness of folk and class differentiation—linked to high levels of educational, commercial, and technical interchange with the non-farm sector—that distinguishes the Midwestern farm family from so many of the world's agricultural producers. Here, as we have seen, "doing" and "becoming" take precedence over "being," and the ethics of openness, friendliness, and equality keep the social spectrum narrow. The farm people are not inclined to look up to "leaders," be they political, intellectual, or any other. With the important exceptions of church and school, social affinities tend to derive from functional roles. If you talk with a group of farmers today, they will probably resemble one another more than any of them does his own ancestor of a generation ago. But if you pass from one type-farming area to the next, or from a less modern to a more modern farm, you are crossing social boundaries. As a matter of ethics and pride, these are not spelled out to a visitor. But the children know.

One of the delights of any tour of the Corn Belt is to see its northern and southern fringes, where the uniform richness of the tall corn country shades toward a diverse bonanza of other valuable crops.

In the fall, in southwestern Wisconsin, or up in picturesque Door County, the bracing air carries the fragrance of fruit-laden trees. Roadside stands and warehouses sell dozens of varieties of snappy, juicy apples that blend so well with the state's renowned cheeses. But apples grow abundantly in other Midwestern states, too—in southern Michigan, and in Ohio, and in the rough, well-drained hills of southern Illinois. Out-of-the-way orchard lands sometimes yield memorable finds: such as the tiny hamlet of Parshallville, east of Detroit, where, in a creaking water mill built in 1837, apple cider is still pressed out in the old-fashioned way.

Before the arrival of the white man, a few types of apples grew wild—such as the Dubuque variety, which flourished along the banks of the upper Mississippi. But the real impetus for commercial apple growing came after 1900, when pioneering associations like the Wisconsin State Horticultural Society introduced scientific grafting, testing, and other research services. Long before that, however, many farms had had their own orchards, large enough to provide for the family and perhaps a little more.

In legend, at least, these early farms owed their treasured orchards to a person named Johnny Appleseed. His real name was Jonathan Chapman, and he was born in Pennsylvania in 1774. Deeply religious, and a follower of the Swedish philosopher Swedenborg, he wandered barefoot through Pennsylvania, Ohio, and Indiana, clad only in a coffee sack, with a tin plate for a hat, which he also used for cooking. Keeping to the rivers, Chapman planted apple trees as he went and returned yearly to tend his little nurseries in the wilderness. Whenever he met newly arrived pioneers, he would regale them with his Biblical and Swedenborgian teachings. And he sold them the young trees with which they started their apple groves. At the age of seventy-one, after a twenty-mile hike near Fort Wayne, Indiana to repair an orchard fence,

he died. Thereafter, the embellished legend of "Johnny Appleseed" captured the hearts of so many thousands that it became a permanent part of Midwestern lore. It contains the wisdom penned by Cicero twenty centuries earlier: "The diligent farmer plants trees of which he himself will never see the fruit." Or, as a Nebraska farmer put it more recently, "I like to think that if I plant a walnut tree, somebody a hundred years from now is going to have a walnut chair to sit in." Today, Lisbon, Ohio, still honors Jonathan Chapman with its yearly Johnny Appleseed Festival; and the state even has a Johnny Appleseed Memorial Highway.

Roadside apple stands also recall the days of a more diversified, less commercial agriculture, before the advent of refrigeration and sophisticated processing, when many farmers, especially those within range of the larger towns, would supplement their slim cash incomes by offering fresh produce along the road. "Egg money" was usually the wife's own: even now, you still see those home-grown egg signs along many of the back roads, especially in areas where the farms remain small.

And in early July, if you are lucky enough to be near Traverse City, in the northwest corner of Michigan's Lower Peninsula, you can stop at any number of roadside stands and buy little baskets of the best eating cherries in the world at bargain prices. The down-to-earth ladies will also sell you their cherry pies—either fully baked, or oven-ready. This is the time of year when Traverse City puts on its Cherry Festival. It is no accident that the town is also the home of Chef Pierre, a young, successful pie-and-pastry firm typical of the hundreds of medium-sized food processors that dot the upper Midwest. The breezes blowing off nearby Lake Michigan have a moderating effect on the climate, delaying the rising of the sap in the spring, lengthening the fall, and giving western Michigan ideal weather for all sorts of fruit growing. The vineyards around Paw Paw, for instance, make the area a major producer of grape juice, jelly, and wine. So Paw Paw, not to be outdone, now celebrates its own yearly Grape Festival.

Over at Le Sueur, Minnesota, lives the Jolly Green Giant. An enterprise very different from the family farm, this large concern is an example of the vertical integration that has come into several non-grain operations. Jolly Green is able to keep close tabs on its products, all the way from fields in which thermometers constantly take the temperature of the soil, up to the clever mass-market packaging and advertising.

Turkey raising is another enterprise to which scientific methods, and the escalating price of beef, have drawn special attention in recent years. The list, in fact, seems endless—from buckwheat, wild rice, and ginseng, in the north, down to honey and popcorn and sugarbeets, and even, on the southern fringes of the Midwest, to cotton and tobacco.

While all modern agriculture is complex and exacting, dairying is even more so. Calves, for instance, must be fed on the basis of extensive knowledge of their nutritional needs and according to precise schedules. Depending on the calf's age, the farmer mixes its "starter" feed from varying percentages of some thirteen different ingredients. And this is but one of hundreds of factors with which he constantly deals, from close temperature controls and the careful cleaning of milk machines, to breeding differentials and lactation records. So complicated has all this become that many dairy cooperatives now provide their members with electronic data-processing services that quickly spit back dozens of tabulations, such as "Concentrate feeding recommendations for each cow in the herd based on milk production, pregnancy and maintenance requirements."

None of this is evident, of course, to the buyer of a quart of milk in a supermarket. More visible, as you drive through the northern fringes of the Corn Belt, are the majestic dairy barns, their rows of lighted windows often gleaming into the night. In these latitudes of hard winters, where fieldstones are more common than in the prairies, the barns often have solid rock foundations that continue as part of the first-story walls. Some barns, especially where the ground is sloping, are built on the old eastern plan of having an earthen ramp communicate with the second story or loft. Throughout the Midwest, the peaked roofs and cupolas of the traditional large barn make it look quite grand. And you see many subregional variants: in one county the windows may all be set in diamond shapes and outlined in white against the red walls, while in another, the windows will be horizontal and the whole bulky affair painted white. Unhappily, however, no specialist seems to have given Midwestern barn styles the careful study they have received in Pennsylvania and the East.

Among the most beautiful of these native structures are the round or many-sided barns. These were particularly associated with dairying, since they allowed the hay to be forked down from the loft into a single area in the center, from which the stalls would radiate like the spokes of a wheel. Round barns reached a peak of popularity between 1910 and 1917, after an agriculture professor at the University of

Wisconsin developed a model whose central core was actually a silo. Such arrangements helped conserve the cattle's natural body heat—by keeping them away from the outside walls and by reducing the surface area per volume enclosed. (A superstition furthermore held that a round barn "kept the devil from hiding in the corners.") Nonetheless, there were problems of lighting, ventilation, and unusable space. The complex interior timbering is wondrous to behold, but it meant that structures like this were far more expensive to build and maintain than rectangular ones.

Because the construction of circular barns was something of a fad, which died out soon after the flush farm days of World War I, the survivors tend to be concentrated in certain areas. There are several polygonal barns along the Lake Michigan coast north of Milwaukee; and there is said to be a thirteen-sided one near Spring Valley, Wisconsin. South of Mankato, Minnesota, are quite a number of round barns which, for the most part, are beautifully maintained. More dilapidated are the few still standing to the south and west of Iowa City, Iowa. But for round barns, as for covered bridges, the queen state seems to be Indiana, where one enthusiast has counted 154 of them. North of Indianapolis, at McCordsville, is the granddaddy of them all, the Kingan barn: it stands 102 feet tall and 102 feet in diameter, and over one hundred gallons of paint are needed to spruce it up. Determined efforts are being made to save these interesting structures from fire and other hazards. In the late 1960s Indiana's Fulton County, which boasts fifteen of them, instituted—what else?—the world's first and only Round Barn Festival.

Beset by profit squeezes, and buffeted by political winds, the dairy industry has not had an easy time in recent years. By contrast, agriculture's rising star has been the soybean. Though cultivated by the Chinese for as long as four thousand years, soybeans were still called "green manure" by American farmers of the 1910s, who simply plowed them under to enrich the soil. But after World War II, many new uses began to be found for the oil and meal crushed from soybeans. So much so that between 1952 and 1972 their acreage leapt from 14 million to 46 million, and the yearly dollar value soared from $811 million to $4.5 billion. Even more dramatic was the contribution to the nation's balance of payments: soybean exports zoomed from $104 million to over $2 billion. Exclaimed Agriculture Secretary Earl Butz: "It's the first time the U.S. has exported two billion dollars' worth of anything." And the trend has continued. Because demand keeps

outracing supply, plantings increased in both 1973 and 1974, assuring the soybean of first place among the nation's cash crops and sparking predictions that export sales could continue rising to as much as $5 billion by 1985.

What lies behind this spectacular performance? Fundamentally, it is the human body's need for protein. Proteins comprise about two thirds of the dry weight of our skin, muscle, and blood and play a crucial role in many other functions—including those all-important, life-directing systems, the antibodies, hormones, and enzymes. The most efficient sources of direct protein intake are animal foods—meat, poultry, fish, and dairy products. Plant foods such as wheat, rice, and corn contain only about 10 per cent protein and peanuts, 25 per cent. But soybeans are far and away the leader, with a whopping 40 per cent. So soybean meal makes the preferred animal feed supplement. Today, with one part of the world getting more affluent and wanting more meat and the other part teetering on the edge of starvation because of the population explosion, a rising demand for soybeans seems inevitable. For the future, various derivatives of the once-lowly bean also hold great potential for direct human consumption. This possibility is particularly interesting in the light of recent medical research linking feedlot beef, various dairy products, eggs, and many of our highly processed foods to a rising incidence of heart disease.

Although the South has been raising its soybean plantings dramatically, most of the American crop still comes from Illinois, Minnesota, Iowa, Indiana, Missouri, and Ohio. Many big Midwestern farmers now carefully divide their acreage between corn and "beans," hoping that any unforeseen price break in one will be offset by the other. The significance of our soybeans as a cash export rests in the fact that the U.S. now harvests some three fourths of the world supply—and accounts for 90 per cent of all the soybeans moving through international trade.

And soybeans are only one among the many products of Midwestern abundance now moving around the globe. It is scarcely surprising, therefore, that today's heartlander is far less of an isolationist than his grandfather was.

Yet the mood of the farm country remains homey and local. While the farmer's grain is being abstractly bought and sold on the ticker tapes of the world, he himself is still primarily on view to his neighbors. Relationships depend on old-fashioned confidence: people dealing face to face and pretty well knowing what folks are up to.

Ride next to a farmer on a lurching wagon, helping him stack heavy bales of hay as they chug up the ramp behind the baler and tractor. Between bales he'll point his gloved finger toward a horizon you can barely see and tell you that that's his neighbor's second son, out looking for arrowheads again; and to look over there, at how they leave *their* bales in the field, then have to go back and pick them up: a silly waste of time, and chancy, too, with this weather. Brushing bits of hay from your perspiring arms, you manage to nod politely—even though you can't make out anything he's pointing at.

Or "dew drop inn" to the local café. Its crossroads hamlet is silent these long summer days while the corn grows. Across the single leafy lane, two dozen houses keep watch on one another: all respectable, none elegant. A single church presides. From the property lines behind the houses, the green stalks march off to infinity. They have been shooting up so fast that they had to send extra roots out from their bases and down into the black earth. Over at the elevator, the owner readies his depleted bins, his massive truckload scales, and his sensitive moisture-analyzing equipment for the long lines of trucks that will be heading his way when picking begins. Then there will be a different atmosphere in the little café. Many farmers who would otherwise go home for their midday meal will come here to save time. Bringing along their seasonal help, they will urgently talk out their machinery problems as they make plans for the afternoon. Right now, though, there are plenty of empty plastic chairs and squeaky counter stools and plenty of slices of homemade pie left on the wooden pass-through shelf. No one to notice the small calendar below the large picture of Jesus, or ask the prices of the card-pak novelty items and lighter sets dropped off by an itinerant salesman three years back. Just a few retirees, who turn their hats in the humid air at the slap of the screen door.

Yet a few miles down the blacktop, in the larger trading center, the cafés are bustling. In the old days the farmers would come clopping into town on Saturdays, hauling most of the family in the wagon. Now they nose their muddy, late-model pickups into the curb any day they can get the time. In the vehicles, as in the life-styles and the thinking, there is more variety than before. Politicians no longer count on a solid block of grassroots opinion, translatable into a monolithic "farm vote." Nevertheless, like the other changes out here, the shift is more of degree than of kind: in hundreds of communities like this one, you vote however you wish, as long as you vote Republican. To be sure, more of the kids coming into farming will have been to "ag" schools, where they may have been exposed to the Keynesians and atheists. On the other hand, these are the boys who *did* come home again, and they've come back to more costly farms. With more to conserve, they are likely to think more conservatively. They'll need a good, Christian reputation around town to get that all-important nod from the locally owned bank.

Lunchtime at the café: you can watch the refueling of the men who've come to town after tractor parts or seed corn, or to see the commodities broker, or to auction off a few hogs. Some of the faces look petrified from too much association of like with like. Some are numbed from heavy toil. But others are hearty—animated by the chance to get together with friends after long hours of working alone. Most contain the eternal mix of hope and disillusion. Unlike the miners and mill hands in the next town south—where the landscape and the people both get rougher—they do not flirt with taboos, or with the waitress.

Sprawling in the plastic booths, some wear overalls; some wear matching work shirts and trousers. Breast pockets bulge with notebooks and pens. Most of the caps are promotional gifts from the seed companies, bearing patches with names like *Pioneer* or *Funk's Hybrids.* Muscled arms, heavy shoulders, blunt hands; bulky ways of moving, standing, leaning. Some eat alone. Others, in threes or fours. Laughter erupts through the country reserve, a kind of humor more in the man than in the words. Always the men's moods are affected by the weather and what it is doing to the crops.

Paper place mats vary. In Michigan they may be imprinted with pencil-puzzles. In Wisconsin, with ice hockey rules and diagrams. In southern Indiana, with a basketball court. At truck stops, with a road-signal quiz. In western Iowa, with folded hands and a prayer. Sometimes, too, there will be inspirational words framed on the wall: *Home is where each lives for the other, and all live for Christ.* Some plastic flowers. And a calendar, with the town slogan: *Life offers more in Sycamore.* or: *Osceola, the town on the Go.*

A dollar buys a heaping plate of spaghetti, salad, and bread. Good

meat dishes cost a little more. But don't take the bread if you don't intend to eat it—wasting food is a minor sin in this part of the world, where its producers believe their occupation to be an especially moral one. Most people take coffee *with* their meal. Sometimes the salads have walnuts in them. And, depending on what time of day it is, there may be six or more freshly baked pies to choose from—such as rhubarb, apple, raisin, blueberry, apricot, and pumpkin.

Meeting the farmers' schedule, Mom and Pop have been open since five. This afternoon, they may get some relief from a high school girl. But by early evening the farmers' café is a gloomy place. It serves no alcohol—it would lose too many customers if it did—and may well close before seven. So, if you're planning on having supper here, it's safest to arrive by 5:30 or 6:00.

Now, however, at "dinner" time, the farmers are still revved up, ready to go back to work. Climbing to their feet, they wipe their mouths with their hip-pocket bandanas, then head for the register.

"And we thank you," says Mom.

"You betcha."

Just as the trading center was once a crossroads, so the crossroads hamlet was once a modest trading village. In the general stretching-out of the countryside, the trading centers, like the farms, have been getting fewer and farther between. Yet many country churches have resisted this century-old process of consolidation and still cling tenaciously to their original sites. Many contain a churchyard, for one thing, and no one wants to plow up the graves of his ancestors. But in even more immediate ways, the local frame church still embodies much that the farmers have always held sacred.

To appreciate this, it is worth recalling the atmosphere in which the inland Garden was planted. Religious freedom was then much more of an issue than now. Although tolerance had become traditional in the Middle Colonies, it was hardly the rule in New England and had only recently been made law by the loose confederation calling itself a nation. In moving west, the Scotch-Irish Presbyterians, hinterland Puritans, Quakers, Mormons, Amish, Pennsylvania Dutch, and other native groups had clear hopes of religious as well as economic freedoms. And since religious repression was severe in parts of Europe, the immigrant shared the determination of the native-born to worship as he chose. In the far-flung forests and prairies, this spelled a lively grassroots diversity and resolute independence from traditional institutions. Amid the lonely disorder of the frontier and post-frontier eras, the local church glowed with an inspired sense of belonging and with the righteous thought that it was bringing civilization to the wilderness. For many years it also served as the chief center of social life and entertainment.

It was no accident, therefore, that newly emergent sects like the Methodists and Baptists scored great gains in the Middle West. They emphasized simplicity of form and thought, fervor of spirit, evangelistic zeal, organizational flexibility, and democratic localism. Less successful in attracting converts were the more traditional Protestant sects, such as the education-minded Presbyterians; the eastward-looking Episcopalians; and the once-prominent Congregationalists, whose eighteenth century rationalism could scarcely gather up roughhewn hearts and souls the way camp meetings did. Large Catholic groups, such as the Irish and Italians, tended to arrive somewhat later and to flow into the urban-industrial belt forming along the shores of the Great Lakes.

The splintering of sects into ever-smaller, ever-more-locally autonomous units proceeded at a stupendous rate in the Mississippi Valley—a tendency that is still quite evident. Even those deeply doctrinaire German and Scandinavian Lutherans, who have long dominated the northern Corn Belt counties as well as most of Wisconsin, Minnesota, and the Dakotas, found it necessary to break away from the parent body and establish their own, stoutly conservative Missouri Synod. The tendency for Midwestern Lutherans to split over theological differences has continued.

Such grassroots fire was fanned by the "begin-again" spirit gripping the pioneers and their followers: by the pride they took in voluntarily joining hands to create their own institutions, and from their permanent distrust of creeping eastern fingers, intellectualism, and broadly based polities in general. In the twentieth century, one of the loudest cries became, "They're trying to take our schools away from us!" And, of course, they did.

So the little country churches, set among the rustling corn stalks, are among the last visible signs of the old localism. Hard economic realities have denuded some of a pastor, and hence of a congregation.

Russell Lee

Yet enough of the faithful are usually left to mend the roof, weed the cemetery, and sometimes even conduct their own services. More typically, a pastor will divide his time among two or three country churches—an idea first devised by that natural organizer, John Wesley, and a Midwest tradition since the days of the old circuit riders. Still other rural churches are today whole, well, and thriving, thank you—perhaps even celebrating their centennials.

As you drive the country roads, you notice small signs directing you to these unpretentious clapboard buildings. On Sunday mornings the cars cluster around them like the flock itself receiving its sustenance. Out here, indeed, the agricultural/pastoral metaphors of Christianity seem more than metaphoric.

Should you wish to go inside, no one will have the bad manners to leave you alone. An open hymnal will be instantly shared. From the pulpit, the preacher welcomes you with a matter-of-fact nod. He may even ask you to introduce yourself to the thirty or forty bronzed faces, the inevitable weather marks at the corners of their eyes, come together this day in His name, bringing along diapers and coloring books and Kleenex and clinging with pride to well-thumbed Bibles. You will be gratefully noticed by the polo-shirted boy who lights the candles and the erstwhile lady who rocks the ancient upright and the demure teen-age girl who thinly and courageously wavers out, "All You Got To Do Is Pray."

The sermon involves a certain amount of hell-fire and finger-pointing, but no surprises. Its underlying intent is not to excite the mind, but to reassure the heart: on these lonely prairies, the church's "belonging" function has always been as important as its "meaning" function. Rachel Peden brings this out in a sketch of a typical weekday gathering:

> The Council women have brought their own ladders, soap, dust mops, vacuum cleaners and brooms. They have a good time visiting while they wash the blue-flowered glass chandeliers, the glass on the framed picture of Christ praying in the garden of Gethsemane. They shake the dust out of the American and Christian flags that stand properly at right and left of the preacher. They close and dust the big old Bible on the pulpit, and put the minister's sermon notes, left there from last week, into the catch-all cabinet of the pulpit. They dust the blue-upholstered chairs and set them stiffly to the right and left of the preacher's larger chair . . .
>
> They clean off the long, gray-painted benches, and one woman, finally giving way to a long curiosity, crawls under a bench to see how much is cherry and how much is poplar. One woman stands on a ladder to wind and set the big wall clock. Then the women leave their mops and brooms and buckets sitting around while they take time for dinner and after that for a short business meeting.

Is the Midwestern farmer an individualist or a conformist?

As early as 1835, Alexis de Tocqueville wrote of America: "I very clearly discern two tendencies; one leading the mind of every man to untried thoughts, the other prohibiting him from thinking at all." Tocqueville attributed the admixture to our experiment with democracy—to the evident contradiction between the ideals of individual freedom and social equality. What he failed to add was that every human being is part individualist, part conformist, and that differences in national character often amount to differences in how much originality we expect to exercise in each of the various areas of our lives. In our day, as in Tocqueville's, Frenchmen think more independently than we do in some ways (choice of cheeses or political parties), but less so in others (TV programing, religion). Viewed in this way, gloomy reports that modern Americans have forsaken their frontier individualism—joined the "other-directed" crowd and become gray-flannel organization men—turn out to be false alarms. On reflection, one can see that we are more and less individualistic than our ancestors.

Similarly, today's Corn Belt farmer is both more and less individualistic than his urban cousin. Less so, in the sense that he is locked into a system of family and neighborhood crop production in which everyone depends on everyone else, knows what everyone else is doing, is preoccupied with many of the same things, and enforces uniform moral, social, religious, and ideological codes. Literal frankness—the farmer's habit of saying what he means and meaning what he says—and instant, first-name informality are guarantees that good neighbors do not build social fences. Verbal subtlety is not interpreted as a virtue but as a lack of genuineness—a sign of tainted urbanity. Aesthetic leanings in an otherwise perfectly normal child bring expressions of condolence. A truly good man neither puffs up nor conceals his assets—he just leaves them safely outdoors, under the blazing sky, for all to see.

And though neighbors do not build fences, they do guard their shared perimeter against outside influence. Many farmers who live near one of the fine Midwestern universities, such as Purdue, or Indiana University, or the University of Michigan, may be abstractly proud of the quality of those institutions, and may even send their sons and daughters there, but they cannot really identify with such centers of learning. For one thing, they fear them as dens of depravity. This is the peasant in the farmer—the adherence to a mental gold standard. Fearing the inquiring Greek, he clings, like the Hebrew, to a received heritage and a revealed book.

Yet the very proliferation of independent country churches shows his urge to read the fundamentals his own way. A distinguished black minister who, as a guest lecturer at the University of Iowa, gave a series of talks on the local station, remembers how one farmer, after hearing the broadcasts on his tractor radio, unabashedly drove straight in from the fields in order to lay eyes on the man and ask him some straight questions. As author Donald Peattie says of these paradoxical prairie tillers: "It is part of the knot twist in their mental timber that they are refractory to a great deal of bosh and even more to decadence. They turn the edge of many blades. They are steadfast, but they grow, yet not so that you can predict them. Because they are free, you never know what they will accept next."

It is this "hybrid vigor" that makes the Midwestern farmer anything

but a peasant. His forefathers, detaching themselves from feudal restraints, sank proud new roots—at a time, and in a place, where strenuous effort paid rich dividends. If the uninhabited forests and fields taught neighborliness, mutual aid, and obstinate endurance, the physical frontier also taught the farmer to experiment, innovate, speculate. So he habituated himself to the future rather than to the past—to kinetics rather than to statics. His sons learned some very unpeasantlike words: progress, opportunity, initiative. Among the world's agricultural systems, such mental assets are indeed rare. And it would be as hard for an Illinois farm boy to try to give these assets away as for a Pakistani or Spaniard or Egyptian *fedayeen* to suddenly acquire them. Regional character endures like the land itself.

On winter evenings, you may find this bourgeois-peasant-capitalist attending an extension course given by one of the land-grant universities, where he learns the latest results of agronomic research. Or back in his shop, puttering and fixing things—he is a confirmed "do-it-yourselfer." Or at a meeting of one of the farm organizations, or taking in the high school game. Or punching the calculator, or whittling, or moonlighting. His is the pragmatic mind, given not to quiet contemplation but to constant physical activity and invention. You may even find him trying farther-out experiments—like saying "no" to rural electrification and generating all his own power with a windmill. Those whirling blades atop their towers were a standard feature of Midwestern farms early in this century. John Lorenzen of Woodward, Iowa, has kept his going for the past fifty years. Like many farmers, Lorenzen is less educated than he is astute—"a genius with his hands" who "just plain enjoys the fact that he can run his own electrical-power plant . . . He chuckled as he looked up and saw the wind turning the propellers."

If the farmer seems a conformist in the social and ideological areas, it is perhaps because he doesn't have time to be an inventor at everything. His neighbor watches how he runs his farm, and he watches his neighbor's farm: and both pride themselves on running their own farm exactly as they wish. In this he finds far greater scope for his individuality than he could ever do as a wage earner. He will tell you that he feels free (except, of course, for the meddlesome bureaucrats). He lives contentedly within the local mores. The regimens of city life—the traffic lights, the clocks, the cubicles, the hierarchical relationships, the constant need to impress strangers—these would make him feel very unfree.

While you may hear an echo of old-fashioned agrarianism in his voice, he'd be the last one to worry about seeming anachronistic. To his way of thinking, the identification of virtue and independence is an absolute. Proud of his calling to an extent that few other men-of-the-soil ever have been, he will happily carry the Jeffersonian banner into the computer room. Right or wrong, his outlook is charged with the power of myth, "a form of reasoning which transcends reasoning in that it wants to bring about the truth it proclaims," which proceeds by "simplifying problems and issues to a single factor and then magnifying it to an absolute." Within a society of pluralists and relativists, the farmer thus lives on an island of monism and absolutism.

Can ideals conquer reals? Can the simplistic model hold? Even in the tough years of the fifties, while government programs, by favoring the larger farmer, were helping push thousands of smaller ones off the agricultural ladder, Dwight Eisenhower spoke with bland reassurance: "In America, agriculture is more than an industry; it is a way of life. Throughout our history the family farm has given strength and vitality to our entire social order. We must keep it healthy and vigorous." Through a century and a half of progress and disappointment, the heartland farmer has learned not only that he must obey nature in order to command it, but that he must also obey the total market, which means carefully adjusting his decisions to ever more complex social, economic, and political realities. For the farmer, as for all of us, freedom and conformity are eternally mingled.

When you cross the threshold of the farmhouse itself, you are getting near the heart of country life. Ken Guen, eighteen years old, talks about his family situation:

"See, our other landlord, he passed away, and left it in an estate, so they decided to sell the farm we're on. And it's kind of ironic, because the people you're going to visit tonight are the people that bought our farm. My dad, he hates to move to town as bad as I do. He really isn't that old, in his early fifties, you know, but he's at the age where he's too young to retire and too old to start over again. So we'll try to rent another farm, and his main purpose in that is to get me started in farming which I really want to do. But the farms around here are pretty scarce, and they want an ungodly price for the few that are for rent. Our farm, we've had it on a sharecrop

basis. So as far as I know we're gonna have to buy a house in town. Already Dad's had a half a dozen offers in ag-related jobs, like at the implement house or at the bank. It's not the income that worries us. He just hates to get away from the farm. And I do too. There's nothin' I hate more than havin' to move to town.

"But, as it looks right now, if we can't find a farm and I can't start farming, I'd like to be an extension advisor, or perhaps an ag teacher in a high school, or even an animal science instructor at a college. I'm a freshman right now at Blackhawk East Junior College, and after that I've narrowed it down to a four-year ag course at either Illinois State University or Western Illinois University. I've got my high school ag teacher to thank quite a bit. I've got a lifetime indebted to him because he's got me on the road to a future.

"I guess I'm a bug on the livestock end of the agricultural field. There's quite a few county fairs that we show livestock at, and right now I'm showing beef cattle. We were just out to the show in Kansas City, and right now I'm getting some steers ready for this International Livestock Exposition in Chicago, which is supposed to be one of the biggest livestock shows in the whole world. We've been fortunate in the last three to four years in that we've had quite a few champions, and reserve champions, but it's a lot of luck and a lot of hard work. Like tonight, I got home from school about four o'clock and helped Dad with the chores and then I spent about two hours brushing steers and combin' up the hair and figuring out feed rations, gettin' them to look just as nice as they possibly can.

"A lot of 4-H programs, a lot of parents, they give their kids the feed, and not have to worry about any costs or anything, but that's far from the truth at our place. My brother and I, we buy our own steers, pay the entire feed bills and vet costs. Dad's trying to prove to us that feeding cattle isn't the rosiest side of the picture that everyone thinks it is.

"And we've won shows without being crooked. Showing cattle you can be as crooked as in anything else. If you've got a calf that's limpin', or maybe bad on a foot, you can give them cortisone or any number of medications. But that's against the ethics of showing cattle. In this international show in Chicago, we'll probably come across some of the crookedest people in the whole world. But we feel if you're gonna win, you better win it fair. That's something Dad's always stressed to us, and I couldn't get much satisfaction out of it any other way.

"What I enjoy most is that actual showing. Here's this gargantuously

big place. You get in there with maybe sixty steers in a class from all over the country. Imagine us just coming from a small farm like ours, two hundred and seventy-six acres, up against people like from way out west with those huge ranches. You sit there, and I mean you sweat and worry about it.

"And, like, everybody kind of laughs at our state and national Future Farmers of America convention—they see a kid on stage getting an award for outstanding livestock production in the whole country, and they say that's not possible, and when I was a freshman I said the same thing. But here, three years later, out of ten shows we've had six champions, and I was president one year and vice president one year of our chapter, and pretty active in the state association, and I was in the livestock judging contests and the soil judging contests, and went to the national convention. So now we've got a reputation pretty high in the state, and a lot of people ask our advice on how to get a steer ready.

"I've been a Catholic all my life and I'm not ashamed to admit it to anybody. My dad, he's probably one of the strongest Catholic men around this area, and he'd do anything to get to church on Sundays. I don't suppose he's ever missed church more than—you could count 'em on one hand and that's because he's got a heart condition, and there's just been times when he couldn't get to church. Sure, I pray a lot and just ask for God's help, and it seems like He always comes through. And I just pray that I never lose my dad, or at least for a while, or my mother or any member of my family. And He has never let me down.

"But in today's agriculture there's just no place for the little guy. Like our three hundred is considered small around here. I'll argue it up and down until tomorrow morning that people are trying to discourage what we call the family farm. Like these people I'll take you to meet tonight, we feel they're guilty because they're trying to get as much land as they can, and they try and snuff out the small fella. But I feel that if you can't go big, you better stay out, so that's why I feel that I'll go the teaching route—there's always going to be

a need for teachers. Sure, I'd like to farm more than anything else, but it's just something that you've got to face. Or maybe teach part time, plus farm. Like Dad is a salesman for the De Kalb seed company, part time. Equipment costs have gotten so far out of line, it goes back to inflation, this country's whole economics. All it is is a monopoly on the farms. It seems like the corporations are just killing the families. You could have a family farm on a thousand or twelve hundred acres, don't get me wrong, but anybody that has that much money, they need a whole lot of backing, from the bank or something.

"If I have to move to town, I really truthfully don't know what I'll do. There's just something about it, when you're on the farm you're your own boss. It's been a good life for us. In teaching, there's the principal telling you what to do, the school board telling the principal, the people telling the school board. Just like clockwork, everybody's pushin' somebody. No, you do a better job if you *want* to do it. And we've had a good life out of it—you see I didn't come to town in rags or anything. But when that day comes to move, I'm sure my dad, he'll sit down and he'll just break down . . ."

After dark Ken shows the way to Bernard's house. At the door, Bernard, a tall, husky, bearded man of thirty, insists Ken come in too. The boy accepts reluctantly. Bernard understands his feelings, tries to be nice to him. He even offers him a job. Ken tries to look appreciative: thanks, but he's busy with school, etc. Everyone sits down around the kitchen table.

What is the most important quality for a farmer to have?

"Common sense," says Bernard. "Common sense and balance."

Ken nods.

Carol, Bernard's wife, says, "Like you said once that you're not a real deep thinker, but you can make on-the-spot decisions that usually turn out right. Like when you take cows through a gate you have to decide right now which one needs to go to market and which doesn't. You're good at that."

Bernard says, "You find these book farmers, they got all the right answers, but when it comes to practicality, it doesn't work. They can sit here with a piece of paper and prove you can put gain on cattle for seventeen or eighteen cents. But they leave out too many variables. They don't forecast this four or five weeks of rainy weather we've been having—which increases your cost-of-gain. You might lose four or five new feeder cattle you've had shipped in. Sure, it's an extreme, but it happens. Farming isn't a battle plan—it's in your blood."

Ken puts in, "Each steer is different. You just know what you gotta do, and you do it. It's not an eight-hour-a-day job, it's twenty-four hours a day, seven days a week. And everything on a farm is related to everything else. It's not a factory."

Bernard shakes his head. "You can't believe what goes on in a factory until you've worked in one. I did for two years when we were first married. The stuff they throw away in an hour, why, it would take me a year to make. They junk stuff like brand new harrows. They had one guy that was cuttin' up harrows. Cost you four or five hundred dollars to buy one. I asked the foreman, can I buy a harrow? No, can't do that, he says, got to cut 'em up, got to scrap 'em, they're the old models. How can you take pride in a job like that?"

Do things get a little tense around here when it's been raining so long?

"They do," Carol agrees. "On both sides. I've got kids in the house, and he's got cows in the slop."

Bernard says, "Well, you know, you learn to live with nature. And sometimes it's not too easy to live with. That corn blight we had two years ago is the best lesson I ever got on that. I think I got more upset over that . . . But the bad part is that we live here on a hill, most of it lays this way, see, it's bottom ground. So you get up at dawn, and you look out of that window, and the first thing you see is about twenty acres of water. Well, you know," he chuckles, "that just isn't any way to start the day."

Ken smiles sympathetically, in spite of himself.

Bernard continues, "This is where I really started usin' the hedging market. I seen we weren't gonna have a corn crop, so I started buying corn futures. Normally we buy between sixty and eighty thousand bushels of corn a year to feed our livestock. But then, if you don't have any corn yourself, that can get pretty expensive. Sometimes you're in a position to see it a little ahead of the speculators. But when you call that guy in Chicago, and he says, 'Well, these big money men are goin' the other way,' you think, what the hell, those guys know more'n what I do. But if you just stick with what you think is right, ninety per cent of the time you'll turn out right. These days a fair percentage of the farmers that have a large production are using the hedging markets. This is one of the things that's changed so much just in the last ten years. Oh, it's changed so doggone much, you wouldn't even recognize it. It takes so much more money to operate, for one thing. The physical fatigue isn't as great as it used to be, but the mental fatigue is greater."

Outside, a truck motor roars. Headlights glare in the window. "That's my steers, comin' in from Wyoming!" Bernard leaps up, hurries out. Ken follows him.

Carol pours another cup of coffee and sits down. "At first, when we moved back here, I was ashamed of farming. Now I'm proud of it. I grew up in suburbia—my dad's a lawyer. And although I think I married Bernard because his family was secure, now it's for himself. He was kind of a pain-in-the-neck at first—expecting me to be like farm women, you know, if anybody was coming over he'd worry I wouldn't have a big huge meal and desserts all prepared in advance. Now that I don't *have* to do it, I enjoy it.

"Farm women like heartiness and naturalness. But they're afraid to open their minds. They just give simple moralistic answers to things. They're defensive about their way of life, and they judge other life-styles. They won't talk about voting—that's not their job—and they won't read a book about child psychology. I like to talk with my farm friends about kids and down-home things. But for the other type of

Grant Heilman

thing I have my town friends. I value our independence here—we can *choose* our friends. That rat race in town does funny things to your insides. And here we can raise a family where the children will be able to come back and have good memories. In town a woman changes her clothes and acts different when her husband comes home. But when, I ask you, is the moment Bernard 'comes home'? You see, I feel this way is more honest. And then, he's always around. He's busy, but he's there. I value this family life-style. But I want my children to be aware of other things in the world, too.

"A lot of farm couples are kind of a team as far as running the farm. But Bernard likes running his own business. And he's *proud.* I can't imagine him working in a place where you have to take orders, 'cause he sure doesn't do that very well. Do you, Bernard?"

Bernard, exhilarated by the sight of the new livestock, bulks the doorway. "Nope," he laughs. "Ken said to say goodbye—he had to get on home." Settling into a chair, Bernard takes some time to collect his indoor thoughts. Then he goes on:

"If you own the land, you get up in the morning and look out the window—and it's yours. And you can tell anybody to go to hell if you feel like it. My dad, he started out as a hired man, and he has done well. There were bad years after World War II, and from around fifty-four to sixty-four you'd wonder why you were farming. And if it wasn't for me, there's no way he would have taken on all this amount of land, all the big figures and big machinery. But you've got to get big or get out. There's a lot of times I don't like it, either. But when you have more land, you can run your machinery more hours. This is where the opportunity is. That ground of Ken's dad's has to be taken over by somebody. People say, what the hell you buying another farm for? You got enough already. Well, maybe you do and maybe you don't. I know one thing, if my dad hadn't done what he done twenty years ago, I wouldn't be where I'm at today. And maybe my boys won't want to farm, and maybe they will, but they're gonna have the opportunity anyway. I wouldn't say I'm doin' this all for them, but fifteen years from now I'd hate to estimate what it's gonna take to farm. It's gonna take a lot of acreage and a lot of capital. And if you don't prepare for that in some way, they're not gonna have the opportunity. There's no better investment, I don't think, than farmland. I think we'll see the day, twenty years from now, that this land we're buying today'll look so cheap—I hope anyway—but I really believe that."

Chapter Six

First and Elm

And so the farmer seeks purity in isolation, only to find himself woven into an ever wider network. Out of this polar tension flows a yield that is often rich, and sometimes ironic.

The prairie town, too, depends on the ocean of grasses and grains, not only for trade, but as a buffer, to preserve its quiet purity. Yet what proves true for the farmer also proves true for the trading center. Isolation may be in its marrow, but interchange remains its lifeblood. So the town, like the farmer, feels the tension between interior stillness and arterial motion.

In the towns, as in the landscape, there remains a great sameness—and a surprising variety. Much of the external sameness derives from the uniform conditions of settlement, the available building materials, the unanimity of taste among the builders. The internal sameness is subtler, but it is characteristic: across the countryside, town after town seems knitted from the same social yarn. Yet there are also "other" towns, where physical or psychological distance from the farm centers is related to their differing economic functions.

In the 1850s, while urban centers swelled along the lake and river shores, the locomotives were plunging onto the prairies. Granted immense parcels of real estate along their rights-of-way as an inducement to track construction, the railroad companies became major promoters of instant towns in the grassy wilderness. They would plant a depot every few miles and sell subdivided lots around it. This policy not only netted them quick cash but tended to increase the value of all the prairie land in the general "building up of the country." Rich as the soils were, the farmer depended heavily on the railroad to get his crop to market and to bring back the machinery and supplies he needed. Thus, the railroads promoted settlement not just for the land profits but in order to assure themselves of an increasing volume of freight and passenger business.

Best known of these "colonizing" railroads was the Illinois Central. Spacing its depots at ten-mile intervals, it established new villages whose lots were priced according to their nearness to the train station. North-south streets were numbered, east-west streets were named for trees, and a "Main Street" was all but inevitable. Add some standardized downtown architecture, and, perhaps later on, a water tower bearing the town name, and you have today's typical prairie community. Its right-angled uniformity seems a perfect complement to the mile-square grid pattern of the fields and homesteads: both town and country express the Yankee-cum-Corn-Belt view of life as orderly, rational, and commercial.

Elsewhere, particularly in older states like Ohio and Michigan, the towns had preceded the railroads, typically growing cumulatively along

Wheatland, South Dakota, late 1800s

J. R. Hamlin

a stream used for grist-milling, or beside a main road. Yet here the same orderliness and conservatism, the same tendency to aesthetic imitation, was evident. The village might begin not at a depot but around a New England–style square. It might well have more native trees than the pure prairie towns. The habit of giving new villages classical or inspirational names was widespread throughout much of the nineteenth century, as was the "Philadelphia" plan of numbering the streets one way and naming them the other. So both tendencies are highly evident all through the Midwest.

The towns' most typical architecture, still to be seen, is the continuous row of downtown brick buildings, two or three stories in height, their plain fronts sometimes softened by decorations such as roof or window cornices. This uniform, vaguely Late Victorian style was hardly original to the region. But, like the townspeople, it was durable and respectable. Replacing more ramshackle predecessors, such commercial blocks were generally put up in the 1880s and 1890s, a period when cast-iron structural elements and flat asphalt roofs were in vogue and when the advent of commercial agriculture had brought a cash flow through the towns, enabling them to afford such improvements. By then, too, many of the old, dusty, and muddy thoroughfares were paved in brick, which can still be seen in many places.

Some years earlier, the balloon-frame house had been invented. It quickly proved ideal for the rapidly growing Midwest, where old-fashioned craftsmen were in short supply. Stronger, cheaper, easier to build, and utilizing the plentiful lumber brought by rail from the Michigan and Wisconsin forests, it became the standard prairie dwelling, particularly in its white, two-story version.

Equally important in "building up the country" was another commodity: publicity. From St. Louis to Stockholm, the railroads puffed up their new prairie communities. So did the state immigration agencies, the land corporations, the wealthy speculators, and sundry others —including the local residents themselves, who had sunk their emotions into the town along with their cash. Continuous bootstraps rallying was necessary because the civic loyalties of the early settlers were, as Daniel Boorstin remarks, "intense and transferable," as well as being "in inverse ratio to the antiquity of their communities." Hundreds of little towns sprang up within a few days' journey of Cincinnati or Chicago or Omaha. Each projected magnificent visions of the future; each saw itself as the epitome of those virtues thought to be embedded in the very landscape of America. And so, though threatened by very real hazards and uncertainties, the Midwestern towns started life on a strong dose of boosterism.

At times the puffery was the work of faraway interests. Nininger, Minnesota, was planned and promoted all the way from Philadelphia by Ignatius Donnelly, whose popular *Emigrant Aid Journal* sang the town's praises while it was still a cornfield. In 1856, Nininger was settled—and became a boomtown almost overnight. When its Boys Lyceum debated the question, "Has Hastings grown more than Nininger during the past year?" the right answer was obvious to all. Equally obvious, five years later, was that Nininger had entirely disappeared. Its buildings were dismantled and moved to Hastings and other nearby communities, including Cottage Grove, whose population had just doubled, but which was destined to vanish as quickly as Nininger. And these were not isolated examples. The state of Iowa alone has amassed some 2200 abandoned places. So high a mortality rate among prairie towns was a sharp reminder that the romantic brouhaha of westernward expansionism could easily turn into its opposite—disillusionment.

Still, boosterism did reassure the citizens and help to attract more. It also helped the town compete for tangible improvements that would transform the dream into a reality. Rival communities fought hard for the favors of governments willing to finance not only railways but also roads, canals, and other improvements. Early on, the Commissioners for the National Road had encountered that rivalry in "the solicitude and importunities of the inhabitants . . . who severally considered their grounds entitled to preference."

Furious battles raged over the selection of county seats. Indicative of the mingling of southern and northern influences, the Midwest evolved a combination of the southern county system and the New England township system—an odd, variable blend that was later carried farther west. For rural areas the county generally proved the more workable form. In the central square of the typical county seat stood a Greek Revival courthouse, the grandest building for miles around. Its impressive cupcake dome presided over the deeds and other official records, the courts, administrative and tax offices, and a jail. With some justification, everyone assumed that so visible a magnet would attract legal and other firms, reinforce civic pride, and guarantee a rosy future. So each new village campaigned to become the county seat.

Ideally, the choice was made at the ballot box. The real lines of

influence, however, were murky and complex. Since the state legislatures were vested with the power to create, enlarge, diminish, or abolish counties, the legislators were vulnerable to all sorts of bribes and threats from vested interests like the land promoters. One result was that counties often multiplied like rabbits. Indiana ended up with ninety-two, leaving that thinly populated state with a jurisdictional legacy as costly as it is cumbersome. And merely becoming a county seat was no guarantee of staying that way. Thirty-nine of Indiana's counties have moved their seats at least once, and some as many as seven times. Out in Kansas, the "county-seat wars," as they came to be called, reached their climax when gangs of hired gunmen began moseying around town about the time the ballot boxes appeared. Back in the more civilized Corn Belt, a few towns confined themselves to raiding the courthouse of their rival, capturing the records, and declaring themselves the new county seat.

Today, the old courthouses and their squares remain among the most visible features of many country towns. Because the central courthouse squares were most in vogue during the years when the middle

Horton, Kansas, late 1930s

J. W. McManigal

portion of the Mississippi Valley was being settled, their frequency is greatest in Indiana, Illinois, Iowa, Missouri, Kentucky, and Tennessee. To the east, west, and north of these states, the courthouses seem less prominent because they are located away from the center of town. Architecturally, a few of these stolid structures are real gems—such as the courthouse at Cambridge, in Illinois' rich-soiled Henry County, a building that has been impeccably maintained. Other, less notable Midwestern courthouses are full of obsolete space and have consequently been treated like white elephants for generations. In 1974, however, the National Trust for Historic Preservation opened a campaign to find ways of restoring their usefulness.

As for boosterism itself, local journalists caught the bug instantly and have been passing it on ever since. Dear to the checkbooks of local advertisers, the down-home press never mentions business failures, arrests, or shotgun weddings. (It doesn't need to.) Instead, its reporters always remember to list as many nice folks' names as possible and to plump for Plainville. In the early days, such vital functions seemed reason enough for every locality to have its own paper. The very first issue of one Iowa sheet pointed out: "The fact that the population of Cedar county is not now vastly larger than it is can only be attributable to the want of a public journal, to unfold its resources, and make known its advantages to the emigrant." But journalistic hyperbole, like the paper boomtowns, helped pave the way for its opposite—the lampooning and muckraking styles developing in the lively pages of such urban and statewide papers as the Chicago *Tribune,* the Des Moines *Register,* the Minneapolis *Tribune,* the Detroit *Free Press,* the Cleveland *Plain Dealer,* and the Cincinnati *Enquirer.* A syndicated reporter named Mark Twain, on looking into the origins of St. Paul, Minnesota, was moved to announce a frontier hypothesis all his own:

How solemn and beautiful is the thought that the earliest pioneer of civilization, the van leader, is never the steamboat, never the railroad, never the newspaper, never the Sabbath School, but always whiskey! The missionary comes after whiskey—I mean he arrives after the whiskey has arrived; next the trader, next the miscellaneous rush; next the gambler, the desperado, the highwayman, and all their kindred of sin of both sexes, and next the smart chap who has bought up an old grant that covers all the land, this brings the lawyer tribe, the vigilante committees, and this brings the undertaker. All these interests bring the newspaper; the newspaper starts up politics and a railroad; all hands turn to and build a church and a jail and behold! Civilization is established forever in the land. Westward the jug of Empire takes its way!

Disenchantment took deeper forms, too. The plain fact was that as the glamorous frontier rolled west, many a hamlet, left in its wake, turned into a depressing backwater. In 1883, Edgar W. Howe, who had grown up in two such villages in northern Missouri, depicted their gloomy atmosphere in his novel *The Story of a Country Town.* Marking, as J. W. Ward says, "the moment when the myth of the garden in America gave way to the wasteland of broken dreams," the book initiated, in this country, the tandem literary movements known as realism and naturalism. While these are usually thought of as signaling the end of romanticism, they can also be seen as a logical culmination of that illusion-disillusion cycle inherent in the romantic temper and in the prairie experience itself. In Howe's opening pages the rose-colored mythology of the boosters falls under the weight of heavy pessimism:

Ours was the prairie district out West, where we had gone to grow up with the country . . .

In the dusty tramp of civilization westward—which seems to have always been justified by a tradition that men grow up by reason of it—our section was not a favorite, and remained new and unsettled after counties and States farther west had grown old . . .

When I see Fairview in my fancy now, it is always from a high place, and looking down upon it the shadow is denser around the house where I lived than anywhere else, so that I feel to this day that should I visit it, and receive permission from the new owners to walk through the rooms, I should find the walls damp and mouldy because the bright sun and the free air of Heaven had deserted them as a curse.

Howe's dim view of life in the Middle West country was soon echoed in the varied writings of Hamlin Garland:

How poor and dull and sleepy and squalid it seemed! The one main street ended at the hillside at his left and stretched away to the north, between two rows of the usual village stores, unrelieved by a tree or a touch of beauty. An unpaved street, drab-colored, miserable, rotting wooden buildings, with the inevitable battlements—the same, only worse, was the town.

Far happier pictures emerged from the fiction of Willa Cather and others. But the dark mood would reappear in Edgar Lee Masters' famous *Spoon River Anthology* and in the well-known novels of Sinclair Lewis. Were the towns as bad as these authors make them out to be? The townspeople in Lewis' own *Main Street* do not think so. They remain full of optimism and "pep." It is only Carol Kennicott, with her artistic aspirations, who sees Gopher Prairie as hopelessly dull and complacent, and who, after trying desperately to change things, is forced to leave her husband in order to leave the town. Yet it is she who speaks for the author. In other words, it is the few who differ, rather than the majority of just-plain-folks, who are dismayed by small-town life.

Having an education has been a strong Midwestern value almost from the beginning. The Northwest Ordinance of 1787 had provided that "religion, morality, and knowledge being necessary to good government and the happiness of mankind, schools and the means of education shall forever be encouraged." The region's basic political document, framed in the East, thus reflected the new nation's twin concerns of pursuing happiness and establishing a democratic state. And in the spirit of the Puritans, who equated ignorance with deviltry, education was taken to comprise religion and morality, as well as knowledge.

Throughout the nineteenth century, the Yankees, midlanders, and immigrants who poured into the Middle West made education one

of their first concerns. After the farms and churches, the one-room log schoolhouses were generally the first buildings to appear. Most of these were replaced by one-room white frame buildings by 1870. At first, the students sat on log and plank benches and at roughhewn desks, shouting their lessons at the tops of their lungs. The "loud" method gave way to slates and blackboards by the 1860s.

Except for the Bible, and perhaps a few classics, the rural child would find few intellectual stimuli outside the classroom. Since most teachers were themselves only minimally qualified, and because rote memorization was heavily stressed, the content of the schoolbooks was of prime importance.

One specialist, Ruth M. Elson, has analyzed the ideological content of over a thousand such books used all over America throughout the nineteenth century. Because the Middle West, more than any other section, was molded during that period, and because its rural population remained relatively homogeneous and insulated, the mental and social climate of its small towns would long reflect those ideas and values.

As implied by the Northwest Ordinance, the broad aims of education were those of nation-building and of middle-class life. Specifically, these included the implanting of moral character, preparation for democratic citizenship, and the imparting of knowledge that would be materially useful. The prevailing orientation was to authority, virtue, and outward success, rather than to scholarly distinction, creative originality, or intellectual freedom. Typical texts advise the pupil:

> Little children, you must seek Rather to be good than wise.
>
> We do not blame a man who is proud of his success, so much as one who is vain of his learning.
>
> How little of our peace and security depends on Reason and how much on *religion and government.*

In a democratic and moral America, usefulness prevails. The love of abstract, useless knowledge belongs to an aristocratic and immoral Europe:

> The colleges and universities of Europe differ materially from those of the United States. They are rather places of study for such as wish to acquire knowledge. Scarcely any control or care is exercised over the character and conduct of the students . . .
>
> . . . those splendid establishments such as Oxford or Cambridge in which immense salaries maintain the professors of literature in monastic idleness.
>
> While many other nations are wasting the brilliant efforts of genius on monuments of ingenious folly, to perpetuate their pride, the Americans, according to the true spirit of Republicanism, are employed almost entirely in works of public and private utility.

Against such a background, and in view of the very real physical challenges of the frontier period, it is not hard to see why the large state university—an institution that took shape in the Middle West—acquired a more utilitarian and democratic cast than its eastern predecessors. While the inventions of Benjamin Franklin had exemplified an earlier brand of American practicality, the cult of the immediately useful rose to a zenith in a time and place in which the nation was overwhelmingly preoccupied with physical growth. By 1873, the Midwest's habit of yoking the mind to simplistic formulas had impressed at least one English visitor to whom a resident had revealed that "all religious, political, social, and historical teaching could be reduced to three subjects—the Sermon on the Mount, the Declaration of American Independence, and the Chicago Republican Platform of 1860."

Indeed, romantic nationalism was much in the air. Wrote one schoolbook author:

Q. What is the national character of the United States?
A. More elevated and refined than that of any nation on earth.

Sprung full-blown from the American Revolution, the nation's magical quality is Liberty. Like most magical qualities, it is, however, never defined. Elson looks hard for examples of what Liberty might have meant to the textbook authors, but can find only a few vague references to freedom of the individual from government interference. Liberty is mystically identified with the American landscape, particularly the western landscape. Thus, nationalism merges with the agrarian myth, and with the romantic heroism of the frontier.

Of particular significance for the Middle West were the famous Readers of William H. McGuffey. Although the great majority of the textbook authors lived in New England, McGuffey, who became the most popular of them all, hailed from Ohio and remained there most of his life. After 1836, when the first McGuffey primer came off the presses, some 123 million McGuffeys were sold—100 million of these between 1850 and 1900. Although their appeal was universal, the McGuffey Readers were thematically oriented to the Midwestern farm village, and it was in the Middle West that they achieved their greatest sales concentration.

While the McGuffeys contain many of the same broad assumptions about education, America, man, and God as the other schoolbooks, their most striking feature is their advocacy of the middle-class view of life as a constant moral struggle. *McGuffey's Third Eclectic Reader,* for example, which was used as late as the 1920s, consists of seventy-nine brief stories and poems, each introducing a few new words and nearly all teaching a moral lesson. A careful reading of this book shows that the McGuffey virtues fall into two general groups: those that promote economic advancement and those that restrain and socialize the passions and ego. The underlying aim of the Readers is to internalize the authority of God and parents—to develop the conscience. The main economic virtues are industry, education, respect for property, perseverance, thrift, frugality, and the avoidance of tempting diversions.

The restraining-socializing virtues are altruism, helpfulness, kindness, humility, gentleness, contentment, forgiveness, forbearance, generosity, and peaceableness. Relating to conscience-development are obedience, honesty, gratitude, prayer, and moral courage.

The stories prove that virtue is always rewarded, vice always punished. McGuffey's payoffs are mainly physical: a boy who plays hooky and lies to his mother nearly drowns as a result; a girl who is meek and well-behaved is astonished to receive a pile of silver coins baked into a loaf of bread. Virtue is also rewarded by parental love and a good conscience. Vice causes shame, to which the authority figure adds either punishment or—once the lesson has been sufficiently learned—forgiveness or a moral dictum:

BEAUTIFUL HANDS.

1. "O Miss Roberts! what coarse-looking hands Mary Jessup has!" said Daisy Marvin, as she walked home from school with her teacher . . .

4. Miss Roberts took Daisy's hands in hers, and said, "Your hands are very soft and white, Daisy—just the hands to look beautiful on a piano; yet they lack one beauty that Mary's hands have . . . Mary's hands are always busy. They wash dishes; they make fires; they hang out clothes, and help to wash them, too; they sweep, and dust, and sew; they are always trying to help her poor, hard-working mother . . ."

11. "O Miss Roberts! I feel so ashamed of myself, and so sorry," said Daisy, looking into her teacher's face with tearful eyes.

12. "Then, my dear, show your sorrow by deeds of kindness. The good alone are really beautiful."

For McGuffey, man is highly perfectible as well as highly corruptible. Therefore, he needs careful molding from the outside. Thus the Readers became an extension of the kinds of controls exerted by the farm family and the local community. McGuffey never encourages the pupil to acquire the kind of soaring ambition that could lead to too much sophistication, or carry him off to the tainted city—a fate already being experienced by millions of rural youths. Instead of kindling visions of excellence, McGuffey recommends the middling, homebound path:

Then contented with my State,
Let me not envy the great;
Since true pleasures may be seen,
On a cheerful village green.

Financiers, cattle drovers, actors, coal miners, politicians, steamboat captains, railroad magnates, factory stewards, westering farmers, runaway slaves, California gold seekers—all of these were familiar figures in nineteenth century America. But none ever appears in McGuffey. His adults are limited to moderately prosperous small-town craftsmen and businessmen, humble rustics, school teachers, and poor widows. Except for idle tramps—men ruined forever by a single taste of alcohol —adults are perfect. Character is simply good or bad, never interestingly personal, or idiosyncratic, or visionary, or a mixture of good and bad. Thus, in a century of unparalleled egoism, independence, and motion, he went on teaching America to be altruistic, humble, and stationary. One wonders how a model McGuffey graduate would have fared in a business world growing ever more competitive, ever more ready to laugh at do-gooders—or in a labor force growing increasingly class-conscious and militant. One wonders whether, during that half-century when a hundred million McGuffeys were read and reread, the peaceful village green had not already become something of a period piece.

Much of McGuffey's appeal, in other words, came from his way of reassuring small-town America that its values were right at a time

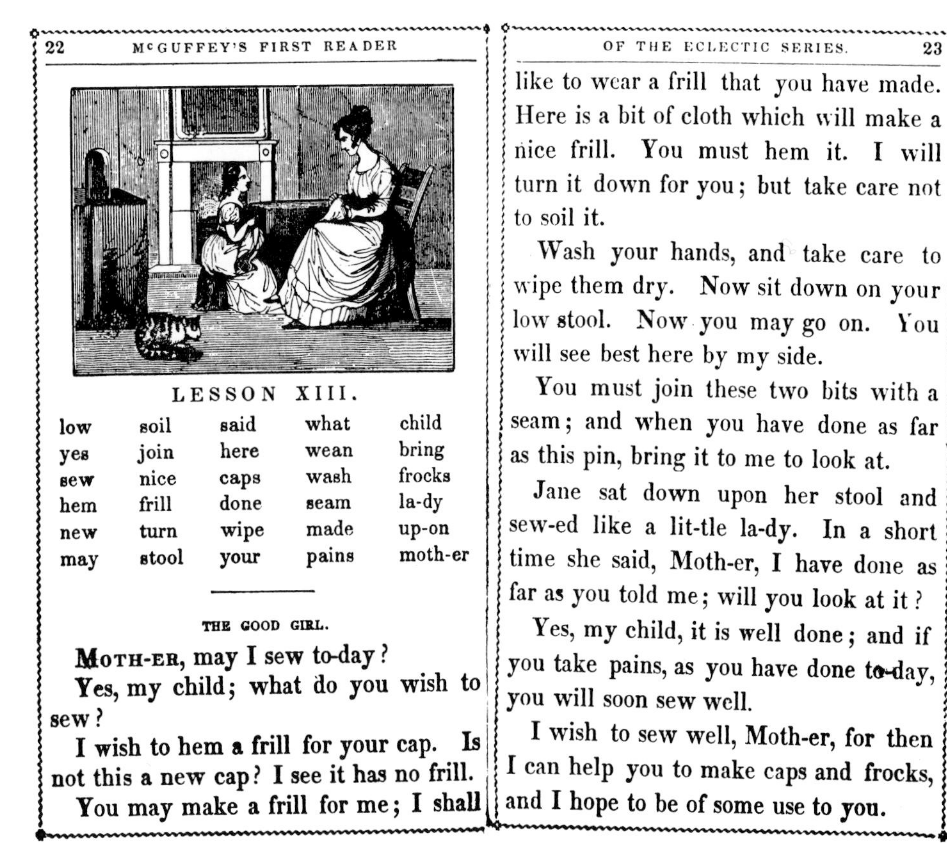
22 McGUFFEY'S FIRST READER

LESSON XIII.

low	soil	said	what	child
yes	join	here	wean	bring
sew	nice	caps	wash	frocks
hem	frill	done	seam	la-dy
new	turn	wipe	made	up-on
may	stool	your	pains	moth-er

THE GOOD GIRL.

MOTH-ER, may I sew to-day?

Yes, my child; what do you wish to sew?

I wish to hem a frill for your cap. Is not this a new cap? I see it has no frill.

You may make a frill for me; I shall

OF THE ECLECTIC SERIES. 23

like to wear a frill that you have made. Here is a bit of cloth which will make a nice frill. You must hem it. I will turn it down for you; but take care not to soil it.

Wash your hands, and take care to wipe them dry. Now sit down on your low stool. Now you may go on. You will see best here by my side.

You must join these two bits with a seam; and when you have done as far as this pin, bring it to me to look at.

Jane sat down upon her stool and sew-ed like a lit-tle la-dy. In a short time she said, Moth-er, I have done as far as you told me; will you look at it?

Yes, my child, it is well done; and if you take pains, as you have done to-day, you will soon sew well.

I wish to sew well, Moth-er, for then I can help you to make caps and frocks, and I hope to be of some use to you.

Pages from a McGuffey Reader

when those values were being sharply challenged by the new urbanity. In the late nineteenth century, this ascendant urbanity showed itself in a vast outpouring of city-oriented "How to Succeed" books, and in the deification of business tycoons like Andrew Carnegie. It was embodied in the rapidly growing urban upper middle class, who, championing rugged individualism and economic libertarianism, fought hard to achieve inequalities of wealth and prestige. As against this type of rough-and-tumble liberty, McGuffey continued to preach rustic equality. His village is classless. It promotes peace and harmony, not ruthless competition. Nature is benevolent, not a Darwinian jungle. Too much of anything that distinguishes the individual, be it wealth or wisdom, is to be discouraged. Ceaseless, dogged, honest effort—not genius or a burning desire to excel—will bring prosperity. And that prosperity, once achieved, does not yield relaxed enjoyment, the refinement of the senses, the pleasures of detachment, the release of energies for higher pursuits, or anything that might appear ostentatious. So deeply ingrained are the scarcity habits—self-denial and unremitting toil—that the middle-class McGuffeyite can never graduate into "decadent" urban or European cultivation. Too little money reveals laziness, or perhaps misfortune. But too much of it, like too much wisdom or talent or fashionable sparkle, separates you from the dominant middle group. You must rise to their standard, but not surpass it. Thus, equality means opportunity—within limits.

Today, the contrast between McGuffey's still, protected village and the strident world of the upper middle class remains very much the atmospheric difference between the downstate town and the lakeshore metropolis. Yet, while McGuffey-style equality has always typified the small communities of the Middle West, it is hardly exclusive to them. Flaubert and others showed how bourgeois conformity permeated the villages of Europe. And Emerson was referring to all of America when he remarked, "our prevailing equality makes a prairie tameness." Santayana ascribed our leveling pressures to moral immaturity, combined with the "contagion" of democratic opinion: "The sphere of unanimity tends to grow larger, and to reduce the margin of diversity to insignificance. The result is an ever-increasing moral unison, which is the simplest form of moral harmony and emotionally the most coercive." Prescient old Tocqueville had spotted the syndrome far earlier: after watching our two main ideals in practice, he had concluded that America preferred equality to liberty.

In *Main Street on the Middle Border,* a definitive study of the small Midwestern town from 1865 to 1950, historian Lewis Atherton shows that class divisions typified the towns from the beginning, but that the strong egalitarian ethic kept people from saying so, and that the barriers were usually low enough to permit considerable mobility. There were three main layers:

> At any one time, a small inner group of people based on varying combinations of wealth, length of residence, occupation, and breeding stood at the top. God-fearing, middle-class people devoted to church and lodge formed still another layer. And, always, a lower class of common day laborers, generally indifferent to dominant ideals, could be distinguished. Like sex, these divisions were not discussed openly. Ideals of a classless society and social purity ranked too high in the small-town code to permit open doubts.

The recollections of a contemporary ex-Midwesterner show how the class system and the egalitarian ethic have been well preserved down to the present day:

"My father was in the oil business, which was transient, and we didn't have a lot of money, so we rented this little house beside the

tracks. That was close enough to be tainted, and I walked to school with children from the wrong side of the tracks. They were very rough-talking and used all kinds of four-letter words. On weekends the oil field people did a lot of drinking and card playing, and the women smoked—all the stuff the nice people in town supposedly didn't do.

"When I was in the first grade I went to a little girl's birthday party in a different neighborhood. It seemed fancy, like in the movies. I could tell I was looked down on. They were nice, but I didn't fit in, and they rathered their daughter hadn't invited me. From my upbringing I was much more outspoken and direct. But it didn't take me long to see that everything was supposed to be done a certain way all the time. Like, you don't let your mind or feelings get out of hand, and you aren't supposed to get carried away with enthusiasm about anything, or say you really hate anything, either. Your own opinions aren't what matter, because there's only one right way to do things anyway. When I used to ask my mother, 'How does everybody *know* what to do?' she'd just say she didn't know what I was talking about.

"By the time I was in junior high my father had become part owner of an oil field business, and we had moved to another town and graduated into the middle category. We bought a house near the high school in the nice part of town and were accepted right in with the church people, who were most of the town. There wasn't any drinking of any kind, and their whole social life was the church. They went to church suppers, and picnics, and there was the woman's group in the church, and the men's group in the church, and the teen-agers' group in the church, and the ladies' aid society, and the deacons' meetings and the other meetings—plenty to fill up a whole week. It was supposed to fill up your whole life. But that didn't mean being saintly: it meant being busy doing things.

"And the clubs that these church people went to—the Kiwanis and Rotary—they could feel right about going because they told themselves they were being useful, not just having fun. But the Elks Club and the VFW, that was the lower echelon crowd, they didn't see anything wrong with having fun. They went to their dances and they drank, and they had the Blue Lounge and a couple of beer bars. The people in the top financial strata belonged to a country club which was considered uppity. They drank and gambled and played cards and golf and all, whether it was Sunday or not, which the general small businessmen and farmers thought was wicked and sinful. But none of this was ever open warfare. In fact these differences would be denied right down the line. That's the whole thing of it—it's never spelled out. Lying and conforming is better than telling the truth and not conforming. So I learned to be quiet. I learned to go underground. They would think I was conforming, but in my head I wasn't.

"There were these two very pretty girls who were condemned, first of all, because they came from the wrong side of the tracks. And they had the double offense of being pretty. In a small town, the plainer you are, the safer and more virtuous you are.

"This other girl friend of mine was in the upper level, and when her family got the first dishwasher in town, and the first television, they were considered lacking in character, to be courting labor-saving devices and leisure. The woman must be out playing bridge, and not be a very good wife, that she should want such things. And when they had professional photographs taken of their children, the whole town was horrified that they would spend that kind of money just to get pictures of their kids. My friend got to design her own clothes and have a dressmaker make them, and that was shocking, that she didn't buy her clothes like everybody else. The mother wore a fur

stole to church, too, and that was unforgivable. She tried for twenty years to be accepted by the middle group, and never was. Oh, they let her be on one of the church committees—but they'd always say her name a special way.

"There had been a doctor the whole town loved. He'd died before I moved there, but I felt like I'd known him from the way they talked about him. Everybody bragged on how he kept the same car for twenty years. He qualified for the top group, but he didn't claim it.

"The uppers tried to have an Episcopal Church, but because there weren't enough of them, it didn't work out. So then they went to the Methodist or Presbyterian churches, which were mainly middle-middle. A few went to the Christian Science Church, but most of the town considered that devil-worship. The Presbyterians thought they themselves were the most intellectual. The Baptists were definitely lower-middle. The others were really the bottom of the barrel—Church of the Nazarene, Latter-day Saints, Seventh-Day Adventists, some other small ones.

"Anybody who didn't fit the pattern was out of it as much as the others could keep them out. The low-income people mostly didn't want in, either, because they wanted to have more fun than the middles. But the upper income ones did conform outwardly because they were trying to get business. Like if a doctor was scandalous and indiscreet—if he drove down Main Street with the woman the town suspected he was having an affair with—they'd all quit going to him. So the uppers paid lip service to the Methodist and Presbyterian code. When they were alone, they went ahead and had their cocktail parties and had their fun, but on Sunday they sat in the pews and pretended to accept the middle-class code. Everybody knew *all* of that. But if you spoke openly about it you were really in hot water. 'It doesn't exist and we all know it doesn't exist and we don't talk about it. Just don't go out with one of them.'

"If a lot of kids were parked and necking, or driving fast or whatever, the policeman could definitely look the other way if it was the son of the head of the schoolboard or president of the bank. The others, they'd really get it. Actually, the town liked to have somebody get caught breaking the law so everyone could point at him and feel self-righteous. This one family have been the bank presidents for four generations, and, man, they've got that thing nailed down. Their son was a spoiled brat, a troublemaker. He raced his convertible around, and the police always chased him and always figured out why to let him go. He was considered a great catch for an upper girl, but my mother wouldn't have wanted me to go with him. That's the kind of thing the uppers wouldn't understand about the middles.

"I don't mean the banker could just say, 'Look, I'm gonna tell you what to do in this town.' But he did have all the power because he could make the loans, and if he didn't like you, he could wreck everything you were trying to do. I remember, when we went in for a loan, he seemed like a god. Or if a man from the wrong side of the tracks worked his way up in the bank for years, they'd never make him a vice-president—the town would always say he didn't deserve it.

"Yet if somebody showed outstanding scholastic achievement or talent, the top group were always anxious to lift them out of the middle-middle. They had to be very careful to do it without opposing the parents or offending the town. In school I was the head of everything—head of the debate team, Queen of the Band, accompanist for everybody, got the DAR award for scholarship, went to Girls' State. So there were these lures out, from some of the uppers and teachers, to get me to go to college. To the middle group, college was no virtue—in fact, too much book-learning was suspect. All through high school, my parents and their friends and mine were relieved when I said I wasn't going. That's a nice sensible girl, girls should get a job, or go to nurses' training, or, mainly, get married. But these others quietly saw to it that I knew the right courses to take. Then, the month I graduated, when I suddenly announced I was going to college, they really galvanized. They moved heaven and earth to get my applications into the state university in time to be accepted at a scholarship hall. My mother wanted me to go to a small church school, because to her the university was the worst place I could go, a place of the devil for sure. The people who came back from there were really ruined. And from her standpoint it was true. The people I graduated from high school with, who did go to college—well, I don't know of any who are still in the town. College broke them away.

"Today, the town has grown from six to eight thousand. But the overall structure is the same—just maybe a little more disguised because of television and travel. More of the people have been to Europe; but that doesn't seem to affect the silent code they live by."

In the rural towns, then, as on the farms, the inward pull of the home place tends to neutralize the outward tug of modern life. Yet the town reveals its awareness of the spin-off threat by the mechanisms it uses to ensure its own survival. Since centrifugal force derives from motion, the aim of these mechanisms is to reduce mobility. Thus, in the girl's remembrance, a negative value is assigned to the transcience of the oil field people, whereas putting down roots—buying a house in the "middle" part of town—is rewarded. Yet mobility within the town is discouraged. The best way to move up from the wrong side of the tracks, therefore, is to change towns. Presumably, this would hold equally true for a "middle" boy eager to move up in banking, either on his merits or by marrying a banker's daughter he might meet in college.

But, of course, the middles do not encourage college, particularly at the large universities, which lack religious affiliation, encourage the questioning of fundamentals, and promote a cosmopolitan outlook—a cluster of forces sure to accelerate one's motion away from local values. And while the uppers may enjoy their more cosmopolitan tastes, they can never leave the town's gravitational influence, but only move sometimes nearer, sometimes farther, within a kind of elliptical orbit.

The nucleus of social realities is defended by rendering it invisible. This highly effective defense mechanism is not confined to small towns, but is, in fact, one of the ways in which our emotional structures are kept intact. If you give a thing a name, you differentiate it from what it is not—thereby making it available for acceptance or rejection.

So the townspeople, jealously guarding their nuclear secrets, do

not name names. The mother does not hear the daughter's question, the policeman looks the other way, the teachers do not appear to oppose the parents, the class structure does not exist. Oscillations are damped; the system remains stable.

But the Middle West is America, and America is motion. So the town's tripartite-but-leveling purity is threatened by interchange. That buffering ocean of grass and grain cannot prevent the arteries of motion from carrying away sons and daughters and bringing back new ideas, new moralities.

Worldly wisest of those arteries is the Mississippi River. Murky and meandering, shipping out whiskey and bringing in foreigners, hauling bargefuls of industrial materials to the wide-open cities along its shores, its unpredictable current has long frightened and fascinated the right-angled towns of the hinterland. During World War I, for instance, the Father of Waters caught an incurable infection in New Orleans and carried it north. The resulting epidemic was bewailed by the *Ladies' Home Journal,* right next to an ad for Pond's Vanishing Cream:

OUR JAZZ-SPOTTED MIDDLE WEST

Small Towns and Rural Districts Need Clean-Up as Well as Chicago and Kansas City

by John R. McMahon

It is an accepted axiom that big cities are wicked, but small towns and rural districts are clean . . . Our Middle West is supposed to be a citadel of Americanism and righteousness. Probably it is. Yet a survey of its length and breadth shows that it is badly spotted with the moral smallpox known as jazz . . .

At Marshalltown, Iowa, a town of fifteen thousand inhabitants, a country club was organized last spring and some nice dances were held. It was a great success until the young people came home from college and introduced the jazz, which utterly shocked the elders and resulted in breaking up the club . . .

"Why are rural women, the guardians of American purity, apparently so complacent in regard to the modern dance?"

"Simply because they do not accompany their girls and boys to, through and from these dances . . . Boy-and-girl couples leave the hall in a state of dangerous disturbance. Any worker who has gone into the night to gather the facts of the activities outside the hall is appalled . . ."

River towns along the Mississippi maintain to a degree their traditional reputation with modern trimmings of jazz and bootleg liquor . . .

We are dancing on an inclined platform that slopes into the bottomless pit of impotent and inferior races. Let's quit! Safety first! Let us find excitement in straight and wholesome activities. Every human being can enroll in the big struggle of enormous consequences now going on—to keep from wobbling and upon an even keel the world, America, one's own neighborhood and oneself!

Not to be outdone by the *Ladies' Home Journal,* a reporter from *Collier's* was dispatched to Oskaloosa, Iowa, where, in 1923, he uncovered alarming evidence of moral slippage. But since Oskaloosa was "almost 100 per cent American . . . a village of retired farmers and of tradespeople," its problems did not appear to stem from jazz or sexual derangement but rather from irreligion, modern life, and the flivver. "The law and the gospel working in perfect harmony could hardly compete with Six-cylinder Sin."

This came near the heart of the matter. Even in horse-drawn days, youthful impertinences and escapes had centered around the instruments of motion. Writes Lewis Atherton: "The carriage with its fast team, yellow fly nets, linen lap robe, and beribboned whip lifted the spirit of the young blade as he drove up and down Main Street with one foot hanging over the body bed and a cigar at an angle in his mouth . . . Men loved a fast horse and a reputation for permitting no rival to pass." And the livery stable, with its "mingled smell of horse urine and manure, harness oil, feed and cured hay," was a center of racy humor, profanity, liquor, card-playing, sexual information, and general male indolence. The stable was therefore about as intriguing to young boys as it was repulsive to their mothers.

Indeed, the agencies of transportation were rapidly reducing the hallowed independence of country towns. Railroads and trucks made mass-produced, brand-name merchandise directly available at low cost. This drove old-fashioned local artisans out of business. Mail-order and chain-store merchandising undercut local merchants, just as supermarkets would eventually undercut the Mom-and-Pop groceries.

But no vehicle reduced the localness of the small-town citizen so dramatically as that most American of products, the automobile. In the late thirties, Sherwood Anderson, having earlier observed that "Nothing in America stands still very long," gave an account of how intimately the car and truck had threaded their way into the life of the mid-American village:

> Life in the towns spreading out in a new way, the old tight close life broken up by the coming of the new big paved highways, the streams of cars always flowing through the towns, endless rivers of cars, American restlessness . . .

The strict moralities of the countryside helped spur an offbeat commerce in the forbidden and fantastic.

. . . the mother of a family, when her children do not demand it, is out in the family car. She picks up a woman friend. They park the car on Main Street and sit and watch the life of the street . . .

Always now, through the long summer days and through summer evenings, the rivers of cars flow through the towns. At night the headlights of the cars make a moving stream of light. If there is a big highway passing through the town, the streets are lined with tourist houses and tourist camps have been built at the town's edge. On summer nights as you lie on your bed in your house in the American town, you hear the heavy rumble of goods trucks. If there is a steep grade through your town the heavily loaded trucks, in low gear, shake the walls of your house . . .

In the Middlewest it is corn cutting time and at the edge of some of the towns, corn husking contests are held. Champion corn huskers come to town to win prizes. Trucks loaded with yellow corn run swiftly through the streets of Middlewestern towns, some of the yellow ears falling in the streets. There are yellow ears, fallen from trucks along the sides of roads leading into town . . .

The small towns are and will remain close to the land. Modern machine-driven life has brought the land and the people of the land closer to the towns.

And so, while the instruments of motion threatened the stillness and inviolability of the countryside, they also helped the farmer by reducing his physical and psychological distance from the trade center. The automobile was, of course, but one phase in a technological revolution that was transforming the farmer's whole way of life—and that would eventually change his image, on Main Street, from poky hayseed to acute business manager.

Fundamentally, the values of the village green and of the blast furnace seem irreconcilable. And yet, during the era when America was shifting from one to the other, both were firmly anchored in the personality of the only Midwesterner whose fame has ever rivaled Lincoln's.

It was just two years before Abe's death that Henry Ford was born on an obscure Michigan farm. Sixty years later, he was the richest man in the country—and a hometown hero to millions of just-plain-folks. His name was not only in the newspapers—it was right there in their driveways and barnyards. He suited their style. They loved him, they trusted him, and they wrote him about a thousand letters

a day. From a farmer's wife in Georgia: "You know, Henry, your car lifted us out of the mud. It brought joy into our lives. We loved every rattle in its bones." From a neighborly Texan: "We had good rain here last night, and I hope you had rain over your way." From Maryland came a joyful word: "I just had a baby girl, and since your wife's name is Mary and yours being Henry, I am going to name it Mary Henryetta Ford, if you don't mind." Many wrote asking for financial help in some form. But a western cattleman pleaded for a higher cause: "Mr. Ford, you have the confidence of the common people. You command publicity. You have the money. You can accomplish the abolition of the gold standard. Do it Henry. The way to do it is to do it. The time is now." An Ohio farmer, evidently willing to overlook the moral rot inherent in horseless transportation, rhapsodized on the liberating effects the Model T had on his neighborhood, then seemed to sum up the gratitude of everyone by saying simply, "God bless Henry Ford."

These and many another glowing missive are quoted by Reynold M. Wik in his book *Henry Ford and Grass-Roots America.* The letters are housed in the Ford Archives at Dearborn, Michigan, which contain over fourteen million documents—enough, it is estimated, to be stacked six times higher than the Empire State Building. That agglomeration, in itself, is a clue to the Ford personality.

With a farm boy's abhorrence of waste, he hated to destroy anything.

He was constantly working on practical and impractical schemes for converting the useless into the useful—such as the recycling of scrap metal. But his fundamental contribution was in teaching American industry how to save *time.* Ford did not actually invent the assembly line—Ransom Olds employed one ten years before he did—but he perfected flow technology with such ingenuity that by 1924 he had cut the time needed to build one car from thirteen hours to one. America was now hatching cars faster than babies, and the Ford Motor Company was building half the automobiles in the entire world.

Nothing better demonstrated Ford's ability to weld the slow-old-rural to the fast-new-urban than his application of a farmer's habit—saving—to a new dimension—time. This brought about a notion of time-work that was deeply alien to static agrarian traditions. Daniel Boorstin describes the new concept:

> "Efficiency," an American gospel in the twentieth century, meant packaging work into units of time. . . . An effective America was a speedy America. Time became a series of homogeneous—precisely measured and precisely repeatable—units. The working day was no longer measured by daylight, and electric lights kept factories going "around the clock." Refrigeration and central heating and air conditioning had begun to abolish nature's seasons. One unit of work time became more like another.

Just as the production line leveled time into equal units, it also leveled matter into interchangeable parts. Indeed, out in rural America, the simplicity, cheapness, and wide availability of those parts were among Ford's major selling points. But the production line also leveled people into interchangeable units. And perfect repeatability implied zero uniqueness. Of course, a certain small variability was inevitable; the engineer controlled this by giving it a name—tolerance. There had to be more of it in Ford parts, which rattled, than in Rolls Royce parts, which had been lovingly fitted together by an old-fashioned craftsman. Such a system of flow technology made the individual feel far less indispensable than he had felt on the family farm or in cottage industry. The inevitable results—industrial "anomie" and the emotional separation of the man from his work—would be abetted by the unions, satirized by Charlie Chaplin, and countered by Ford's own nostalgia for the Greenfield of his youth. Almost unconsciously, he had become a leading actor in a drama whose theme would resound ever more widely: in Boorstin's words, experience loses its uniqueness as it becomes repeatable.

But this was not the Ford his customers knew, any more than they knew the Ford who was skeptical toward religion. Theirs was the hometown Henry, the local boy who had gone to town and made good, and who still came back to visit without putting on highfalutin airs. Who spoke plainly, mixing a country shyness with a flair for P.R. in just the right proportions. Who loudly decried the enemies of the common man—the railroads, the big eastern bankers, the villains on Wall Street. Who spent his millions, not on fancy European paintings, but on useful projects that would benefit everybody. Who opposed jazz, booze, Jews, installment buying, internationalism, and war—and paid the working man an unheard-of five dollars a day. Who, rather than hobnobbing with the Carnegies and Mellons, headed up into the clean mountain air of the West with earthy pals like Thomas Edison and Harvey Firestone and Luther Burbank. And who fervently believed that there need be no gulf between the village green and the blast furnace, since the basis of both was, or ought to be, the moral code of William H. McGuffey.

The world's troubles could be traced to laziness and idleness. Self-reliance and hard, practical work were the answer—not charity or highbrow intellectualism. "Did you ever see dishonest callouses on a man's hands?" demanded Ford. "Hardly. When a man's hands are calloused and womens' are worn, you may be sure honesty is there. That's more than you can say about many soft white hands." Here, indeed, was a complex figure. Here was a rural youth, having forsaken the family farm because he disliked manual labor, assuring us that McGuffey's Daisy Marvin and Miss Roberts were alive and well and

Henry Ford talking with farmers

living right there with him and Mary in their fifty-six-room Dearborn mansion. After paying a visit to J. P. Morgan, Ford casually remarked, "It is very interesting to see how the rich live." He meant it.

Later he said, "America is out there among the old village sites, the small towns, and the farms." He meant that too. And he acted on it. He was constantly funding agricultural research, agrarian improvement schemes, and rural schools. He stocked his classrooms with McGuffey Readers because, he declared, these had been the greatest intellectual influence on his life. He built tractors that, like the cars, were simple, cheap, and lightweight (but that sold with limited success). He attended state fairs and plowing contests, marched through fields chatting with farmers, jumped aboard hay wagons, and took delight in personally driving starstruck pilgrims around his own seven-thousand-acre farm at Dearborn. In 1922 he wired a sales meeting, FARMING IS AND ALWAYS WILL BE THE FOUNDATION UPON WHICH THE ECONOMIC GROWTH OF OUR NATION DEPENDS. Of course, it was all priceless publicity—the company made sure of that. And in an age when America worshiped its business heroes as oracles, the reporters gobbled it up.

That age ended rather abruptly in the fall of 1929. Predictably, Ford blamed the Depression on the stock market and the eastern banking establishment. Bankers, he thundered, should be compelled to obey the Ten Commandments. But as the gloom deepened, his bland reassurances sounded more and more hollow. When Ford claimed the Depression was actually beneficial because it taught people to appreciate the simple things in life, a hungry family in rural Michigan snapped back, "He makes light of ills he never felt." When he advised the jobless simply to go back to the land, an Indiana farmer scribbled angrily, "Are you so ignorant that you can't see that we can't buy land held by real estate companies because we are broke, dead broke." When Ford said farm prices could never get too low, a farmer hollered, "I will not take any lip from you after we have been buying your cars and tractors. How do you suppose we can buy anything if we are working for nothing? Don't you know we are losing our farms." Disillusioned with capitalism, more and more Americans were turning, instead, to Washington. The oracle had lost his audience.

He was also losing money. The sale of Fords to farmers plummeted from 650,000 in 1929 to 55,000 in 1932; between 1931 and 1934, the closely held concern lost $125 million. And there was more to those fading fortunes than the Crash. Like hometown Henry, the Ford Motor Company had failed to keep pace with America's changing values.

Ben Shahn

Booze, jazz, and pretty flivvers *did* go together. And while the Depression might delay the quest for newness and glamour, that quest, well planted during the flapper era, was not about to die out. True, the beloved Tin Lizzie, which never changed its style, and which was available only in black, had resoundingly beaten its costly early competitors. Fulfilling the static values and physical needs of the countryside, the Model T had indeed lifted America out of the mud. Once out, however, America turned more and more to what canny General Motors was offering: installment buying, urbane advertising, and the annual model.

In 1922 Henry Ford could still say, "It does not please us to have a buyer's car wear out or become obsolete." But by 1926 he was starting to complain, "A fever of newness has been everywhere confused with the spirit of progress." The next year, the battle lines were drawn as GM's Alfred P. Sloan wrote to Fisher Bodies' Lawrence P. Fisher: "The great problem of the future is to have our cars different from each other and different from year to year." The auto giant's several divisions were deliberately conceived as a ladder of status symbolism. Planned obsolescence took the wheel of American industry. Declared GM's researchers in 1932: "The simplest way to assure safe production is to keep changing the product . . . One of the fundamental purposes of research is to foster a healthy dissatisfaction."

From then on, the Ford Motor Company found itself hurrying to catch up. With the urban upper-middles now squarely in the driver's seat, anxious modernity had replaced country simplicity. The stillness of McGuffey's country village had been overtaken by the very mobility his famous disciple had helped create.

Chapter Seven

Park Street

GENESEO, ILLINOIS. Dawn flares in the puddles along Park Street. Bundled up in caps and hoods, four little boys scuffle along the curbless asphalt, toting their lunch pails. An enormous school bus groans past. The low sun reddens the windows of Mrs. Burnside's small frame house. In the garret, Dan, a traveling seed salesman, has just finished retying his tie. He starts down the steep narrow stairs. Later Mrs. Burnside, eighty-six, will shakily mount those steps and make his bed. In her spacious white wooden kitchen, she has been making cookies. She never knows when a few of her seventeen great-grandchildren might stop in. Mrs. Burnside's daughter, who lives two blocks down, thinks she should move to a "home." She steadfastly refuses. The grandchildren covet the antique furniture in her modest parlor, but she smiles and says it is too practical to part with. Just now, a feminist spokesperson in a New York television studio is addressing the empty platform rocker.

Front porch, Grand Tower, Illinois

From the parlor, Dan enters the bathroom. Later, Mrs. Burnside will stoop carefully over the huge, four-legged bathtub to rinse out the odd black stuff the young man uses on his hair. Working the Henry County territory, he stays here because Mrs. Burnside only charges twelve dollars a week. These days, most everyone else uses the motels out on the Interstate.

A green maple leaf, emblem of Geneseo High School, is painted in the middle of the main intersection. Above it dangles a four-way traffic light. Above that, birds wheel and soar, land and take off from the uniform three-story roof line. Jutting into the intersection from the modernistic Central Bank, a digital sign alternately flashes *8:45* and *37°*.

Metal marquees roof the sidewalks. The town is almost as proud of its marquees and its off-street parking lots as it is of its winning football team: the downtown improvements represent the local merchants' bootstrap response to a new shopping center twenty minutes up the highway. Someone has suggested bumper stickers saying SHOP GENESEO. People know they pay a few cents more to shop locally, but it's handier, and it makes them feel better.

The small retail stores are concentrated within these four brick Victorian blocks. Scattered a little back from the center are the auto agencies, feed brokers, farm implement dealers, and supermarkets. One central block houses the Municipal Utilities, The Book Store (which carries cards and novelties but no books), Ace Hardware, the Moline *Dispatch* newspaper office, Farber and Larimer Appliances, Ward's Catalogue Sales Agcy., Hornsby's dime store, Hanford Insurance, Palace Café, The Raquet men's shop, Guzzardo's novelties and sundries, Little's Cleaners (whose sign last week advised LIFT DON'T LEAN and this week proclaims A WORD TO THE WISE IS ENOUGH) and The Geneseo Hotel, which has been closed and converted into offices, but has retained its good restaurant, The Cellar.

In front of The Book Store, two middle-aged ladies are vigorously sweeping the sidewalk. A retired gent, out for a walk, stops and chats with them. In the next block, in front of Walter's Men's Wear, a tall blond football player sweeps very slowly, his mind elsewhere. Blair's Café, across from Walter's, is crowded. Above county political posters, and between two old-fashioned milk cans, the steamy windows are full of moving silhouettes.

9:00 A.M. As if by a stage director's signal, the street springs to life. Three cronies who have been chatting in the window of the Western Auto Store scatter like birds—one north across the railroad tracks, one south into the Neuleib Insurance Agency, the other into the depths of the store past ladders and strollers and barbecues. Under the mar-

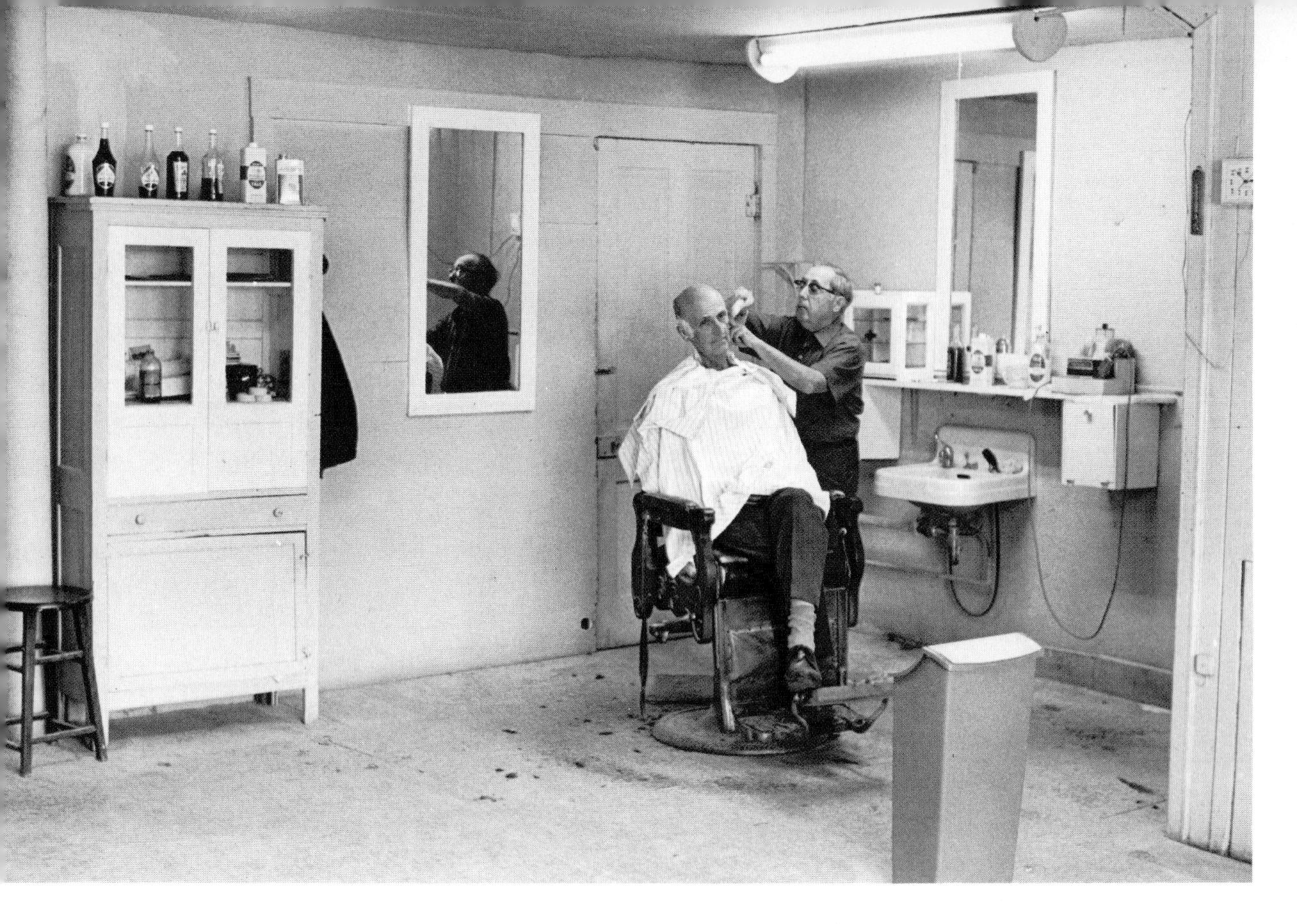

Rockport, Indiana

quees, shoppers materialize. An aging policeman steps along, eyeing the parking meters. A young woman carries a baby across the maple leaf. A fancy blond lady in a red wool dress with a beauty parlor hairdo gets out of a Lincoln Continental and hurries into the office of Harry and Mabel Brown, Attorneys. Here comes the postman, his pants too short, his rubbers protruding from one corner of his three-wheeled cart. Rushing out of Blair's, Clyde Walter distractedly removes his glasses on his way across the street, hollers back over his shoulder at a man getting into a car marked HULTING HYBRIDS—GENESEO, ILL., and then disappears into Walter's Men's Wear.

Soon the cars outnumber the birds.

"You have to fertilize and nurture a town like the soil," says the banker, hurrying through his lunch at The Deck, a large new truck-stop complex at the Geneseo turnoff on Interstate 80. "Our merchants are young and progressive, and there's hardly any absentee ownership. If one improves his storefront, the others all rush to do it. Confidence in our future has a snowball effect. Even though the population is held to about six thousand by the city limits, the trading area keeps on growing. There's this new development out at Hazelwood, for instance. And the farmland around here is some of the richest in the world, so the per capita income of the farmers and townspeople is relatively high. Less than half the high school students are farmers, and yet seventy-five per cent of our bank loans are farm loans. The farm influence helps give the community economic and emotional stability. Geneseo has a fine new hospital, our schools are excellent, and our real estate taxes are much lower than in Moline and Davenport and the other Quad Cities. So, even though the town doesn't have any industry, people who work in Moline are attracted to come here and live. There's 'old money' here too, as you can see from some of the homes. But these younger people coming in are the key to the future. If their kids go to school here, they'll do business here."

In the Corn Belt, at least two large and excellent historical farms are open to the public: Conner Prairie, near Indianapolis and Living History Farms, near Des Moines. Here and there the traveler will also find some smaller sites with an intimate atmosphere all their own.

One of the best of these is the Johnson Living Farm, four miles east of Geneseo on Route 6. A pet project of Clyde Walter, the energetic bachelor who owns Walter's Men's Wear, it re-creates a typical prairie farmstead of the 1910 era. There are a ten-room house, a barn and other outbuildings, all kinds of old farm machinery and tools, a variety of mooing and snorting and honking barnyard creatures, prairie sod, and an authentic "little red schoolhouse" where Clyde likes to talk to visiting groups of schoolchildren. The Johnson Farm is open from spring through fall. As a climax to the final week, invited guests enjoy an old-fashioned Sunday dinner with all the trimmings.

The Grid Club convenes at noon in the back room of the Palace Café. Twenty-eight sober faces. Lunch is downed quickly. Happy Birthday is sung. A slotted cigar box is passed from hand to hand, each member depositing a quarter for the Pick-the-Winners List. Faces turn intent as Coach Reade rises to analyze last week's varsity and freshman games.

Coach Reade is venerated as a winner and as a character builder. Later he confides to a visitor: "We place too much emphasis on winning. The purpose of sport should be to teach a boy to extend himself to his best self, to play with pain, to overcome obstacles. A boy can play a game in which he has extended himself far beyond his capabilities, yet the scoreboard and the crowd may call him a loser. I have said that the scoreboard is the biggest crime in America. We need all-state boys more than we need all-state players. Sure, we had two high school

Johnson Farm, Geneseo, Illinois

all-Americans in the last two years. But I refuse willingly to make a robot out of a player. The boys must learn that athletics is only a phase of life and that fame is, at best, temporary. A winning streak can be one of the worst things that can happen to you if it means some other values are forgotten.

"Off the field we have a man-to-man relationship. Helping a young man with his girl problems is as important as teaching him how to block. We urge them to participate in different school functions. In 1966 we were unbeaten—yet three of our all-conference players missed the early part of practice because they wanted to sing in the chorus.

"The young people in town look up to our varsity. Playing football in the yard, they'll yell, 'Hey, I'm so-and-so.' Being a gentleman is our number one training rule. Most other areas of society have copped out on emphasizing discipline, but I'm old-fashioned enough to believe we need discipline. We insist that our players keep their hair short. It's a conservative community, and we represent it. When you're sweating, short hair is also neater and cleaner. And if our boys didn't act well downtown, the town would pull the rug out from under us.

"We stress discipline, execution, and maximum individual performance. We're a basic ball-control team. No garbage plays. We do very few things and try to do them well. Play simple, play tough, and hang onto the ball—that's everything we ever teach."

To the north of town, rows of experimental cornstalks and a cluster of warehouses announce Sieben Hybrids. Unlike such national seed companies as Pioneer and De Kalb, Sieben is a family-owned business.

"I planted my first seed crop on my dad's farm near here in nineteen thirty-nine," remembers Art Sieben. "The farmers first used those seeds in nineteen forty. Hybrids had been developed experimentally in the twenties, and farmers had started using them in the early thirties. By the time I came into it, the improvement in corn yields was so obvious that I'd say about ninety per cent of our farmers were using hybrid seeds. A hybrid is a first-generation cross between two pure lines. We keep improving the inbred strains for yield, disease resistance, insect resistance, and stamina. Then, when two of these separate strains

are crossed you get 'hybrid vigor,' a maximization of the good qualities. But the seeds of *that* generation will be inferior. So the farmers keep coming back to us every year to buy newly crossed hybrids.

"Even though the big national concerns have the advantage of saturation advertising, we have the advantage of being able to give our customers more personal attention. We're one of, I'd say, three or four hundred independent seed companies in America. Operating within a seventy-five-mile radius, we can get to our customers within hours, or they can call us on the phone and talk to me, or to Chan or Todd, here, personally. And that means a lot to a farmer. Plus, we like the close relationship between all phases of the business that you get in a smaller operation like ours.

"Same as the majors, though, we put out these caps and jackets, with our name on them, that have gotten so popular with the farmers. The caps alone cost us about twenty-five hundred dollars last year! We do some of our own research and breeding, and we belong to Illinois Foundation Seeds at Urbana. It has about a hundred members like us, who pool their money for research. And the seeds developed by the land grant colleges and by the Department of Agriculture are available to everybody. We try to improve on those, checking our results against the old-standby varieties. Right now we're working on some specialized seeds for sandy and mucky ground."

Sieben Hybrids' office is as roughhewn and unpretentious as they come. The talk is straight, the desks plain. Employees, farmers, and Art Sieben and his two sons move in and out with no noticeable awareness of status differences. "Work patterns are different in a small town than in a city," Art continues. "People work longer hours—eight to five and a lot of Saturdays. But the pace is more leisurely. There's less pressure and less commute time. Out here, you don't do any business in bars. Cocktails at lunch are looked down on. Lunches are short. Social life isn't as stratified as it is in some places, and it's easy for people to get involved in community affairs. That helps to counteract the divided allegiance of the folks who live in Geneseo but work somewhere else. In a town like this, virtually everyone owns their own home."

Art's son Todd is glad he spent time elsewhere before returning to the family business. "This community is like being on an island. There is wealth—and a fund of ignorance about minority problems. People talk about Chicago and St. Louis with no awareness of the true situation in the inner cities. In Geneseo, the slum problem consists

Bank president, Sioux Center, Iowa

Gordon Gammack

of about three houses. People apply the standards of Geneseo and come up with simplistic solutions to the outside world.

"But the Quad Cities are nearby, so we can have the advantages of both country and city. You can go fishing and hunting and boating not far from here, and you can go to the Quad Cities and hear a pop concert or a musical like *Hair.* Sure, we're cast in the family mold, and for me to try to live a different life-style would be difficult. Or a very social person from somewhere else, who needs a lot of glittery social activity, would probably find it boring. Most of the social life takes place in the home—ten or twenty people at a time, typically. That suits us. I like the security and serenity of small-town living."

At home, Jean Sieben, Todd's mother, is working with her pens and paints. She has a lively eye and a sprightly wit. "When I came here with my paint box, people said, 'You're going to be our artist!' I had no choice! When I gave a little talk to the women at the Columbian Club in nineteen forty, they came up afterward to feel the brushes and touch the paints—they'd never seen any. Oh, long before, there'd been one other artist, but they didn't claim her. Now we have the Gallery and concentrated workshops and other art events several times a year.

"The Columbian Club has a culture division, a garden division, and a patriotism division. The Junior Women have various benevolent projects. We have the Federated Women's Clubs. We're clubbed to death! There's also the music club: there's no age limit to that, you just have to be able to perform something. Ah, that vocal trio the other night!" She laughs. "That was the gem of the evening!"

"I'm from Elkhart, Indiana, which wasn't overly artistic. It's famous for three things: trailers, musical instruments, and Alka-Seltzer. The biggest excitements I can remember here in Geneseo were the train wreck and the tornado. When that funnel cloud came through, it yanked a seventy-foot buckeye tree right out of our yard by the roots.

"I'm selling reproductions of these large drawings. Later they'll come out as greeting cards. I find people buy the best of my work. People are attracted to the universal subjects. But I'm a kept woman—things would have been very different if I'd had to try to make a living at art. My function is to be productive in my particular way, and I don't have to go out and plow the dirt for it.

"I think it's nice that the kids can see their dad three times a day. For good or bad, there's more parental impact on the child in a small town. And the man and wife aren't so separated by living in different environments. A town like Geneseo makes for more stable relationships all around. The other day Todd came home and asked me, 'Mom, how do you know *everything?*' It's because parents watch out for one another's kids. They'll call up and say 'I saw so-and-so crossing diagonally on such-and-such a street.' Or they'll ask the boy or girl, 'Do your folks know you're out?'

Mayor, Geneseo, Illinois

"I like the simplicity. I like having the time to think, the time to watch the leaves fall, the leisurely pace. I'm inclined to think we have a pretty nice ivory tower."

Unexpectedly, Dan, the traveling salesman, stops back at Mrs. Burnside's in the middle of the afternoon.

"We're havin' a card game!" she cries in a gay, quivery voice.

"So I see!"

A foursome of mature ladies occupies the parlor. Four more sit at a card table in the kitchen.

Under a veil of polite nods, the seasoned eyes give the startled young man the once-over. He edges toward the stairs. Every face but Mrs. Burnside's wears the same thought: "*I* don't have to take in roomers."

Sherwood Anderson wrote: "The characters of the towns give the towns their color. In the small towns you know every man's idiosyncrasies. They cannot escape you. Life in the towns can be at times terrible or it can be infinitely amusing and absorbing.

"The life in the town is a test of man's ability to adjust himself. It tells the story of his skill in living with others, his ability to go out to others and to let others be a part of his own life. You have to go on living with your neighbors. If they are sometimes queer it may be that they also think of you as queer. Without quite knowing it, you may yourself be one of the 'characters of your town.' "

A damp day, mid-October. Soon it will be dark. Oaks rustle under a heavy sky. Trees of many kinds line the grassy square. A third of their branches are bare. Some of the fallen leaves have been swept into neat piles. More leaves shower down, whirl in eddies, race along the curbs.

Facing the square is a hulking brick building—the junior high. Its tall flagpole is empty. The wind shivers its taut ropes. Metal fasteners twang against the silvery pole. In summer, on Tuesday evenings, there are ice cream socials in the square. But now the band shell is mute. Three hours ago an army of giant yellow buses churned around the park's perimeter, hauling farm kids home in every direction. Now the only sound is a car starting, far away. Somewhere else two dogs begin to bark—one baritone, one tenor. Stolid, two-story homes face the square. Bikes lie unattended on wide lawns. Porch lights wink on.

The Congregational church faces the square. It was built by abolitionist families who, in the 1830s, had migrated from New York's Geneseo River Valley to found this town on the Illinois prairie. From the bases of its pillars to the top of its high steeple, the church is proudly spotlighted. But for many Geneseoans, the denomination's New England-based doctrines are too liberal, the preacher too intellectual, the tone too formal—so attendance is not impressive. Some of those who do attend live in the town but are not of it. They commute to their executive desks at the sleek, Saarinen-designed international headquarters of Deere & Company, half an hour down Interstate 80. Last Sunday, just before the sermon, the preacher gently reminded his fashionably dressed listeners that the Sunday School, downstairs, was not a baby sitting service for parents who were not themselves present upstairs.

On another corner of the square, at the clapboard Baptist church, no such admonition is needed. The Baptists comprise a fervent, earthy slice of the Geneseo populace. In a few minutes naked bulbs will come on in their meeting rooms. Above the front door, a red neon message is already beaming into the night: JESUS SAVES—ARE YOU READY?

7:17 P.M. A freight train from Chicago thunders through the center of town. Several like it pass Geneseo each day, but only the morning passenger train stops. For a block or so back from the tracks there is the familiar railroad smell. But in this town no stigma is attached to living near the tracks, or on a particular side of them.

Dan is a strange and lonely person. Although he never gets to know anyone in the towns he visits, he often goes, in the evening, to one

Greenfield, Illinois

General store, Grand Tower, Illinois

of Geneseo's three small bars. There he slowly sips a beer and observes his fellow man.

The bartender at the Korner Tap has a large paunch and nervous, unhappy eyes that brighten whenever he engages in small talk. Behind him, the wall is hung with trinkets and ads and calendars and clocks. In another corner, between the juke box and the player piano, a brown furnace bulks large. The men along the bar wear checkered Mackinaws, blue workshirts, poplin jackets, billed caps. Next to Dan, a painter and a sandblaster have been having a good time. The sandblaster gets up to leave.

"I'll see you in church."

"Yours or mine?" Laughter.

"Really, you ought to come and hear this preacher."

"Don't be surprised if you see me come in the door. I won't be drunk, though."

"I might not be there."

Sentimentally, the painter tells the bartender, "He and I grew up together. He introduced me to Coffee Royale. Lots of times, we have two Coffee Royales and then go out hunting all morning."

Dan emerges from the Korner Tap. He goes up to Park Street and turns right toward Mrs. Burnside's. As he passes the massive shape of the Methodist church, lights go off in the basement. The Kiwanis Club has finished its meeting. The Methodist Women have cleared away the thirty-two plates and the plastic flowers. "All Hail the Power of Jesus' Name" and "Onward in Kiwanis" have been sung; a discussion about the upcoming Pancake Day has concluded; a member has finished showing his slides of Europe. Now, under a porch light, the men are coming out. An older one tells a guest, "We think we have pretty good meals. They always pass everything around twice."

Dan hurries on into the shadows. Two blocks down he comes to the elegant corner mansion owned by Frieda Myers, the same Frieda Myers who owns Myers' Furniture Store. Long after everyone has gone to bed, the sign on the lawn will shine brightly through the darkness to remind Geneseoans of their destiny: MYERS' FUNERAL HOME.

In the dim interior of the corrugated metal bin, the husky boy glances up anxiously. His father's head is silhouetted against the bright hole at the peak of the conical roof.

"Keep some tension on it." The father's voice booms in the hollow bin. "Take the rope outside and fasten it. *And keep some tension on it.*"

High above, the agile figure shifts position, sending a shiver through the whole drumlike structure. The head vanishes. A pole of sunlight stabs down through the dank air.

Holding tight to the rope, the son moves to a small window and climbs out gingerly. He secures the rope. He wipes his brow. At the other end of the rope dangles a brand-new "stirator," a two-thousand-dollar piece of machinery that will circulate the moist corn after the bin is full, preventing it from rotting and enabling the family to hold this fall's crop until the market price rises.

By raising calves, the boy has managed to save $4000 for college. He's not going to play football there: it would take too much time away from his studies. "But I'll miss Coach Reade—that's for sure."

The tractor's blinking red taillight makes the faces in the wagon appear and disappear. The boys toss hay at the girls. The loudest shrieks come from those who are not targets. One girl falls off. The father, who has been driving a tractor all day, stops; waits; starts again.

Most of the passengers are high school seniors. One couple is engaged. Above the roar of the tractor the girl yells in the ear of her friend, "He writes poems. Once he sat by the railroad tracks waiting for a train and wrote a great big long poem about the train."

Everyone sings "Old MacDonald Had a Farm." In the blinking red light, under the fresh-smelling hay, some body-jostling appears to be going on.

"Hey, you guys, that's not funny!"

At the end of the ride, the mother and three girls hurry toward the kitchen. The father gets a bonfire roaring. The boys chase each other with water bags. The girls face the warming flames, dangling their legs from the wagon. Suddenly the son grabs his dad, hoists him over his shoulder, and races across the yard with him. This draws applause and whoops of laughter. Then screams, as other boys try it with the girls.

The mother and her helpers bring the food: hot chocolate, homemade donuts, pop, and hot dogs to roast on sticks. Quieter now, the kids poke the fire, stare glassily at the flames. A plastic wrapper crinkles, vanishes.

All form a circle around the fire. Joining hands, they sing the Doxology. At the perimeter of light, tumbling maple leaves. Dewy black earth. Fragrance of embers. Bits of hay stuck to sweaters.

Tailpipes roar off into the night.

Rex Milliken, for whom the new Milliken Elementary School was named, was Geneseo's superintendent of schools for thirty-six years. He is optimistic. "What is the age of the most influential residents? That's the question. Whether or not a town is active and growing depends on whether it has aggressive young people. And our young people are coming back.

"Partly, we're becoming a bedroom town for the Quad Cities. And when an outsider moves in, we try to get him on our side. We want to accept him, make him part of the community. But he must accept our ways. People here have a tendency to be friendly right away—then to sit back and see what kind you really are.

"The churches and schools make a big difference to any town. In our high school we have excellent personnel and a good salary scale. The great majority of the kids go on to college, and we've found that they tend to get better grades after they get there than they do here.

But our yearly cost per student is over eight hundred dollars. For a family with three children, you don't get that back in taxes, even if they buy a fifty-thousand-dollar house. So, although we do get some state and federal aid, we'd like to get some industry. Light, highly skilled industry—not heavy industry. Of course, there is some controversy about this. We do have Illini Beef Packers to the north of town. Another outfit tried to buy land near the high school for a trailer park. But the town didn't want them. When they had a sewer problem, the town was able to stop the project by refusing to help them with their sewer.

"So you see, we're growing—but we refuse to give up our character."

Park Street, 5:55 P.M. A hidden sun sets the western clouds ablaze. Yellow leaves brighten on shadowless lawns. Wet asphalt turns to orange.

Then leafless sticks, a dying sky. Wires dissolve in mist.

Geneseo's positive outlook is not universal among the small towns of the prairies. Go a little farther from the Quad Cities, and the "bed-

Overlooking the Mississippi, Bellevue, Iowa

room town" factor vanishes. Go some distance from Interstate 80 and the railroad line, and you'll find less optimism among the bankers and merchants. Even at the county seat of Cambridge, twelve miles south of Geneseo, there is indolence in a business community whose storefronts have not been improved for half a century. Galva, in the southeast corner of the county, remains a prosperous farm trade center, though it lacks Geneseo's old money and profitable relation to the Quad Cities. Kewanee, not far from Galva, is twice Geneseo's size, industrial, and more motley. Tiny Woodhull, beside U.S. 74, has a fancy new truck stop but a creaking, boarded-up downtown. Orion, an easy commute from the Quad Cities, is being transformed into a pure bedroom town, its stately old two-story houses abutted by expanses of tract bungalows.

This picture of Henry County, Illinois, is rather typical of the Midwest country as a whole. The stronger towns get stronger; the weaker ones get weaker. Faster highways and the diminishing number of farmers spell trouble for some communities, while those same highways, plus the steadily rising overall capital expenditures of agriculture, bring prosperity to others. These days, distribution follows an ever-widening system of service areas, rather than a static map of isolated trade centers.

The Middle West is also a leading participant in a new national trend: the resurgence of the small town. The 1950s witnessed a net flow of 5.5 million people from the country to the city. But during the 1960s this drain slowed to 2.2 million. And in the early seventies, the trend reversed itself, with a small net flow from metropolitan areas (including suburbs) to non-metropolitan areas. "This is a major, historic turning point," said Calvin L. Beale, the U.S.D.A.'s top authority on population studies; "you'd have to go back to the pre-1890 period to find anything like it, when the corn-belt and Great Plains states were being actively settled by the Germans and the Scandinavians . . . It is not a back-to-the-farm movement. It is, in many cases, a back-to-the-country movement, with modern conveniences and good roads and nearby small-scale urban facilities."

Why the reversal? A young doctor returning to Hendricks, Minnesota, says he feels more appreciated there. One couple, after experiencing "the usual sort of urban malaise," moved their antique business from Chicago to Galena, Illinois—thereby reducing their rental costs by 67 per cent. Others cite clean air, the relaxed pace, safer streets, work satisfaction, a better family environment. In a small town, people can feel an important part of their community and identify

Abandoned house, Port Wing, Wisconsin

with it. "What do my county and my home town mean to me?" asks Cecil Beeson, a retired postman in Hartford City, Indiana. "Here I have lived, worked, made my home, and reared my family. So to me they mean everything." The nationwide newsletter *Small Town* cites the potential for "intimate human relationships, the security of settled home and associations, for spiritual unity and for orderly transmission of the basic cultural inheritance."

But the quiescent equality of the typical mid-American town is not for everyone. Those in their twenties often say they miss the bright lights and cultural stimulation of the city. "Everybody mows their lawn on the same day and they take down their Christmas decorations by July and wash their cars on Saturday evenings so they can drive over to the Dairy Queen and 'see who's in town,' " says Iowa collegian Mary Perhall; "it's hard to return to Baxter." To be sure, the rural-urban value gap has narrowed, and relationships have become somewhat more voluntary. But urban women who grew up in small towns learning to play prescribed, unliberated roles are particularly loath to return. Kathleen Fury remembers how, in Plainfield, Indiana, "Marriage was the indisputable proof of our worth, the inevitable conclusion to our desperate search for 'popularity' and acceptance . . . we did not really exist as *people* in high school, but as clay to be molded into the shapes most pleasing to our elders; therefore, many of our organizations started with the word 'future.' . . . We ended up causing trouble for nobody but ourselves, leading half-empty lives that were not, as promised, made entirely full by having children."

Many people would like to move to a country town but find that the restricted job market is a major barrier. However, Midwestern

Edgar Lee Masters home, Petersburg, Illinois

communities are striving to lower that barrier by broadening their economic bases. Competing successfully as a farm service center depends, as it always has, on adapting to shifting patterns of transportation and agriculture and on maintaining a general level of business activity high enough for the local store owners to display varied and competitively priced merchandise. While such factors are difficult to control directly, the town can attract certain kinds of industry by offering lower taxes, cheaper land and utilities, and fewer union problems than elsewhere. Once begun, the growth process can have a multiplier effect: rising prosperity creates expanded facilities which, in turn, attract more industry. Today, even a highly rural state like Iowa receives more of its income from industry than from agriculture (though much of that industry is ag-based).

But painful lessons have also been learned—about pollution; about "footloose" industries that can vanish overnight; about the rising deficits of local government in the wake of too many tax concessions; and about unbalanced or too-rapid growth, which can spoil the congenial atmosphere it was meant to enhance. Some towns have gone so far as to say "no" to further growth while others simply stagnate under an ingrown, fearful leadership. Still others, however, are embracing the Geneseo formula of carefully managed growth, underwritten by vigorous boosterism.

"Thinking-makes-it-so" is an old habit in the small towns of mid-America. Get-together rituals raise money and enthusiasm, assure everyone of his own importance, and become a soft-sell celebration of the McGuffey virtues. The town reinforces its pride by sprucing up its downtown buildings and sending its offspring to the regional playoffs or to Girls' State, where they learn to dissolve individual quirks in the higher cause of loyalty to the Home Team. Unsavory books are kept out of the library so that the idea that people are basically good, strong, and rational can tone the whole community and become a self-fulfilling prophecy. There is no need to consult your minister or a psychiatrist about personal problems, because there is no need for personal problems. Nourished by a blend of simplistic idealism and pervasive pragmatism, every town creates itself in the image of that middle-century, middle-ground America which, as historian Richard Hofstadter remarked, "was the only country in the world that began with perfection and aspired to progress."

Chapter Eight

The Flow

THE OLD SWIMMING HOLE, the river, and the skating pond were tempting places in McGuffey's day. But since most Midwestern boys and girls never really learned to swim, the *Readers* dutifully warned the pupil to resist the allurements of water.

Yet it was on the Father of Waters that Huck Finn escaped the torpor of the town. When he poled his raft out far enough, he could sit back and chuckle at the foibles of mankind. Life on the river held high adventure and high risk: sharp snags and unplumbed depths, shifting shorelines, flooded farms, the hard wisdom that comes of meeting every breed of humanity. Unlike the sunny atomism of the prairie settlements, the chemistry of the river was as dark and ambiguous as its own gumbo mud.

The Mississippi River near Cape Girardeau, Missouri, showing Illinois floodplain in foreground

Indeed, the umbilical current has always brought unWASPish types into the heartland. In the centuries when mid-America was dominated by France, the Mississippi carried black-robed priests and wizened Gallic traders. Along the shores they sprinkled their Catholic influence, their saints' names, and a distinctive architecture. Some of the early French structures can still be seen in southern Illinois and at Missouri's Ste. Genevieve, an Old-Worldly village founded about 1723 and tucked into the rolling ground above the Mississippi. By the nineteenth century the river was teeming with colorful flatboats, keelboats, and steamboats whose seasoned hands lent their rollicking spirit to the waterfront towns. One eyewitness wrote this account:

> The boisterous gaiety of the hands, the congratulations, the moving picture of life on board the boats, in the numerous animals, large and small, which they carry, their different loads, the evidence of the increasing agriculture of the country above, and more than all, the immense distances which they have already come . . . Dunghill fowls are fluttering over the roofs, as an invariable appendage. The chanticleer raises his piercing note. The swine utter their cries. The cattle low. The horses trample, as in their stables. There are boats fitted on purpose, and loaded entirely with turkeys, that, having little else to do, gobble most furiously. The hands travel about from boat to boat, making inquiries, and acquaintances, and form alliances to yield mutual assistance to each other, on their descent from this to New Orleans. After an hour or two passed this way, they spring on shore or raise the wind in town. It is well for the people of the village, if they do not become riotous in the course of the evening; in which case I have often seen the most summary and strong measures taken. About midnight the uproar is all hushed. The fleet unites once more at Natchez, or New Orleans, and, although they live on the same river, they may, perhaps, never meet each other again on the earth . . .

Like the harbors of Naples or Bombay or Beirut, the ports of the Ohio, the Mississippi, the Missouri, and the Great Lakes looked out on a worldly world, rather than inward to a holy hinterland. Pent-up hog and cattle drovers reaching the slaughterhouses of Kansas City or Cincinnati or Chicago could have themselves quite a fling while they were at it. And as midsized river towns like Omaha and Sioux City became manufacturing and distribution centers to the new inland empire, they, too, drew an unMcGuffeylike populace that included traveling salesmen and dancing instructors and Jewish wholesalers.

In a farm town, every person is known, accounted for, essential. But out on the brawling river, life is cheap. Nobody knows how many bodies may lie interred in its secret depths. Like other boulevards, the major waterways have always attracted a plentiful supply of sharpies and desperadoes. The place most feared by Midwestern travelers of the nineteenth century was not the treacherous Falls of the Ohio at Louisville, Kentucky, but a point farther downstream known as Cave-in-Rock. Devolving from an enterprise called Wilson's Liquor Vault & House for Entertainment, this natural cave on the Illinois shore became an unassailable robbers' roost. Its denizens specialized

Brown County, southern Indiana

Hartley Alley

in murdering families of emigrants on their flatboats and divvying up the loot. Meanwhile, down in Cairo (pronounced "Karo"), where the Ohio met the Mississippi, one Colonel Fluger, alias Colonel Plug, was making it his business to rob traders and boatmen while his wife lavished them with her favors. In his later years Mark Twain, lamenting the arrival of a more sober commercial atmosphere, continued to take delight in the river's roguish and idiosyncratic ways. In *Life on the Mississippi* he tells, for instance, of a cave in a bluff near his home town of Hannibal, Missouri:

> In my time the person who then owned it turned it into a mausoleum for his daughter, aged fourteen. The body of this poor child was put into a copper cylinder filled with alcohol, and this was suspended in one of the dismal avenues of the cave. The top of the cylinder was removable; and it was said to be a common thing for the baser order of tourists to drag the dead face into view and examine it and comment upon it.

Amid cardsharps and exploding steamboats, the cosmopolitanism of the rivers inevitably pushed hostile groups toe-to-toe, leading to further explosions. Yet the mercurial streams also fostered just the opposite quality: drowsy serenity. What four-square Babbitt could have dreamed up the folly, the fantasy, the indulgence of steamboat Gothic architecture? Examples of this extravagant style still dot the meandering Ohio shoreline. It reaches its most literal at tiny Alton, Indiana, whose sagging Paar house is said to have been built in 1889 by a steamboat captain to remind him of his beloved vessels. Newburgh, Indiana, advertises itself with a pun no prairie town would use: "The best little town by a dam site." And venerable riverside communities like Madison and Vevay, with their lush trees and century-old brick houses, exude a heavy perfume of the past.

Southern Indianans, of course, are nothing if not sentimental. They can prove up and down that the catfish from their bee-you-tee-full Ohio taste much better than those from the muddy and polluted Mississippi. But do Hoosiers really talk differently from other Midwesterners? "No," one insists, "we just talk *more.*" Nostalgia for southern Indiana's log cabins, stone fences, barn-side basketball hoops, and one-lane bridges is nothing new, either. As early as the turn of the century, and for many years thereafter, *Indianapolis News* writer Kin Hubbard helped Hoosiers celebrate Hoosierdom by reporting the crackerbarrel humor and wisdom of his Brown County alter-ego, "Abe Martin":

Miss Fawn Lippincut went up t' Indynoplus t' see "Pollyanna" yesterday, but had t' leave before th' last act, as she run out o' yarn.

A young lady o' Vevay writes t'know if its proper t' double back after reachin' th' end of a roastin' ear.

Absence makes th' neck grow longer.

Th' longer it takes you t' select a cantaloupe th' worse it is.

It's jest like havin' some one return from th' grave t'have a daughter come home from a canoe ride.

Th' ole time mother who used t' wonder where her boy wuz now has a grandson who wonders where his mother is.

I never knowed a successful man that could quote poetry.

Some fellers worry so much about ther rights that they fergit t' make a livin'.

If ever'buddy wuz as pleasant as th' feller that's tryin' t' skin you wouldn't this be a swell world?

When a speaker lays his watch on th' table prepare fer th' worst.

Ever notice how an office seeker's eyesight fails after he gits what he wants?

Think before you applaud.

The southern counties of Indiana, Ohio, and Illinois are affected, to this day, by a twining of hillbilly ways with the murky wisdom of the streams. Explains one southern Illinoisan: "Up in central Illinois,

Geneseo, Illinois

it's every town for itself. If you're from Charleston, you don't promote Mattoon. But down here it's like one big county. We've developed a closeness that's quite distinctive—and a fierce loyalty. If we had a cause and someone to lead us, we'd secede from the rest of Illinois." Tommy Hale, who runs a justly famous home-style restaurant known as "Ma Hale's" in Grand Tower, Illinois, on the Mississippi, lives there because he likes the mood. "The minute I turn off Route 3, I feel a load off my shoulders. It's a slower, easier pace. You take off your shoes and you get a little of that gumbo between your toes, and you're comin' back. People around here go out looking for wolf dens and join the Jackson County Anti-Horse-and-Mule-Thief Association and just such silliness as that. Our river towns don't depend on any marshal or law. In the old days, boatmen by the hundreds would come in here and raise all kinds a' hell, fightin' and stabbin' and carryin' on. So we learned to straighten things out ourselves. If somebody gets *too* far out of line, someone will just go on over to his house and let him know he better move away."

Meanings are less explicit, eye contact more fleeting, overtones more significant than in the right-angled prairie towns. The constant selling of charm and quasi-sex helps to dissolve whatever cut-and-dried efficiency might spring up. Girls with double names like Anita-Jane drawl their honey-drippin' "bye-bye, now." Slow-going policemen throw in plenty of "sirs" and "ma'ams," talk of "them boys over to the rester'nt," and say, "I do believe I'll open me a Doctor Pepper." Goods cost about the same as farther north, but services tend to cost less. Almost every transaction comes with a long-handled story attached. And author Baker Brownell cites still another hillbilly quality: hard-bitten willfulness. The southern Illinoisan "may find symbols for his pride and stubbornness in lonely squirrel hunting, in strange, creative profanity, or sometimes in revival 'meetings.'"

Surprisingly, the old migration between the southern uplands and the heartland has not ended. Come spring and summer weekends, the bridges at Cincinnati are jammed with the cars of urban factory workers heading back to the old home places of Appalachia. Ohio newspaperwoman Betty Garrett confesses her nostalgia: "I know, as all hill people do, that dogwood trees will bloom until they resemble a froth of white lace dashed over a breastline gasping with redbud-purple. And it will be glorious. So I must testify to the absolute truth of a cliché: you can take the woman out of the hill country, but you can't take the hill country out of the woman."

Lancaster, Wisconsin

But if dappled atmospherics divide the towns of the southern counties from those of the prairies, so does an opposite heritage: toughness, suspicion, and quick tempers. Like a dark reflection of the rainbow images painted by the schoolbook authors and town boosters, the hill country carries a legacy of social backwardness and industrial strife.

Before the Civil War, Illinois' arrowheadlike lower tip, known as "Egypt," was its cutting edge. The state's first two capitals were established here: first at Kaskaskia, then at Vandalia. Shawneetown became a thriving port, and more than 4800 steamboats called at Cairo in the year 1857 alone. A minor cotton-and-tobacco culture even sprang up (and is still visible across the river near Sikeston, Missouri). Confederate sympathies ran high. Yet Egypt was bound politically to the North, and Grant used it as a salient for his western assault. After the war, this "land between the rivers" was hard hit by the northward shift of commerce—brought on by the expansion of the railroads to the Great Lakes and prairies and by the huge influx of people into the upper Midwest. Earlier, the state capital had been moved to Springfield. Towns like Vandalia and Cairo and Shawneetown entered an economic and psychological decline that has lasted down to the present day.

There was just one hope: coal. The puffing locomotives and whistling factories were hungry for it. And although the ancient seas and glaciers had spread coal under most of Illinois, Egypt's deposits lay conveniently near the surface—and below soils that were relatively poor for farming. By 1900 the southern mines had become the richest in the state. But Egypt's population was dominated by southern upland farmers, eking out a submarginal living yet reluctant to change their ingrown ways. So the managers brought in experienced miners from all over Europe, plus black miners from Tennessee and Kentucky. Which spelled progress—and strife.

Like other extractive industries, coal mining, by its very nature, fostered an atmosphere of danger, transience, and cynicism. Steep economic ups and downs were chronic. Violence was no stranger to the hot-blooded hill folk; their murderous family feuds stretched back for generations. And these agrarian fundamentalists deeply resented the wage-earning newcomers, many of whom were Catholics. Before long, open gun battles broke out. Raging on for years, Egypt's social and industrial strife culminated in the infamous Herrin massacre of 1922, a cold-blooded multiple murder that shocked the nation. After a few years, as the coal began to give out, the violence slackened. But the atmosphere of alienation, suspicion, and resignation lingered on. In declining towns where all groups were, in effect, minority groups and where class lines were firmly, even contemptuously drawn, it would take many years before any true sense of community could develop.

Odd remnants of those tough times still dot the landscape. In the near-ghost-town of Du Bois, for instance, stands a magnificent, spotlessly maintained Catholic cathedral. Not far away, the earth is ruptured and strewn with the remnants of old underground mines. Yet strip mining has brought economic revival to other parts of southern Illinois' central plateau. Here and there the denuded mine lands have

been restored to productive use as parks or orchards, offering hope that future operators will act more responsibly than some of their predecessors.

Mingled with the industrial problems of the 1920s were the wider social stresses that prompted thousands to enlist in the Ku Klux Klan. Its aims were to restore "the highest ideals of the native-born white Gentile American." The movement represented a last-ditch stand of many small-town, lower-middle-class WASPs who felt threatened not only by immigrants and blacks but also by the increasingly powerful upper-middle-class WASPs. The mores of the newer groups were embedded not in villagey isolation and purity but in urban stimulation and competition—not in the Methodist church supper but in the downtown blues parlor, the Croatian miners' picnic, the country club tennis ladder. Thus the hooded knights' voodoo raids on private homes in the name of "one hundred per cent Americanism" sprang from many of the same frustrations that had inspired other superpatriots to endorse ax-swinging Carrie Nation and the Prohibitionists. Both coercive movements drew sizable followings in downstate Illinois and Indiana. And in the long run both only helped to strengthen the very forces they sought to oppose, including the gangster element operating out of rough towns like East St. Louis.

Thus, the close harmony of the village green was being threatened not merely by the automobile and other instruments of mobility but by the steady march of urban and industrial values, and in some cases by the violent clash of opposing life-styles. All of this was traceable, in a sense, to that deep fault line in American life whose opening Jefferson had tried to forestall: the conflict between the rural-agrarian and the urban-industrial. It has been the fate and fortune of the Midwestern mixing bowl that both tendencies were highly developed here. If they often helped reinforce each other, the fault line between them also sometimes yawned into a frightening chasm.

One type of community that is highly typical of the Middle West is the midsized town. Mankato, Minnesota; Decatur, Illinois; and Marion, Ohio, are examples. Such communities are too large to be called small towns and too small to be called cities. In general, they have some small, specialized industries, some farm and transportation functions, and perhaps a small college. Their character usually mingles zest, dullness, charm, and ticky-tackiness:

Marion, northeast of Raymond, is better off [than Raymond] (four railroads), bigger (about 40,000 people including Mr. and Mrs. Obal Gearhiser), more historical (Warren G. Harding is buried there), and more likely to succeed (a triangular park contains a machine gun for small fry to practice on). In Marion you will find the Harding Memorial, a not-too-exciting business district, and street after street of one-family houses, many with front porches, all lined neatly in a compact row. The bank looks like a castle. Some sides of Marion, the near-in south, for example, have seen better days, but here, there, and everywhere the developers have worked their quasi-magic, sometimes creating monotony, sometimes creating beauty. In other words, Marion is the busy, prosperous, ordinary, bland Ohio city that has drive-ins, a sense of history, and growing pains. How much industry? The chamber says 67 different varieties . . . Marion turns out a lot of popcorn, one of the companies doing same being Betty Zane Corn Products, Incorporated. The Houghton-Sulky Company on North State Street makes racing sulkies . . . You might consider Marion as the all-purpose county with Marion being its all-purpose city.

In most of the histories and guidebooks, the story of towns like these is a missing chapter. So is that of their natural ancestor, the small factory community of the early industrial period. Yet such medium-sized communities helped spark the quick growth of both industry and unions a century ago. And it is these all-purpose towns that some

Crossing the Ohio at Vevay, Indiana

Plying the Mississippi near Prairie du Chien, Wisconsin

forecasters believe will set the pattern for a decentralized, "rurban" type of national growth pattern in the "post-industrial" period ahead.

From about 1870 to 1900, as we noted, the libertarian-capitalist ethic reached a peak in America's rapidly expanding metropolises. Lacking any personal identification with the laboring classes, the cities' dominant middle and upper-middle groups believed in a pure Darwinian society. Immutable natural laws were thought to govern not just economics but all of life. The proper working of these laws depended on maintaining the absolute sanctity of private property, contracts, and capital. The view that America's progress had proven the correctness of the laissez-faire system, and that any tampering with it would court disaster, was endorsed wholeheartedly by the urban news media. "The man who lays up not for the morrow, perishes on the morrow," the *Chicago Times* told workers clamoring for reform. "It is the inexorable law of God, which neither legislatures nor communistic blatherskites can repeal. The fittest alone survive, and those are fittest, as the result always proves, who provide for their own survival."

In the smaller industrial towns, such strident Darwinism was tempered by the egalitarian ethic. The workers were real people whose faces you saw every day. They were apt to have lived in the town a long time, and their problems drew more sympathy from the shopkeepers and professionals than in the cities. Here the old-fashioned dignity of the craftsman had not yet been obliterated by automation. The town was slow to accept the assumption that things or people could be made into interchangeable parts. Therefore, small-town industrialists often found their freedom of action impaired when they cut wages, or refused to negotiate with a union, or went outside the community for help in maintaining their authority. For one thing, in these early years the worker had a stronger and more direct voice in small-town politics than he did in city politics. For another, the local newspaper was more sensitive to his point of view. But whether it was a matter of an ironmongers' dispute in Ohio's Hocking Valley or three workers getting seats on the city council of Joliet, Illinois, the central difference in the small industrial town was the balancing effect of the nonlaboring middle group, who were inclined to apply leveling standards of equality and fair play:

> They could judge the troubles and complaints of both workers and employers by personal experience and by what happened around them and did not have to rely on secondary accounts. While they invariably accepted the concepts of private property and free entrepreneurship, their judgments about the *social* behavior of industrialists often drew upon noneconomic considerations and values. They saw no necessary contradiction between private enterprise and gain on the one hand, and decent, humane social relations between workers and employers on the other.

But as the industrial system matured, the values and relationships prevailing in even these smaller industrial communities were destined to change. In-depth studies of Muncie, Indiana, from 1890 to 1935 showed that the arrival of mass production and mass consumption brought deep changes to every aspect of community life. As the population of the town grew from eleven thousand to over forty thousand, its chief industry remained the production of glass products, particularly glass jars. The town's leading entrepreneurs were the Ball family, who gave their name not only to the well-known jars and the factory but to Ball State Teachers College and a host of other local institutions. In the early years the glass workers enjoyed the respectability, pay, and influence of a tightly knit craft hierarchy. But, as everywhere, their skills were gradually outmoded by the assembly line. Boredom, alienation, and social isolation increased. Intrinsic satisfactions gave way to extrinsic affluence. Older forms of status placement, including age and experience, were overtaken by the yardstick of success, calibrated as the ability to own mass-produced goods. Unionization abetted this process by further dividing the man from his work *per se* and by offering to help him in his dollar-oriented climb.

As part of the race, parents of all classes implanted rising educational ambitions in their children. Muncie grew larger and more heterogeneous, new forms of leisure proliferated, family ties weakened. The Balls' business interests spread across Indiana and beyond. After they sent their children out of state to be educated, the family's preoccupation with the town diminished. The Depression accented the isolation of individual families and underlined the growing diffuseness of the community. Far from halting the consumption race, the hard times redoubled everyone's resolve to subordinate all other values to that of "success." By 1937 the authors of the Muncie studies, Robert and Helen Lynd, could write that "going to church becomes a kind of moral life-insurance policy and one's children go to school and college so that they can get a better job and know the right people. Bit by bit in a culture devoted to movement and progress these permanent things of life become themselves adjuncts to the central business of getting ahead, dependent symbols about the central acquisitive symbols of the community's life."

In the mid-sized town, then, the transformation of values and relationships toward those of the mass society was well under way before World War II. Today, Muncie's population has reached about seventy thousand. Countless places like it are destined to remain key switching centers for the forces propelling our national life away from the quiescent village green.

Nowhere are the dynamics of flow more striking than along the urban corridor that runs between northern Ohio and eastern Michigan. From Youngstown and Akron and Cleveland around to Toledo and Detroit, this blast furnace of mid-America has long mixed a molten brew of iron, commerce, and humanity. In the narrow crescent live nearly ten million people—half the total population of the two states. Accenting the urban sense of flux, many are wage earners who draw high pay in boom times but often find themselves jobless during slack periods.

This industrial corridor's special advantage is its access to the waterborne transport of heavy raw materials and finished goods. Penetrating the continent's deep interior via the St. Lawrence Seaway, ships of many flags slip down along Lake Erie, then up into the giant jigsaw of Lakes Huron, Ontario, Michigan, and Superior. The combined shoreline is some four thousand miles long—longer than the nation's Atlantic or Pacific coasts. The mammoth vessels may be disgorging Volkswagens at Toledo, then receiving trucks at Detroit; dropping Swedish pulpwood at Green Bay before taking on grain at Duluth; or delivering Honduran bananas to Milwaukee prior to picking up Illinois earthmovers at Chicago. Even more vital is the domestic commerce. Iron ore and limestone are hauled from remote U.S. and Canadian ports down to the great steel centers on the lower lakeshores. Coal, fuel oil, cement, and other bulky commodities circle about in a bewildering maze of motion.

From the Pennsylvania border the Ohio shoreline slants evenly west and south. Quiet, sometimes scrubby beaches are interrupted by the grimy smokestacks and thundering ore-unloaders of Conneaut and Ashtabula. Down at Akron, the Midwest's industrial might is on view at the Goodyear plant and at Stan Hywet Hall, the monumental Tudor mansion erected by rubber czar Frank A. Seiberling. Cleveland, though lacking a natural harbor, is the point where the winding, deep-gorged Cuyahoga River empties into Lake Erie. Cutting through the thumping heart of Ohio's number-one metropolis, the churning lake freighters slide beneath a lacework of bridges and past mile after mile of unloading docks and mill yards.

West of Cleveland the shoreline turns quiet again—except when lashed by an Erie storm—and is marked by beaches, billboards, and industrial ports like Lorain and Sandusky. Offshore, the Bass Islands recall the days before Lake Erie was deadened by pollution and when the crowded waterfront of little Sandusky was known as the largest freshwater fishing market in the world. It was from South Bass Island's Put-in-Bay that Commodore Oliver Perry sailed in 1813 to beat the British in the decisive Battle of Lake Erie. A century later, Middle Bass' grand summer hotels hosted the nation's elite, including four Presidents. But today those glories, like so much of the lakes' colorful past, have been submerged by the tides of commerce, trailer camps, and yachting regattas.

Erie's rim angles northwest, then makes a ninety-degree right turn at the broad and discolored Maumee River. Here is booming Toledo. Home to Owens-Illinois Glass, Champion Spark Plugs, and innumerable other manufacturers, Toledo ranks as the Great Lakes' second largest port, after Duluth, in tonnage handled.

Just north of Maumee Bay is the Michigan border. Of the two separate pieces into which the Wolverine State is divided, this, the Lower Peninsula, is by far the largest and most productive. Its shape has been aptly likened to that of a big mitten. Functionally, the mitten is divided into two halves. Western Michigan is a slower-paced land of fruit orchards and modest farms, of fashionable vacation beaches, and of careful burghers like the stolid Dutch-Americans who have always dominated Gerald Ford's home town of Grand Rapids. Eastern

4th of July powwow at Ponemah, Minnesota

Michigan is eastern—crowded, boisterous, industrial, a whirring money-machine whose citizens work hard, play hard, vote a liberal ticket, root passionately for the Tigers and Lions, and never forget to lock their doors.

Of a sultry summer afternoon, Detroit's sparkling Lake St. Clair blooms with bright sails. Lively national groups like the Poles of the Hamtramck section throw beer-guzzling, sausage-gulping wingdings along the concrete banks of the Detroit River. It is a bewildering, disorienting city, one of the first in America to go determinedly suburban. Depressed inner Detroit can no longer risk even a first-run movie theater. At night, dark figures drift like shadows through its ominous canyons. Farther out, in the bland gravy of suburbia, there are more reassuring sights and sounds: TVs blaring, hard-hat dads racing to work, air conditioners humming steadily in totally enclosed shopping malls.

In such environs it takes a lively imagination to re-create the seventeenth century wilderness through which La Salle and Hennepin passed in their famous sailing ship, the *Griffin.* Or the eighteenth, when Antoine de la Mothe Cadillac, the "caustic-tongued Gascon," raised a fort and founded a village of happy-go-lucky French colonial farmers along what they termed *le détroit*—the strait linking Lakes Huron and Erie. Or that morning of August 26, 1818, when the first steamboat to ply the Great Lakes, the *Walk-in-the-Water,* entered the Detroit River, causing one astonished French farmer to dash home crying, "Jean! Jean! Look at the river! What are those Yankees sending us now but a sawmill!"

The remark was a strangely prescient one. Ninety per cent of Michigan's land area was blanketed with magnificent trees—thick pineries to the north, dense hardwood stands to the south. By midcentury the Saginaw River country had launched the first large-scale logging operation in the Middle West. The silence of centuries was broken by the throaty cries of burly Maine lumberjacks as the Saginaw's three million acres of tall white pines crashed to earth. Floated down hundreds of miles of rivers, the virgin logs fed screaming mills that spewed out a hundred million board feet of lumber yearly by the 1850s and a billion by the 1880s. Giant logjams drew swarms of onlookers—and killed many a daring "driver" who loosened the crucial log. Immense forest fires, licking unchecked through the dry slash, cut a wide swath of death and destruction and burned up more usable timber than was ever harvested.

Betty Carter

Boundary Waters Canoe Area, northern Minnesota

This hell-for-leather logging business quickly spread to western Michigan, to the Upper Peninsula, and on to Wisconsin and Minnesota. Grand Rapids and other towns boomed as furniture-making centers. From the Civil War until after the turn of the century, Michigan's economy was dominated by lumber. Shipped east, south, and west on tall-masted lake schooners, many of which were built at the town of Saginaw, the precious pine boards were soon hammered together into prairie farmhouses, orderly towns, and teeming city blocks.

Denuded of their hardwoods, the southern halves of Michigan, Wisconsin, and Minnesota were transformed mainly into farms and orchards. But as the sawyers and lumber barons abandoned the northern "stumplands" and moved on to the Pacific Northwest, these slaughtered pineries remained barren and fire-ridden. Half again as large as all of New England, the Midwestern "cutover" has more recently made a comeback as the site of newly seeded timber plantations, largely of quick-growing pulp for the paper mills.

It has also been turned into a recreational wonderland. Today, Michigan's second-growth woods resound not only to the rasp of the chain saw but to the crack of the deer rifle, the whisper of the bird watcher, the whoosh of the skier. Behind cozy vacation cottages, snub-nosed snowmobiles peek out from under their covers. Sport fishing for walleye, northern pike, bass, musky, and steelhead is excellent all across the north country. Off-the-beaten-track enthusiasts may compete in the Great Lakes Sled Dog Association races in western Michigan, discover old-time logging camps in Wisconsin, or join wolf researchers in northern Minnesota on their spooky midnight "wolf howls."

There are innumerable fine bays and lakes on the western coast of Michigan. The area around Lake Charlevoix and Petoskey is known for its rustic inns and boat harbors and for restaurants specializing in fresh Lake Michigan fish—smelt, whitefish, coho salmon. It was here that Ernest Hemingway spent his boyhood summers in the family cottage on Walloon Lake and here that he picked up the old Midwestern habit of escaping the painful complexities of civilization by plunging into the great outdoors. Later, he set several of his short stories amid the woods and streams of northern Michigan. These narratives emphasized the curative power of nature:

> When he awoke in the night he heard the wind in the hemlock trees outside the cottage and the waves of the lake coming in on the shore, and he went back to sleep. In the morning there was a big wind blowing and the waves were running high up on the beach and he was awake a long time before he remembered that his heart was broken.

Up in Mackinaw City, at the apex of the Michigan mitten, the gentle mood of the state's western half collides with the toughness of the industrial east. High-priced motels cope with a summer population explosion. Leggy shoppers grab up postcard sets and genuine Indian moccasins made in Taiwan. Perspiring attendants with megaphones wave drivers toward the parking lots for the ferryboat rides to Mackinac Island. Thankfully, on Mackinac itself (pronounced "mackinaw") there are no automobiles. And the picturesque island is pervaded with a sense of its long, seminal history.

Two years before the Pilgrims landed at Plymouth, the first European set foot in Michigan. He was Etienne Brulé, a lusty young protégé of the seasoned explorer, Samuel de Champlain. Having established the settlement of Quebec on the St. Lawrence River, Champlain was engaged in pushing the frontiers of New France ever deeper into the continent. Brulé's assignment was to explore the wilderness and to learn the customs and languages of the Indians. Hunting, traveling, and warring with the tribes, eating and dressing as they did, and happily reciprocating the advances of the women, Brulé embraced the role with gusto. Ranging far and wide, he gave Champlain valuable reports of his adventures. He discovered Lakes Huron and Superior and spent the winter of 1618–19 near the site of present-day Sault Ste. Marie. But Brulé went more and more native. Finally he forgot his patrimony so entirely as to side briefly with the hostile British, helping them capture Champlain himself and the town of Quebec. Before long, this independent soul made himself unloved by the British, as well—and by the Huron Indians, who taught him one last custom: they tortured, quartered, broiled, and ate him.

In 1634 another of Champlain's protégés, Jean Nicolet, passed through the Straits of Mackinac from Lake Huron into Lake Michigan on his way to what he thought would be "Cathay on the extreme coast of Asia" but which turned out to be Green Bay, Wisconsin. Nicolet undoubtedly saw Mackinac Island, but it was not until some thirty

Upper Peninsula, Michigan

years later that a roving Jesuit, Père Claude Allouez, left the first written account of it. Père Claude Dablon conducted a mission there in 1670, and this was soon taken over by Père Jacques Marquette. Marquette left in 1673 to join Louis Joliet on their famous exploration of the upper Mississippi region.

Slowly but surely, the French missionaries, traders, and empire builders were developing a vast inland territory to which the Straits of Mackinac were an indispensable key. Robert La Salle traveled extensively through mid-America and in 1682 claimed the whole region drained by the Mississippi for France. Meanwhile, the fur business was becoming highly lucrative. To the Mackinac shores came the famed *voyageurs* and other toughened traders who had paddled their pelt-laden canoes across thousands of square miles of uncharted wilderness. Thus the Straits became a lens through which the spreading rays of east-west commerce and credit were focused. But French progress was being seriously challenged by British competition and by the hostility of the natives. So, to guard the channel, the French built stout Fort Michilimackinac on the southern shore about 1715.

For nearly a century the French and British fought one another in a series of colonial battles known as the French and Indian Wars. This struggle was finally climaxed in 1754 by a British victory that effectively ended the French presence in North America. Britain received Canada and all of the territory east of the Mississippi. Spain took possession of the huge Louisiana Territory west of the Mississippi—which Napoleon would take back in 1800 before selling it, with French New Orleans, to the United States three years later.

In this continuing rivalry for control of the Old Northwest, Mackinac was even more vital. The British had occupied Fort Michilimackinac in 1761. But after the outbreak of the Revolutionary War, George Rogers Clark marched his American musketeers across Illinois and Indiana, storming one British bastion after the next. Fearing that Michilimackinac might also prove vulnerable, the redcoats destroyed this mainland fort and built a stronger one out on Mackinac Island. Then came the American victory at Yorktown, and Independence. In 1783, at the Treaty of Paris, the British were forced to accept an international boundary running through the center of four of the Great Lakes. Today, that boundary remains a prime segment in the longest unfortified frontier in the world.

Contrary to the treaty, however, the redcoats remained at their posts in the remote northwest. Their fur trade still flourished, and it was controlled by the North West Company, whose headquarters were situated under the stone ramparts of Fort Mackinac. In 1796 the Americans succeeded in taking over the island, only to lose it again in the opening weeks of the War of 1812. Not until 1815 did the Stars and Stripes flutter permanently over the much-contested outpost.

Now it was John Jacob Astor's turn to hold a virtual monopoly on the profitable fur business. His American Fur Company made its headquarters in four white frame buildings on Mackinac Island. Here hundreds of clerks worked feverishly to keep up with the comings and goings of thousands of boatmen who, in a good year, received $3 million or more for their pelts. But out in the woods, the beaver and other furry creatures were being trapped nearly to extinction. Soon this ruthlessly extractive industry entered a final decline, and Astor sold out in 1834.

By then the island was becoming what it still is—a summer resort. To escape the humid heat of the central Midwest and East, the wealthy and fashionable flocked to its salubrious air, pleasant hills, and pretty harbors. In 1875 the undeveloped sections became a national park. Two years later the Grand Hotel, a stupendous white edifice featuring the longest front porch in the world, opened for business. Today, horsedrawn carriages still clop regularly to a halt under the wide portico before a long red carpet and a squad of fancy doormen. The clerks gamely struggle to uphold the hotel's tradition of snooty elegance against proletarian armies of day-trippers and conventioneers who storm the wide lawns and mill around in the plush lobby.

Nature trails abound. But the island's real treasures are Fort Mackinac and the town, which comprise a visible slice through four centuries of Midwestern history. In Marquette Park stands a tiny bark chapel resembling the ones the Jesuit *pères* used in their missionary work. The Biddle House, parts of which date from the 1780s, is thought to be the oldest residence in Michigan, if not in the entire Old Northwest. Several of Astor's commercial buildings remain, including the warehouse where the furs were checked and stored. The rambling fort is full of interesting rooms and gun platforms. On the ferry back to the south shore you get an unhurried view of the Mackinac Bridge, the longest suspension bridge in the world. And the old log fort on the mainland, Michilimackinac, has been painstakingly reconstructed.

Along its northern edge, then, as along its southern, the heartland has been chastened by the flow of time, water, and industry.

And yet up around Lake Superior the north country's turbulent past remains subdued by a virginal hush. Purer, deeper, and colder than any of her four sisters, Superior is the biggest freshwater lake in the world. And she is moody. Below brooding headlands, she howls with a white fury through the long winters. In other seasons she turns gray and introspective as freighters bleat through her massive fogs. But under the dark blue dome of summer she stretches herself seductively, her soft breast glittering as with diamonds.

The land is vast, empty, powerful. Near Sault Ste. Marie the westbound highway dips inland to become a ruler-straight, hundred-mile gash through second-growth timber. To the north, Hiawatha's "dark and golden river," the Tahquamenon, winds through cedar swamps, tumbles over Tahquamenon Falls, and finally flows into Gitche Gumee—Lake Superior—at Whitefish Bay. Farther west the lonely coast passes mile after mile of mysterious cliffs and caverns known as the Pictured Rocks. Rejoining the shore at Munising before heading on to Marquette and Ishpeming, the highway plunges through the scarred hills of Michigan's iron mining country. The stark booms and busts of the iron business were not unlike those of the fur and lumber bonanzas.

But for mining lore, ethnic roots, and sheer beauty, the thumblike outcrop of the Keweenaw Peninsula is unique. Geologically, its bumpy surface is possibly the oldest in the New World. For fully three quarters of a century it was a fabulous copper kingdom—site of America's first major mining rush in 1844 and of a sustained boom that lasted well into the 1920s. Spying out fortunes only waiting to be dug up, industrial heroes like Douglass Houghton left their names on the land along with the gaunt headframes that still preside like skeletons over the spent shafts. The long-lived Quincy mine, whose tunnels honeycomb through hundreds of miles and reach a depth of 6400 feet, paid out over $27 million in dividends before closing in 1945. Just below the Quincy, the twin towns of Hancock and Houghton face each other across the narrow channel of Portage Lake, which cuts the spiny peninsula in half. It is characteristic of these steep-sided copper communities, whose streets once rang to the ersatz lingos of European-born miners, that its roomy taverns are among the most lavishly decorated places in town. If such establishments seem a long way from the Corn Belt, so do the Keweenaw's dense stands of northern hardwoods—birches, aspens, beeches, maples. Fall ignites their leaves into a thrilling blaze of scarlet and gold and wakes drowsy vacation hamlets along the lake to a portentous chill sweeping down across the thousands of miles of emptiness that are all that divide the Keweenaw from the North Pole.

Westernmost of Michigan's iron ranges is the Gogebic, where towns like Bessemer and Wakefield and Ironwood reaped millions from the great ore beds a century ago but have since faded to pale versions of their old selves. Just over the Montreal River in Wisconsin is Hurley, whose Silver Street was known far and wide as the hell-raisingest place of all on a raw frontier well used to serving the needs of men who mostly needed what came in corsets and bottles. Countless yarns are still spun about the bawdy Hurley of old and about its later revival as a mecca for rumrunners and gangsters. Even today, Silver Street is dotted with survivors of the eighty-odd saloons that once lined the little town's muddy boardwalks. All across the north country, faded mining and lumbering centers like these are haunted by impoverished, decrepit men, thin as whispers, living out their twilight years among the tottering structures whose memories they share.

At the fine port of Ashland, however, the ongoing present shows itself in the bustle of coal and iron terminals and in modern paper plants like that of the American Can Company. Up at tiny Bayfield, the accent is on fun. Vacationers wander through its arty shops, then scurry down to the marina to catch the ferry out to highly developed Madeline Island, with its chic piano bars, fancy yacht harbor, and old Indian graveyard. The other islands in the Apostle group look, from the mainland, like pumice stones. Mosquito-ridden and primitive, they have recently been declared a National Lakeshore. Red Cliff Indian Reservation occupies the tip of the peninsula above Bayfield. Throughout this part of northern Wisconsin the soil, shores, and stream bottoms have a distinctively red cast that also shows up in some Victorian buildings made of natural stone.

The coast road to Duluth passes through remote hamlets—Cornucopia, Herbster, Port Wing—many of whose white clapboard churches and false-front stores date from the boom times of the nineties. Like so much of the cutover, these recalcitrant soils have been tried by many farmers but largely abandoned. A few hardscrabblers still cling to the land, however, particularly those dairymen able to utilize its grasses for grazing. And for generations, isolated families have been scattered through the second-growth stumplands of Wisconsin and Minnesota, barely managing to survive in their rude shacks and cabins. Such rural poverty, nonexistent in the prairies, enhances that atmosphere of flux and decline that so oddly ties these upper reaches of the Midwest to the hillbilly country lying six hundred miles to the south.

In startling contrast, the contiguous harbors of Duluth and Superior are one of the commercial glories of the Middle West. So huge are the quantities of raw commodities handled at Duluth alone that, in terms of tonnage, it ranks as the nation's second largest port, after New York. Visitors on excursion boats gasp at the tangled skein of jetties, bridges, chutes, and stacks. Steam billows, horns scream, bridges lift and swing as vessels large and small crisscross the broad harbors. Giant elevators shower rivers of yellow grain into the maws of low-slung freighters waiting to make the week-long, 2300-mile journey back to the Atlantic and thence to every corner of the world. Long trains of gondola cars rumble out onto black ore docks to dump their clattering loads into the holds of ships anchored hundreds of feet below. Wharves the size of airports hold mountains of cement, pulpwood, taconite. Nowhere is the gargantuan productivity of mid-America more starkly on view.

Duluth itself is an important wholesaling and manufacturing center. A "string city," it rises by narrow stairsteps into the steep hills that hem it in, yet stretches along the level lakeshore for twenty miles. There is an appealing forthrightness about Duluth: sober, aging brick buildings; this-a-way, that-a-way boardwalks; big square wooden homes anchored to the hillside's rakish tilt; railroad cars screeching and jerking all night long. The faces do not pretend: short Finns, lantern-jawed Swedes, housewives in sensible shorts and halters buying Cornish pasties or talking across picket fences. Dockworkers in their undershirts lounge on curled wooden steps, tip cans of beer, and turn their heads after a pretty blonde on a motorcycle, her arms pressed tight around her boyfriend, her hair flying. If this is Duluth, it is also Minnesota, a rough-and-ready state untouched by eastern complication or southern innuendo or prairie containment.

Northeast of Duluth the North Shore Drive hugs the rocky coast for 150 miles. Dozens of trout streams pour out of the north woods into Lake Superior. Cabins and motels are everywhere. Knife River Village is known for its smoked fish, and Gooseberry River State Park for its waterfalls. Near the Cross River thousands of cords of pulpwood are rafted out into the lake to be floated to the Wisconsin mills. Grand Portage has a restored stockade depicting its historic role in the fur trade, and from here a ferry heads out across Lake Superior to Isle Royale National Park, a deep-woods island shared by moose, wolves, beavers, and back packers.

But in recent years the most widely publicized spot on this scenic coast has been Silver Bay, site of the mammoth iron ore processing facilities of the Reserve Mining Company. In a classic confrontation, environmental and governmental groups joined to argue that Reserve was unreasonably using the public air and water as free garbage dumps. Each day the plant discharged 67,000 tons of taconite ore waste into Lake Superior, speeding algae growth and causing asbestos fibers and other residues to turn up in such places as Duluth's drinking water. Reserve and its owners, Armco and Republic Steel, countered that there was no evidence the wastes were harming the lake or its residents. Having satisfied every official requirement when they made their $350 million investment in the 1950s, they protested it would be unfair to change the rules only twenty years later. And they stressed the economic importance of the plant, which employs thousands of workers and accounts for 15 per cent of America's iron ore output. The complex struggle ended in a compromise decision, upheld by the U.S. Supreme Court in 1975. Reserve was required to stop polluting the air rather quickly but was allowed a longer, vaguer amount of time to locate

Grain elevators and harbor, Duluth, Minnesota

an inland dump for its massive tailings. Nationally, the expensive case was a red flag to would-be polluters. For moody Superior herself, it seemed yet another enactment of her historic double role as virgin and temptress.

With the approach of summer, millions of wild geese flock north along the broad Mississippi flyway. You greet them in twos and threes in cornfields and tamarack bogs. You sight their great V-formations over the brow of distant ridges. And you find yourself surrounded by their flappings and gabblings in sanctuaries like Horseshoe Lake in southern Illinois or Horicon Marsh in Wisconsin.

Man, too, is nudged north by the sun. Cars and campers wind along the spectacular bluffs of the Mississippi's Great River Road, then jam the lot of the Holiday Inn on a marshy island in the middle of the river near the roughhewn old town of La Crosse, Wisconsin. Musing in a rowboat, a fisherman squints through early morning tule fog to watch that venerable sternwheeler, the *Delta Queen,* churn by on her way from Cincinnati to St. Paul. In Prairie du Chien the vacationer checks the gossip at the bait shops and pays a visit to Villa Louis, the lavishly appointed mansion of Astor's fur trade agent, Hercules Dousman. Then he heads past red barns and white steeples to Wisconsin's apple country, to the rocks and watercourses of the Wisconsin Dells, and to Lake Winnebago. Or he turns west to reach Minnesota's Lake Itasca, forest-bound source of the Mississippi.

Year after year, man flows back to these elemental places for replenishment and perspective.

He enters the land of the Chippewa and the Menominee. Yet he cannot know the Indian. He cannot go out to a shattered race whose world was not linear and progressive and pragmatic like his, but holistic, heroic, symbolic. He views their holy site at Pipestone and their fine museum at Mille Lacs. He pays them a dollar a night to camp at Leech Lake. He paddles his aluminum canoe alongside their aluminum canoes in the yearly wild rice harvests. He watches their festive dances at Shakopee or Red Lake—and still he cannot know them. They may be quite friendly, which is not the same thing. They may offer him whiskey and tell jokes against themselves and him, which is not it either. Sometimes he goes home wondering whether the Indian any longer knows himself.

When the Europeans first appeared in the Northwest Territory in the seventeenth century, the Chippewa, or Ojibwa as they were also known, lived in the central-upper Great Lakes area to the east of Lake Superior. But as the French expanded their trading empire, the Chippewa moved gradually westward into the Superior basin. In the eighteenth century they reached present-day Minnesota, then occupied by the Sioux. Because their economy had come to rely on trapping and trading, they already possessed some of the white man's implements, foods, and firewater. And they had guns, which enabled them to drive the Sioux westward into the Dakotas. Expert builders of birchbark canoes, the Chippewa found themselves among a myriad of lakes blooming with wild rice. As they mastered the complex arts of harvesting, storing, and preparing this nutritious food, it became a distinctive part of their economy.

Equally central to their way of life were their social customs and metaphysical outlook. Individualism was stressed over cooperation; yet sharing was also a strong value. The entire natural world was assumed to be threaded with mutual obligations. Hoarding, for instance, or an unnecessary act of cruelty, might invite retaliation in the form of malevolent sorcery. Outward appearances were deceiving and were only an incidental attribute of being. The vital part, the soul, migrated from one body to another, to animals and even to inanimate objects like shells or stones. Nature was never aloof or indifferent, and the Chippewa were on intimate terms with it. Before killing a bear, a young brave might feel constrained to apologize to him; he might even change his mind and tell the animal to run away.

The goal of life was fullness rather than outward achievements. Especially for the men, longevity and fullness could only be realized with the aid of powerful guardian spirits—"the grandfathers"—who attached themselves to a young boy during puberty and whom he would call on for help in later life. On long, bitter-cold winter nights, huddled in their birchbark lodges, the Chippewa would whisper the sacred stories of these immortal beings. This would please the grandfathers, and they would come near to listen.

Between Gitche Gumee's rugged headlands in the east and the spring wheat and sugar beets of the Red River Valley in the west, northern Minnesota is a mosaic of great forests and desolate open country, of tourist lakes and Indian reservations, of spotty farms and the diminished mines of the once-great Mesabi iron range. But the state's northeastern fringe is special. Astride the Canadian border lies a primeval maze of lakes and woods known as the Quetico-Superior. The American half of this two-hundred-mile-wide stretch is the protected Boundary Waters Canoe Area. Here the beaver can still build his dam undisturbed. The moose and the bear and the timber wolf roam free. Otters gambol, dive, and bark back at their dens of yelping pups. Owls and ospreys share the abundance with loons, ravens, kingbirds, and whiskey jacks. Yet the dominant tone is one of silence and serenity. On the glassy surfaces of hundreds of lakes, images of tree-lined shores float upside-down among scudding clouds and lily pads. The rain-pure waters are ruffled only by the splash of a frog or trout, by occasional storms, and by the tugging paddles of thousands of modern-day *voyageurs* who melt into this labyrinth of waterways, portages, and campsites.

The BWCA has also been called the last large, complete ecosystem of northern conifers in the United States. No one appreciates this system's virile and delicate interrelationships better than Bud Heinselman, principal plant ecologist for the U.S. Forest Service in northern Minnesota. At the Heinselmans' tree-shrouded cabin on Burntside Lake, near Ely, Bud and his wife, Fran, treated my wife, Betty, and me to heaping bowls of blueberries and to delicious blueberry muffins. "Later this morning I'll show you where we picked these berries," Bud promised. "There's been quite a profusion of them up in the area of the Little Sioux Fire." Spreading out waterproof maps, the Heinselmans gave us practical tips for our forthcoming canoe trip and showed us where to look for Indian cliff paintings.

After breakfast Bud drove with us along the forest road called the Echo Trail, threading the edge of the BWCA. "There isn't another road north of here until way past the Canadian border," he explained. "The Canoe Area forests are a patchwork of virgin trees and second-growth stands following logging. We've made careful studies of the fires that have periodically swept these woods, from as far back as the sixteenth century right up to this most recent Little Sioux Fire in 1971.

"These scraggly looking trees just ahead, with the rough grayish bark, are jack pines of an 1894 age class. As you can see, they're loaded with cones. The cones stay on the tree indefinitely and are sealed shut with resins. The melting point of the resins is just about the temperature reached briefly during a crown fire. That type of fire burns the tops of the trees and kills them, but it makes the cones open and drop their seeds—and it's the only thing that *will* open them. On the Little Sioux Fire I literally saw this happen. I saw the trees burning in mid-May, and two weeks later I saw the seed fall, and by the end of summer there were twenty thousand jack pine seedlings per acre in some places. Of course, only a small fraction of those will live to maturity. But this beautiful, natural adaptation to fire assures that some will survive."

Bud pointed out the portage where Betty and I would be setting out. Then he continued: "Those pitchy trees are balsam firs. They don't reproduce well after a fire. But then, after a long time without fire, they will come up in the shade as an understory tree and eventually replace the aspens and pines and birches. That process forms fuel for another fire. So, in nature, every hundred or two hundred years a fire comes through and wipes out the balsam and replenishes the pines and aspen, and the cycle starts again. But what are we doing now? We've taken fire out of the system. So we're encouraging the balsam fir everywhere, and this in turn is causing spruce budworm epidemics all over northeastern North America. Meanwhile, more and more fuel is accumulating. Which may mean that our efforts to prevent fire have been so successful that, ironically, we're going to be faced sooner or later with a real holocaust we can't control.

"Two of our other prominent trees are the red and white pine. Both have thick bark and long, clear trunks, which help them survive quite a bit of fire. And some *have* to survive, because, unlike the jack pines, they seed once every few years and don't have sealed cones. So these old fellas—I call them the veterans who've made it through the wars—they become the seed source of a new forest. But if you log off the red and white pine without reseeding or planting, as they did in the early days, then you've lost your seed sources and you're out of business.

"Now we're just coming into the recent fire area. In just two years a lot of these young aspen and paper birch have grown taller than a man. They resprout from the roots or bases of trees, and the wind can also carry their seeds great distances. They are the pioneers—often the first to replace the forest that was there, especially if the old seed sources were destroyed by logging. This is why you see so many aspen and birch now across the northern Middle West."

We headed up a rough dirt track. Amid the blackened skeletons of the burned trunks, new green plants had sprung up in profusion. "A lot of these trees were of the 1755 to 1759 age class, so you can imagine the history they've seen. Right after they burned, revegetation began. And burrowing bugs started knocking off the outside bark, which helped to fertilize the ground. Then the woodpeckers came in after the burrowing bugs. In a couple of weeks most of the herbs and grasses were back and many of the shrubs. Unexpected things happened, too—phenomena not known to occur within hundreds of miles—like bluebirds suddenly showing up from the prairies! It was the darndest thing you ever saw."

We parked and went ahead on foot. "Here's where Fran and I got most of our blueberries," Bud said. "There are many other kinds of berries along here, too. And look. These are a variety of cherry. The birds eat the cherries somewhere off the fire and then come in here, and their droppings contain the seeds. In fact it appears that going through a bird's digestive tract is necessary before the seed can grow." Bud showed us bear and deer tracks and pointed out a family of grouse. He told us more about fire's regenerative effect—the terrific fertilizer shot it gives the soil, the nutrient cycling and energy flow it stimulates, how the seedbeds and rocks change, the effects on parasites and insects, the altered competition for light and space, and how the smaller animals go underground to wait out the blaze.

"That first night of the fire, all the country between here and Meander Lake burned in a few hours. You can imagine what a sight it was when I came through—a pitch dark night with these hills all flaring up! Luckily, no persons were killed or injured. For a while we were worried that the town of Ely might burn. Although we did everything we could to stop the fire, what finally put it out was a snowstorm and a rainstorm.

"We've always tried to prevent forest fires, and for very good reasons, including protecting lives and property and commercial timber. But now that we know that fire is such a prominent factor in the natural system, we need to think more about doing prescribed burning. Because fire, you see, is actually the principal means by which the forest renews itself."

Earth, air, fire, water: the ancients had not been far wrong in assessing the basics, I thought that evening.

Betty and I awoke at dawn. At the portage I hefted the lightweight boat over my head in the typical "canoe carry." Trudging down the trail, I could see only the ground under me and the mottled lower bark of the red pines. Bud's story of how the forest regenerates itself was still vivid in my mind, and I tried to guess which of the larger trunks might be the "veterans" who had reseeded the whole stand.

At the lake we stowed our packsacks, tent, sleeping bags, and camera cases in the bottom of the canoe. Then, balancing carefully, we pushed off. Betty paddled on one side, I on the other. Now and then a cool droplet splashed on my bare arm. Our gliding motion sent low ripples across the blue-black water. It seemed a special time. Neither of us spoke for quite a while.

That idea of prescribed burns had somehow piqued my imagination. Yet when I tried to catch the meaning, it vanished. Never mind, I thought: the drifting clouds, the resistance of the paddle were enough.

Near the center of the lake we stopped to sample the lake water. It tasted cool and good. I glanced at my watch, but the time made no impression on my mind. What registered was that the watch itself looked out of place, part of some alien order we had already left behind. The buzzing of a mosquito, the acute angle of the morning sun on my neck—these were real.

We began rowing again. The sun slipped under the edge of a graying cloud and drifted there like a silver wafer. I thought of the nimble Chippewa who had painted the hieroglyphs on the rock faces of our next lake. And I thought of those singing, red-capped *voyageurs,* their birchbark canoes groaning with pelts, who had traveled these waters in centuries past.

A lichen-encrusted boulder near a tiny island sent my thoughts far back, beyond the comings and goings of man, bison, or dinosaur, to those titanic eruptions and glacial scourings that formed the vast Laurentian Shield of which these rocks are a part. Horace Greeley would doubtless have said of the boulders, as he did of the prairies, that they had been patiently awaiting our advent since Creation. But to me they looked more as if they were patiently waiting out our brief visit.

Was that not the same Creation that was soon followed by man's taking the Knowledge-bite, leaving him out of joint with nature? In Greeley's time man had been passing from the stage of using nature to that of subduing it. But now he has entered a third phase, involving a more sensitive relation to nature. He sees that he cannot exempt himself from her laws, and that "preservation" really means self-preservation. The Indians had known this all along. They had known, too, that there was more than matter to be preserved—that, as Santayana said, nature is material but not materialistic. The scientists of today see matter less as a "thing-ness" than as an energy equivalent. The more we learn about nature, the more elusive she becomes. She runs rings around our time-lines. And as always, she asks us to obey her if we would master her—something the farmer, or anyone else who lives on the uncovered ground, knows by instinct.

I dug the paddle into the water, watched the eddies disperse. And now I saw what had been teasing me about Bud's idea that we give the forest back its fire: Knowledge itself was carrying us the long way home toward the Garden.

The map showed the portage ahead to be a short one. We had intended to cross it and to keep right on going across the next lake before stopping for the night. But black clouds were boiling up in the west. Just as we spotted the trail, thunder rumbled across the sky. We dragged the canoe onto some half-submerged logs. "We'd better look for a place to camp," I said.

We found a good campsite beside the next lake. Hurriedly, Betty made lunch while I struggled with the low, two-man tent. The stakes would not hold on the thickly matted forest floor, so I tightened the ropes on trees. The sky was getting darker by the minute. I chopped some dry firewood and stuck it inside the tent. Betty crawled in. I dug a drainage ditch around the tent, then plunged inside as the storm struck hard.

Dozing on and off, we listened to the pelting rain and blowing pines. Once, a squirrel ran across the canvas roof. Hours passed.

When the rain stopped, we crawled outside and saw the storm had been a blessing. Pearly drops hung from the pine needles. A fine glow radiated from the ferns, the wintergreen, the birch leaves, and the wild mushrooms. Mulchy aromas of decaying stumps wafted through the scrubbed air. Two woodpeckers were back on the job. As Betty and I roamed the outskirts of camp with our cameras, she called me to come and see a spider web. Six inches across, the fancy pattern was so full of glittering droplets that it looked like a queen's tiara.

Leaving the tent and packs, we put the canoe in the water and set out to explore the lake. It had a bend in it, like a boomerang. Just as we reached the bend, Betty pointed out a red fox standing on the far slope, calmly observing us. Soon the narrowing channel was choked with lily pads and rushes, swishing against the boat's thin metal skin. Water bugs scooted from pad to pad. On our left, lumpy and chiseled rocks gradually rose to become an overhanging ridge. And there, some six feet above the water, we saw the Indian pictographs. Deftly executed in natural red iron oxide, they showed a heroic human figure, a small animal, and an elk with proud, enormous antlers.

Toward dusk the fish started jumping all around us. At the far end of the lake a beaver slapped his tail and dove. The western clouds seemed to be on fire. Crows cawed, ducks quacked. Slowly, we paddled back toward camp.

Early the next morning we slid out of the tent into a Japanese-painting world of gray vapor. In the makeshift stone fireplace I got a blaze going, and Betty made coffee. I carried my cup down to a great slab of granite that protruded from the lake and settled myself in the boulder's ancient, crusty lap. The water rose and fell at its flanks. Forty feet out the lake disappeared into the diaphanous mist.

The wilderness, I thought, is a font. Hence our wish to keep it pure. Many motives impel us back to simpler times, simpler places. Writing of the Quetico-Superior, Sigurd Olson says that the wilderness, by reawakening our primal selves, returns us to wholeness and wonder. Surely he is right. Here we seek Edenic connectedness, freshness of eye, regeneration.

Morning fog, Boundary Waters Canoe Area, northern Minnesota

John Karras

But flowing back to the wilderness is only one expression of the need to begin again. I have responded to it, for instance, in garish motel rooms by opening the Gideon Bible to the first verses of Genesis. In a broad sense it was this yearning that stirred the backwoods colonial farmers to breach the Appalachian barrier, the immigrants to make their perilous journeys, the town builders to plant their fundamentalist churches and grassroots schools. Later, it was the need to find sustenance in this first seeding that gave such power to the log cabin myth and that stirred the Midwestern historian, Frederick Jackson Turner, to say: "It is not without significance that when nations have reached a high level of achievement, when the energy of national life is at full tide, they turn with an irresistible longing to learn more of their history." Still later, the quest for an unblemished, storybook past led Grant Wood to paint his tidy landscapes, and mass-producer Henry Ford to create his Greenfield Village. In 1962 the need to touch one's beginnings impelled a Cleveland business executive to pay a bewildered farm family for the privilege of staying on their farm for a week and picking blueberries—something he had not done for thirty-five years. "Nostalgia" is a poor, devalued word, but it seems the only one we have for this basic need. Sherwood Anderson's nostalgia was focused on the prairie town:

> Sometimes the city man, remembering an old hunger, returns to the town of his youth. He walks about the streets.
>
> The town seems strangely changed to him. It is a constant shock to him that the people of his town have also grown older . . .
>
> During all his life in the city, the small town of his boyhood has remained

home to him. Every house in the town, the faces of people seen on the street in his boyhood, have all remained sharply in his mind. How clearly he remembers the hill above the water-works pond, where he, with a troupe of other boys, went along a path beside a wheat field to the town swimming hole . . .

There is something reached for, wanted also by the city man—to be known and recognized by the clerk in the neighboring drug store, the nearby A. & P., or the news dealer at the corner . . .

It is the old hunger for intimacy.

The Japanese-landscape world in front of me had been changing. The gray dome was brightening; the fog was dissolving. Along the near shores, pines and spruces were beginning to poke their tops above the thinning wisps. Out on a little point I could discern two vague shapes—deer, drinking from the lake. Moments later the water was visible all the way out to the boomerang bend.

I was thinking about polarities: about progress and purity, liberty and equality, expediency and morality, illusion and disillusion, stillness and flow. I recalled Superior's sweetness and her rage, the locomotive hurtling onto the slumbering prairie, Chicago's *I Will* versus the small towns' *We Are,* the hell-raising lumbermen outlasted by the silent seeds in their sealed cones, the deep agrarian ethic and the wide vascular sheath of waterborne commerce. What a diversity! I saw the cars clustering summer after summer around the Dairy Queens and fall after fall around the bonfires—and remembered GM's canny status symbolism. I thought of the icemelt flowing from here north to Hudson's Bay, and south on the Father of Waters to the Gulf, and east, down the stairsteps of the Great Lakes and St. Lawrence, to the Atlantic. I thought back to the country hymnals, the fur barons, the cow barns and blast furnaces, the Cincinnati pork packers and the Geneseo Grid Club.

And now, it seemed, I had come full circle and was back to the question with which I had begun: Why the Middle West? For its fibrous muscularity and multiform energies. For what Turner called its "largeness of design." For the gifts Lincoln exemplified: a vision of the spiritual within the physical, of the many within the one, of balance. For the recognition that man is of nature, that nature moves among polarities and is, in the largest sense, stable.

The fog had gone, and the far shore shone clear. I rose to go. Then I stopped. The call of a loon was coming over the lake.

Acknowledgments

People's kindness and helpfulness have been so much a part of the creation of *Middle West Country* that the following list seems a virtual blueprint of the project. If I have forgotten anyone, it is surely not by intention; and any errors in the book are mine alone.

Fundamentally, the project was made possible by the faith of my brother-in-law, John Huneke, and of my friends Moshe Alafi, Dennis King, Dave Lennihan, and Mike Schilling.

If the soul of the Middle West can be said to reside in any one place, it is on the farms. I treasure my memories of the hospitalities extended me by these farm people: Ellen Klemperer, Fritz Klemperer, and Bob and Carol Green, all of Chanticleer Farm near Richmond, Indiana; Bud, Dolores, and Jim Reshke, Barbara, Bruce, and Rod Searle, and Bernard and Carol Francque, all of Henry County, Illinois; and Earl and Phyllis Sorenson of Fennville, Michigan.

In the town of Geneseo, Illinois, a great many people gave generously of their time and interest, particularly Clyde Walter and others mentioned in the text, as well as Jackie Henney. Particular thanks go also to Cecil Beeson of Hartford City, Indiana; Russell Foster and his large family, and Roy Raney, of Mankato, Minnesota; Bob and Sue Fritz of Lake Forest, Illinois; Jack and Mel Brown, and William Blair, of Lake Bluff, Illinois; Russell and Alfreda Soper of Sioux City, Iowa, and Russell's sister Gracie Thompson of San Diego, California; Lee and Kitty Stephens of Aurora, Illinois; and Charles Whitney of Galva, Illinois.

Southern Illinois has a unique spirit, and so do the people who helped me there: Bill Farley, Tommy Hale, Bill Horrell, Dr. William Lewis, Virginia Marmaduke, Jim Seed, Rip Stokes, and Reverend Lloyd Sumner. In northern Minnesota, Bud and Fran Heinselman were extremely kind, as was Stan Carmichael.

There is nothing like the eye of a seasoned regional writer to help guide a rank newcomer. I am, therefore, deeply indebted to these distinguished professionals for their assistance: author and publisher Richard E. Banta; writer and editor Robert Cromie, editor Jack McCutcheon, and president Frederick A. Nichols, all of the Chicago *Tribune;* editor Jill Dean of *Wisconsin Trails;* poet and author Paul Engle of the University of Iowa; columnist Gordon Gammack of the Des Moines *Register;* novelist Fredrick Manfred; Time-Life author William Weber Johnson; editor Ralph Reynolds of *The Furrow;* and editor John Gerstner of *JD Journal.* Special thanks go to writer-farmer Rex Gogarty for reading the farm chapters and making helpful suggestions at several points.

Both in person and by letter, these members of the academic community have given wise advice and potent insights: Lewis Atherton of the University of Missouri; Ray Allen Billington of the Huntington Library; Peter Carroll of the University of Minnesota; Sterling Cook of Miami University (Ohio); Roy Meyer of Mankato State; David Noble of the University of Minnesota; and James Thorpe of Earlham College.

I feel extremely grateful to Deere and Company for making their considerable resources available to me at every phase of the project. Warm welcomes and valuable leads flowed from the offices of William A. Hewitt, Walter Straley, and Tim Henney.

The staffs of nearly every major library and historical society in the corn-growing states were unstinting in their efforts to assist me in my search for pictures and facts. George Talbot, curator of the superb iconography collection at the State Historical Society of Wisconsin, extended courtesies far beyond the call of duty. Much of my basic research was done at the Stanford University Libraries, whose staff remain as personable as they are proficient.

I am grateful also to R. C. Hudson of the H. D. Hudson Manufacturing Company in Chicago; to Bonnie Mickelson of Ohio's fascinating Seiberling family; to Robert W. Murphy, a Midwest buff and vice president of Borg-Warner; and to Howard Thurman, a man of deep spiritual perceptions.

Most seminal of all, in another way, are the inspirations of my many teachers, past and present. My wife Betty, an ex-Midwesterner, made such extensive contributions, from broad understandings through typing and indexing, that it would be impossible to list them all. Our visits to the home of her parents, Dwight and Eleanor Eakin of Larned, Kansas, greatly enriched my appreciation of the Middle West and of its large, loving families. Finally, and as always, my mother and my father have helped me with this project in their own uniquely valuable ways.

Notes on the Sources

FOREWORD

The concept of regionalism has received remarkably little attention from historians and social scientists. Significant exceptions are Wilbur Zelinsky's valuable *The Cultural Geography of the United States* (1973) and Carle C. Zimmerman and Richard E. Du Wors' *Graphic Regional Sociology* (1952). *Regionalism in America* (1965), edited by Merrill Jensen, is an anthology drawn from a wide variety of sources.

"Prairie" and "plain" have been used in so many confusing ways that to insist on a sharp distinction would be to ignore the real world. My usage, however, follows that of many current botanists and ecologists. See, for example, David F. Costello's *The Prairie World* (1969).

Mr. Trillin's article appeared in the New York *Times*, September 9, 1974.

CHAPTER ONE

The quotation on page 11 is from *The Heartland* (1967) by Robert McLaughlin and the editors of Time-Life Books. That on page 18 is from *The Plains States* (1968) by Evan Jones and the same editors. These slender volumes contain some of the most lively and well-researched writing available on the Midwest, even though their picture essays are dated and their institutional-series concept resulted in dividing the region in an unnatural way.

The quotation on page 17 (third paragraph, fifth sentence) is from Graham Hutton's *Midwest at Noon* (1946), a sympathetic study of the region by an Englishman whose insights have enriched my own at several points.

Useful facts on the Great Lakes area are contained in Russell McKee's *Great Lakes Country* (1966) and in William Donohue Ellis' *Land of the Inland Seas* (1974). Roy W. Meyer's *The Middle Western Farm Novel in the Twentieth Century* (1965) provides a comprehensive outline of rural fiction.

CHAPTER TWO

Indispensable sources on the great trek west are Ray Allen Billington's *Westward Expansion* (1967) and Robert E. Riegel and Robert A. Athearn's *America Moves West* (1964). Classic works on immigration include Marcus Lee Hansen's *The Atlantic Migration* (1940) and *The Immigrant in American History* (1940), and Carl Wittke's *We Who Built America* (1964). The emphasis on cultural predetermination has been disputed by Allan G. Bogue and others; see his essay, "Farming in the Prairie Peninsula, 1830–1890," in *The Journal of Economic History,* March, 1963. The quotations on pages 30 and 31 (second and third paragraphs) are from Billington, pp. 266, 92–93 & 164. Those on pages 51 and 61 are from Wittke, pp. 204 & 290.

Descriptive regional writing reached a zenith in the decades surrounding World War II. The guidebooks produced by the WPA remain the best of their kind; of these, the *Illinois Guide* (1939), *Ohio Guide* (1940), and *Indiana Guide* (1941) are among the finest. The Rivers of America series was equally ambitious; among its several Midwestern titles, R. E. Banta's *The Ohio* merits special note. Walter Havighurst's prolific writings, particularly *The Heartland* (1956), are a genre unto themselves. The works of Harlan Hatcher, August Derleth, and Milo M. Quaife, from the same period, should also be mentioned. Holiday Magazine in its flush years commissioned top-notch pieces about each state, then brought them together in *American Panorama* (1960), in which the Midwest is ably treated by Mark Schorer, Bruce Catton, Bentz Plagemann, and others. The quotation on pages 43–44 is as quoted in the *Indiana Guide,* p. 149; those on pages 50 and 53 (third and fourth paragraphs) are from the *Ohio Guide,* pp. 217–18, 79, & 201. The quotation on page 64 is as quoted by Banta, p. 377. Those on pages 32 and 37 are from Havighurst, pp. 153 & 117. That on page 53 (second paragraph) is from *American Panorama,* pp. 242 & 246.

John Bakeless' *The Eyes of Discovery* (1950) nicely threads together many accounts of virgin America. Early descriptions of the Midwest by Morris Birkbeck are valuable, particularly his *Notes on a Journey in America* (1818). So is his follower, John Woods' *Two Years Residence on the English Prairie of Illinois* (1822). O. E. Rölvaag's *Giants in the Earth* (1927) is a great fictional narrative of the settling of the northern grasslands by Norwegian pioneers. The quotations on page 33 are from Bakeless, pp. 283–86 & 306. That on page 40 is from Birkbeck, *op. cit.* That on pages 49–50 is from Woods, *op. cit.,* Donnelley edition (1968), pp. 211–213.

The contrasting lifestyles of the old southern forester and Yankee are fascinatingly documented in Richard L. Power's *Planting Corn Belt Culture* (1953). Harold B. Allen's *The Linguistic Atlas of the Upper Midwest* (1973) is a detailed analysis of subregional word variants. Page Smith's *As a City Upon a Hill* (1966) stresses the colonizing communities from New England. John Bartlow Martin's *Call It North Country* (1944) is a colorful account of the boom years in upper Michigan. Leo Marx' *The Machine in the Garden* portrays the clashing pastoral and mechanical ideals throughout American history. The quotations on pages 37 (last paragraph) and 38 are as quoted by Power, pp. 16–17. That on page 31 (first paragraph) is as quoted by Smith, p. 45. That on page 58 is from Martin, p. 18. Jefferson's famous passage on pages 29–30 is as quoted by Marx, pp. 124–25.

To the extent that the Midwest is indeed "the most American America," studies of the American character have special relevance to this region. A good introduction to the voluminous literature on the subject is a comprehensive anthology, *The Character of Americans* (1970), edited by Michael McGiffert.

CHAPTER THREE

Careful texts on nineteenth century farming include Paul W. Gates' *The Farmer's Age: Agriculture 1815–1860* (1960); Allan G. Bogue's *From Prairie to Corn Belt* (1963); Gilbert C. Fite's *The Farmer's Frontier 1865–1900* (1966); and Fred A. Shannon's *The Farmer's Last Frontier* (1961). The quotations on pages 82, 88, and 89 (third paragraph, second sentence) are from Gates, pp. 159, 210–12, & 217. Those on page 89 (third paragraph, fourth sentence) are from Bogue, p. 106.

The Nowlin quotations are from Donnelley & Sons' Lakeside Press reprint of *The Bark Covered House* (1937). Martin Welker's are from his *Farm Life in Ohio Sixty Years Ago* (1895).

The quotation on page 84 (third paragraph) is from Elizabeth Nowell, *Thomas Wolfe* (1960), p. 395. That on page 84 (second paragraph) is from the letter by Richard H. Beach in *Prairie State* (1968), edited by Paul M. Angle, p. 168. Those on page 86 are as quoted by Power, *op. cit.,* pp. 152 & 154.

Albert Britt's *An America That Was* appeared in 1964; the quotations are from pp. 113–14, 99–100, 104, 129–30, 140, & 141. For further colorful descriptions of daily life in the rural Midwest before 1900, see Logan Esarey's *The Indiana Home* (1947).

CHAPTER FOUR

Prairie descriptions are quoted from the following sources. That on page 97, from Bogue, *op. cit.,* p. 5. Page 98 (second paragraph, second sentence) as quoted by Roger Anderson, *Outdoor Illinois,* February, 1972. Page 98 (second paragraph, fourth sentence), Charles Dickens, *American Notes* (1842). Page 98 (third paragraph), by William Newnham Blane in 1824, as quoted by Ralph H. Brown, *Historical Geography of the United States* (1948), p. 210. Those on pages 98–99 and 100 are as compiled by Angle, *op. cit.,* pp. 174–78 & 15–18. Page 99, Herbert H. Kersten, *American Forests,* June, 1972, p. 17. Pages 101–02, 112, 113, and 121, Herbert Quick, *One Man's Life* (1925), pp. 75–77, 94–95, 217, 211–12, & 206. Page 103, as quoted by Donald Culross Peattie, *A Prairie Grove* (1938), pp. 266–69. Page 104, Costello, *op. cit.,* p. 214.

Editor John J. Murray's *The Heritage of the Middle West* (1958) is a useful collection of essays on a variety of topics. The quotations on pages 106–07 and 111 are from Ray Allen Billington's essay in that volume, pp. 35, 27, & 51 (as amended by permission of Professor Billington). Pages 107–08, as quoted by Gates, *op. cit.,* p. 76. Page 112 (first paragraph), *Farmers Alliance,* August 23, 1890.

A landmark work on the agrarian myth is Henry Nash Smith's *Virgin Land* (1950). Richard Hofstadter's authoritative *The Age of Reform* (1955) includes discussions of farming and agrarianism in the period from Bryan to F.D.R. A vital alternative to the political dimension is Daniel J. Boorstin's series, *The Americans,* which stresses the technological, economic, and grassroots social causes of history; volumes two and three, *The National Experience* (1965) and *The Democratic Experience* (1973) are significant for the Midwest. The quotation on page 122 is as quoted in the latter, p. 124. That on page 112 (second paragraph) is as quoted by Hofstadter, Vintage edition, p. 34. That on pages 121–22 is as quoted by Newell LeRoy Sims in *Elements of Rural Sociology* (1940), pp. 376–77.

Close-in descriptions of farm life are quoted from the following sources. Pages 123–24, Sherwood Anderson, *Poor White* (1920), pp. 130 & 223. Pages 125, 126, 128, and 129, Harvey Jacobs, *We Came Rejoicing* (1967), pp. 88–89, 53, 104, & 148–49. Pages 125–26, Ethel Sabin Smith, *A Furrow Deep and True* (1964), pp. 127–28. Pages 129–30, Hutton, *op. cit.,* pp. 82–91. Pages 132, 132–33, and 133–34, Curtis Harnack, *We Have All Gone Away* (1973), pp. 34–35, 40–41, 75, 76, 163–64, 187–88.

CHAPTER FIVE

Broadly based interpretations of modern Midwestern farming and the rural scene appear to be almost nonexistent. However, Edward Higbee's *Farms and Farmers in an Urban Age* (1963) and *American Agriculture* (1958) are helpful, as are Lowry Nelson's *American Farm Life* (1954) and *The Minnesota Community* (1960). Among sociologists, Carl C. Taylor has shown a rare willingness to look beyond narrow methodologies and bland generalizations; see, for instance, *Rural Life in the United States* (1949), by Taylor and others.

Excellent farm and rural reporting continues to brighten the pages of the Des Moines *Register* and other statewide journals, and of such national papers as the *New York Times* and the *Wall Street Journal.* Impressionistic pieces by the *Times'* Andrew H. Malcolm have been issued as *Unknown America* (1974). Agricultural stories from the *Journal* have been gathered under the title *This Abundant Land* (1975), edited by John A. Prestbo. Portions of my account on page 152 (fifth and sixth paragraphs) are drawn from Gene Meyer's article in the *Journal,* October 14, 1974. The quotation on page 157 is from a story by Richard Doak in the *Register,* May 31, 1973. That on page 174 (first paragraph) is from a story by Gene Raffensperger in the *Register,* February 25, 1973.

Factual publications for the farmer have long been issued in prolific quantities by the U.S.D.A., the land grant universities, and countless farm machinery and agribusiness firms. See, for example, the voluminous U.S.D.A. *Yearbooks,* Iowa State's definitive *Midwest Farm Handbook,* and Deere & Company's excellent magazine, *The Furrow.* The quotation on page 161 is from the *Handbook*'s Seventh Edition, p. 329. The account of Iowa's landscape on pages 154–57 is drawn from the multi-media project, *Land Patterns of Iowa* (1973), developed by Iowa State's Department of Landscape Architecture and written by David Faxlanger, James Sinatra, and C. John Uban. The quotations on pages 151 and 160 (third sentence) are from *The Furrow,* November, 1972 & May–June, 1974.

For the religious history of America and the Midwest, see the extensive works of W. W. Sweet, Edwin Scott Gaustad, Martin E. Marty, and others. David M. Potter's thesis on abundance and the American character is set forth in *People of Plenty* (1954).

Quotations from other sources are as follows. Pages 137–38, as quoted by Rupert B. Vance in the *International Encyclopedia of the Social Sciences* (1968), Vol. 13, p. 379. Page 138, Sherwood Anderson, *The American County Fair* (1930), p. 3. Page 139, Ellsworth Huntington, *Principles of Human Geography,* Sixth Edition (1951), p. 544. Page 143, *Beyond the Suburbs* (1967), edited by Rex R. Campbell and Wayne H. Oberle, Book I, Section II, p. 17. Page 144, as quoted by Kusum Nair, *The Lonely Furrow* (1969), pp. 24–26 & 23. Pages 153–54 and 171, Rachel Peden, *Rural Free* (1961), pp. 345, 182, 94, 51, 216, 331, 87–88, 163, 336, & 304–05. Pages 157–58, American Panorama, *op. cit.,* p. 360. Page 160 (fourth sentence), *National Geographic,* March, 1974, p. 388. Page 171, Alexis de Tocqueville, *Democracy in America,* Vintage edition (1955), Vol. 1, p. 12. Page 172, Peattie, *op. cit.,* p. 160. Page 174 (third paragraph), Frank R. Kramer, *Voices in the Valley* (1964), pp. 8 & 180. Page 175, Dwight D. Eisenhower, "Special Message to the Congress," January 9, 1956.

CHAPTER SIX

Quotations are from the following sources. Pages 187 and 188, *The National Experience, op. cit.,* pp. 122 & 254. Page 191, as quoted by John Szarkowski, *The Face of Minnesota,* p. 165. Pages 191 and 191–92, Edgar W. Howe, *The Story of A Country Town* (1882), Signet edition (1964), pp. 304 & 13–20. Page 192, Hamlin Garland, *Main-Travelled Roads* (1891), Signet edition (1962), p. 261. Pages 194 and 195, Ruth Miller Elson, *Guardians of Tradition* (1964), pp. 226, 230, 225, 224–25, 223–24, 223, & 168. Page 195 (first paragraph), Murray, *op. cit.,* p. 60. Page 196 (third paragraph), *McGuffey's Third Eclectic Reader* (1879/1920), pp. 62–65. Pages 196 (fifth paragraph), 199, and 207 (first paragraph), Lewis Atherton, *Main Street on the Middle Border* (1954), Quadrangle edition, pp. 66, 105, 35, & 37. Page 198, as quoted by Hutton, *op. cit.,* p. 188. Page 198, George Santayana, *Character and Opinion in the United States,* Norton edition (1967), p. 225. Page 206, *Ladies Home Journal,* February, 1922. Page 206, *Colliers,* June 2, 1923. Page 207 (third paragraph), Sherwood Anderson, *Tar: A Midwest Childhood* (1926), Western Reserve edition (1969), p. 16. Pages 207–08, Sherwood Anderson, *Home Town* (1940), pp. 33, 39, 40, & 142. Pages 209–212, Reynold M. Wik, *Henry Ford and Grass-roots America* (1972). Pages 210 and 213, *The Democratic Experience, op. cit.,*pp. 362, 549, 555, & 552.

CHAPTER SEVEN

Helpful aids to anyone exploring Corn Belt byways are county "Atlas and Plat Books," showing not only all the villages and back roads but also the names of the farm owners, their acreage, and many of their buildings.

The quotation on page 224 is from *Home Town, op. cit.,* p. 95. Page 231 (second paragraph, third sentence), Des Moines *Register,* April 30, 1973. Page 231 (second paragraph, sixth sentence), *Redbook,* December, 1972. Page 233, Hofstadter, *op. cit.,* p. 36.

For sociological portraits of a typically stable-yet-changing Missouri farm village community, see James West's *Plainville, U.S.A.* (1945) and Art Gallaher, Jr.'s *Plainville Fifteen Years Later* (1961).

CHAPTER EIGHT

The literature on the Mississippi is, of course, copious. For southern Illinois, see Baker Brownell's *The Other Illinois* (1958), Paul M. Angle's *Bloody Williamson* (1973), Joseph P. Lyford's *The Talk in Vandalia* (1962), Herman R. Lantz' *People of Coal Town* (1958), and C. William Horrell, Henry Dan Piper, and John W. Voight's *Land Between the Rivers* (1973). Many books are available on the KKK and Prohibition; Peter N. Carroll and David W. Noble's *The Restless Centuries* (1973) provocatively attributes these and other phenomena occurring throughout U.S. history to class and ideological conflicts. My account of Muncie is based on *The Eclipse of Community* (1960), in which Maurice R. Stein interprets Robert S. and Helen M. Lynd's *Middletown* (1929) and *Middletown in Transition* (1937). Labor relations in the smaller communities of the early industrial age are described by Herbert G. Gutman in an essay in *The Old Northwest* (1969), edited by Harry N. Scheiber—a useful anthology of writings on the Midwest in the period 1787–1910.

Detailed histories of portions of the upper Midwest include Walter Havighurst's *The Long Ships Passing* (1942), Willis F. Dunbar's *Michigan* (1970), and Theodore C. Blegen's *Minnesota* (1963). The Boundary Waters Canoe Area is lovingly depicted by Sigurd F. Olson in *The Singing Wilderness* (1956) and in many other books and articles. *The North Woods* (1972) by Percy Knauth and the editors of Time-Life Books is exquisitely photographed, reliably researched, and warmly presented.

Quotations are as follows. Page 236, Timothy Flint, *Recollections of the Last Ten Years* (1826), Southern Illinois University Press edition (1968), pp. 76–77. Page 237, Samuel L. Clemens, *Life on the Mississippi* (1883), Magnum/Lancer edition (1968), p. 480. Page 238, Kin Hubbard, *Abe Martin's Primer* and *Abe Martin on the War and Other Things* (undated, unpaged). Page 240, Brownell, *op. cit.,* p. 15. Page 240 (third paragraph), New York *Times,* March 31, 1973. Page 244, Dick Perry, *Ohio: A Personal Portrait of the 17th State* (1969), pp. 78–79. Pages 245 and 246, Gutman in Sheiber, *op. cit.,* pp. 390 & 173. Page 247, as quoted by Stein, *op. cit.,* p. 61. Page 253, Ernest Hemingway, *The Nick Adams Stories,* Bantam edition (1973), p. 21. Page 253, Frederick Jackson Turner, "The Development of American Society" (1908) in *America's Great Frontiers and Sections,* Bison edition (1965), p. 168. Pages 269–270, *Home Town, op. cit.,* pp. 20–22.

Index

(page numbers referring to captions are italicized)